Hawker's Naval Fighters

Sea Harrier FRS.2 ZA195, the first development aircraft, launches from HMS *Ark Royal* during sea trials in November 1990.

Hawker's Naval Fighters

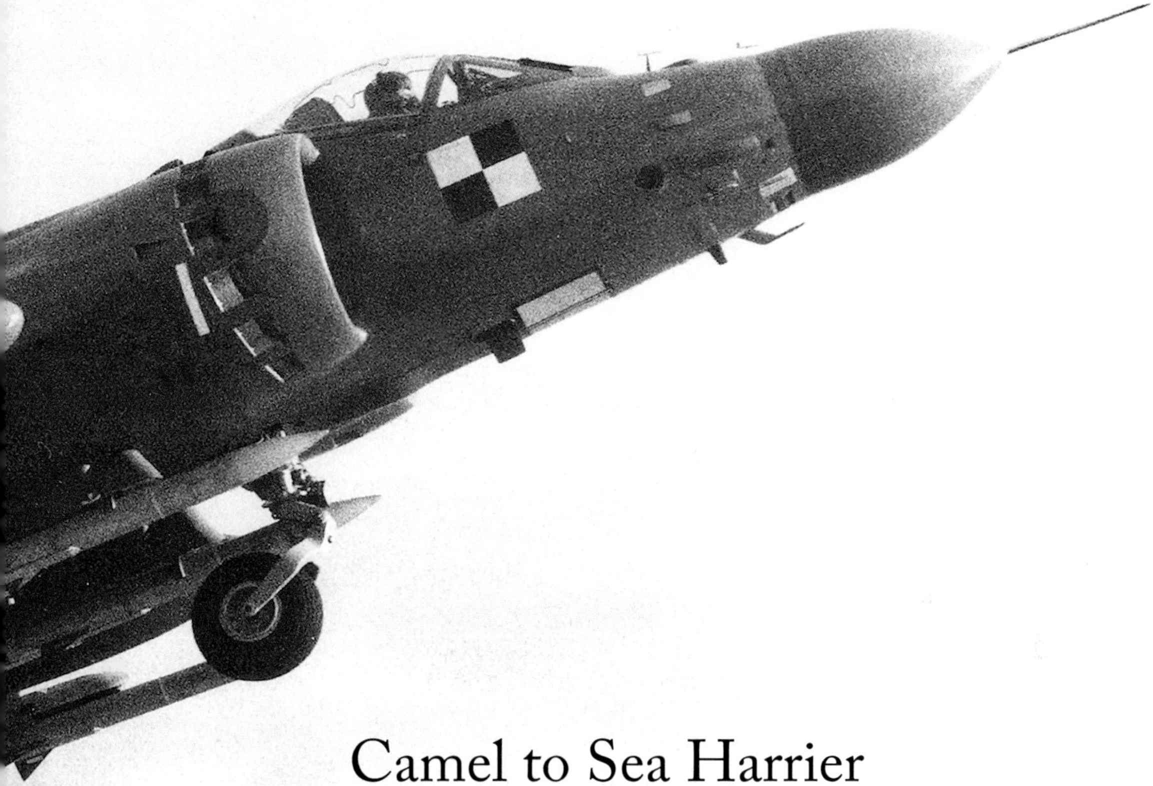

Camel to Sea Harrier

Christopher Budgen

First published in Great Britain in 2025 by
Air World
An imprint of Pen & Sword Books Limited
Yorkshire – Philadelphia

ISBN 978 1 03610 232 6

Typeset by Mac Style
Printed in the UK by CPI Group (UK) Ltd, Croydon, CR0 4YY.

The Publisher's authorised representative in the EU for product
safety is Authorised Rep Compliance Ltd., Ground Floor,
71 Lower Baggot Street, Dublin D02 P593, Ireland.
www.arccompliance.com

For a complete list of Pen & Sword titles please contact

PEN & SWORD BOOKS LIMITED
47 Church Street, Barnsley, South Yorkshire, S70 2AS, England
E-mail: enquiries@pen-and-sword.co.uk
Website: www.pen-and-sword.co.uk
or
PEN AND SWORD BOOKS
1950 Lawrence Road, Havertown, PA 19083, USA
E-mail: uspen-and-sword@casematepublishers.com
Website: www.penandswordbooks.com

Contents

Acknowledgements

My thanks to the following for their assistance in compiling this history: Peter Amos, Ben Dunnell, Frank Chapman, Heinz Frick, Jock Alexander and Chris Gotke, staff at Fly Navy Heritage Trust, Kieron Kirk, Frank Rainsborough, Julian Temple and BAE Systems Archive, and Brooklands Museum staff. Robert Mitchell for his help with the image preparation.

Photographic imagery acknowledgements: BL – courtesy of Brooklands Museum; BAE – courtesy of BAE Systems; BAE/BL – BAE Systems, courtesy of Brooklands Museum; PA – courtesy of Peter Amos; AW – courtesy of Alan Wilson; Author – Author's Collection.

Glossary

A&AEE	Aeroplane and Armament Experimental Establishment
AAM	Air-to-Air Missile
AMRAAM	Advanced Medium Range Air-to-Air Missile
ASM	Air-to-Surface Missile
BAC	British Aircraft Corporation
BAe	British Aerospace
C(A)	Controller (Aircraft)
CG	Centre of Gravity
CTP	Chief Test Pilot
ETPS	Empire Test Pilots' School
DOR	Director/Directorate of Operational Requirements
DTD	Director/Directorate of Technical Development
F/A	Fighter Attack
FAA	Fleet Air Arm
FAW	Fighter All Weather
FB	Fighter Bomber
FGA	Fighter Ground attack
FRADU	Fleet Requirements and Air Direction Unit
FRS	Fighter Reconnaissance Strike
FRU	Fleet Requirements Unit
Gunbus	Design whereby the engine was mounted at the rear of the crew nacelle, allowing a machine gun or similar to be mounted in the nose
HAL	Hawker Aircraft Ltd
HSA	Hawker Siddeley Aviation
INS	Indian Navy Ship
JSF	Joint Strike Fighter
MAEE	Marine Aircraft Experimental Establishment
MAP	Ministry of Aircraft Procurement
MDAP	Mutual Defence Assistance Pact
MoA	Ministry of Aviation
MoS	Ministry of Supply
MU	Maintenance Unit
MWDP	Mutual Weapons Development Pact
NAS	Naval Air Squadron
NATO	North Atlantic Treaty Organisation

NPL	National Physical Laboratory
Pusher	Aircraft design whereby the engine and propeller are mounted at the rear of the fuselage
RAE	Royal Aircraft Establishment
RAF	Royal Air Force
RATO	Rocket Assisted Take Off
RFC	Royal Flying Corps
RNAS	Royal Naval Air Service/Station
SAM	Surface-to-Air Missile
SBAC	Society of British Aircraft Constructors (British Aerospace Companies)
STOVL	Short Take Off and Vertical Landing
Tractor	Aircraft design whereby the engine and propeller are mounted at the front of the fuselage
TSR	Tactical Strike Reconnaissance
USMC	United States Marine Corps
USSR	Union of Soviet Socialist Republics
V/STOL	Vertical/Short Take Off and Landing
VTOL	Vertical Take Off and Landing

Foreword

Some might be asking why a naval helicopter pilot is writing the foreword to a book on some of the finest fixed-wing aircraft to have served with both the Fleet Air Arm and the Royal Air Force. Indeed, I asked that same question when I was initially approached on the subject but was persuaded by the demand for a 'different' viewpoint and also one from the perspective of running Navy Wings for the last eight years. It helped of course that a couple of the Navy Wings collection are covered in this book in the form of the Hawker Sea Fury and Sea Hawk.

For the uninitiated, Navy Wings is the charity which keeps heritage naval aircraft flying, and we believe that the best way to inform current and future generations about the glorious past of naval aviation is by displaying these iconic aircraft around the United Kingdom. As the Royal Navy is largely an 'over the horizon' Service, which struggles to reach the UK hinterland, we aim to inform the general public and hopefully inspire future generations to consider a career in maritime aviation.

To summarise what has been produced, this book is one of a series covering Hawker Aircraft Ltd and Hawker Siddeley Aviation and it has taken almost four years of deep research to reach publication. Although the author does not have a Service background, his thorough knowledge of aviation was imbued from an early age. Dunsfold Airfield was built on land farmed by his great-grandfather and his father worked there most of his life, so he grew up immersed in the world of flight. His own work on the Harrier and Hawk then took him around various service and ministry sites including Yeovilton, Boscombe Down, West Freugh and St Athan as well as a short spell in HMS *Ark Royal* with the development of the Sea Harrier FRS.2.

The author leads us through a fascinating historical journey from the perspective of the Hawker Aircraft company in its different guises, one of the most important aviation companies of its time. We start with land-based aircraft in the form of the world famous Sopwith Pup, 1½ Strutter, Triplane and, perhaps the most iconic, the Sopwith Camel, but at the same time they were developing the maritime base with the Sopwith Baby. Post the Great War, they then produced a litany of different aircraft types in the form of the Woodcock, Hedgehog, Horsley, Hoopoe, Nimrod, Osprey, Sea Hurricane, Sea Fury, Sea Hawk, Hunter and Sea Harrier, all of which are covered herein.

Although this tome covers over 100 years of aviation history, I think from a naval perspective perhaps the most interesting thing was the innovative approach required to operate these aircraft from ships at sea. Operating from the deck in a harsh maritime environment is not for the faint-hearted and the Royal Naval Air Service, followed by the Fleet Air Arm, had to constantly adapt as technology moved quickly forward. This started with the simple use of cranes to get the early aircraft on and off ships, then encompassed float-planes like the Sopwith Baby, before morphing into catapults, angled-flight decks and, finally, ski jumps, all of which were British inventions. Sometimes, of course, this constant innovation and thirst to move forward ended in tragic consequences, but the ethos of naval aviators is to learn and move forward and I truly believe we operate in a far safer way today thanks to the work of our forebears, alongside companies like Hawker.

In my own time in the Service, which covered over 38 years, I saw many aircraft come into and leave operational service and as I reflect on my career, everything I flew, from the Chipmunk and Gazelle through to the Sea King, has now been retired. On a wider scale, all the naval aircraft I served alongside, including the Wasp, Lynx and Sea Harrier, have also gone from the active list and this just demonstrates how quickly technology moves forward, particularly in the aviation world.

I am now lucky enough to be running Navy Wings, which has given me a bit of an insight into some of these beautiful old aircraft. We have a great example of a Hawker Sea Fury in our collection, which is a British carrier-borne fighter aircraft designed and manufactured by Hawker Aircraft. It was developed during the Second World War but did not enter service until 1947 and it was the last, biggest and most powerful propeller-driven fighter to serve with the Royal Navy. However, this was the start of the jet age and although the Sea Fury was probably the pinnacle of the propellor-driven fighters, it was quickly replaced in service by another stalwart from the Hawker stable, namely the Sea Hawk. Navy Wings has also inherited a fine example of this popular fighter from the Royal Navy and we are currently working on a restoration project, with an aim of having her back in the skies within the next couple of years.

For anyone with an interest in iconic British aircraft in the 20th Century, this book will be of real interest. I am delighted to be able to provide this introduction and I commend it to you. Enjoy!

Cdre Jock Alexander OBE MA FRAeS,
Chief Executive - Fly Navy Heritage Trust,
December 2024.

Commodore Jock Alexander joined the Royal Navy as a Seaman Officer and spent his first job as a Ship's Diving Officer before gaining his pilot's 'Wings' in 1984. He joined 820 Naval Air Squadron (NAS), his first front-line squadron, in 1985 embarked in HMS Invincible *before the entire air group transferred to HMS* Ark Royal *in 1986 for her first commission. In 1987 he was appointed to 819 NAS as the Helicopter Warfare Instructor, before going on to take command of HMS* Kellington *in 1989. He then returned to the flying world in 1992 as Senior Pilot of 820 NAS embarked once again in HMS* Ark Royal, *before going onto staff course in 1984 and a staff appointment thereafter. On completion, he was appointed as the Commanding Officer of 819 NAS in 1997 where he remained until promotion to Commander in 1999, whereupon he became the Staff Officer Operations to the Fleet Air Arm (FAA). In 2001 he was appointed as Commander Air in HMS* Illustrious, *where he remained until joining Navy Command HQ in the position of the Staff Aviation Officer in 2002. In 2008 he returned to Navy Command*

HQ in charge of the Carrier Strike Integration Team, responsible for the introduction to service of HMS Queen Elizabeth *and HMS* Prince of Wales. *In 2012 he was appointed OBE for this work and promoted to Commodore before being appointed as the Commanding Officer of Royal Naval Air Station Yeovilton later that year. He retired from the Royal Navy in 2016 and took up his current position as Chief Executive Officer of Navy Wings that same year, as well as becoming Chairman of the Fly Navy Federation, a role he still holds today.*

Introduction

In 1906, the launch of HMS *Dreadnought* changed the face of naval warfare – overnight. The advent of the all-big-gun battleship represented the acme of fighting ships of the line, making all previous battleships (and navies) obsolete, and confirmed the UK as the most powerful naval entity on the planet. *Dreadnought*, the largest and most powerful warship in the world, was quickly followed by an arms race as other naval powers sought to catch up with the Royal Navy by building their own versions, this race coming to a head when the Royal Navy's Grand Fleet and the High Seas Fleet of the German Navy met in the cold waters of the North Sea off Jutland. What should have been the defining moment of battleship power was instead something of a damp squib as neither force was able to land a convincing blow on the enemy. The big-gun battleship was the pre-eminent expression of a nation's power in the first two decades of the twentieth century, yet, within a few years, it was obsolete, rendered so by its vulnerability to aerial attack from the aeroplane. By 1940 the battleship had been all but supplanted as the pre-eminent expression of power at sea; henceforth, its place would be taken by the aircraft carrier.

From uncertain beginnings around 1910, naval aviation would expand as the usefulness of the aircraft at sea was more fully appreciated and its initial unreliability was replaced by efficient machines able to project firepower beyond the horizon to such an extent that opposing fleets could give battle while never sighting the enemy. Today, the aircraft carrier remains THE capital ship of large navies, a symbol of strength and power. However, this is a book about aircraft, not ships, though the two are inextricably intertwined when naval air power is to be considered.

The companies founded by Thomas Octave Murdoch Sopwith – Sopwith Aviation, HG Hawker Engineering and Hawker Aircraft Ltd (and later Hawker Siddeley Aviation) – were fortunate to have been in at the very beginnings of naval aviation, largely thanks to Sopwith's interest in all things nautical and the means to pursue those interests as a young man. His contact with members of the Royal Navy would stand him and his company in good stead when time came to offer his early aircraft to the Senior Service. Sopwith's father was a civil engineer, allowing young Sopwith to grow up exposed to engineering in its broadest sense. As a young adult his enthusiasm for adventure had led him successively to interests in ballooning, sailing, speedboats, motorcycles, motor cars and, latterly, aircraft and it was his half ownership of the schooner *Neva* that led to his employment of a young engineer – Frederick Sigrist – to crew the vessel and attend to its mechanics. This most serendipitous meeting in 1909 would see the two remain in a close working relationship for the next fifty years and become the kernel upon which Sopwith would build his aircraft empire. On Sigrist's death on 10 December 1956, Sopwith wrote:

Fred Sigrist was one of the pioneers of aviation. Although his name does not appear in any Royal Aero Club list of record holders he was one of the best engineers I have ever known and because of this aviation owes a great debt to his memory. He had the priceless gift of getting the best out of all who worked with or under him, partly because he knew his job but principally, I am sure, because he was so completely genuine. Fred Sigrist was a Jerseyman. I first met him when he joined the crew of an auxiliary schooner as engineer in 1909. Within a year we were immersed in the early days of flying and in December 1910, largely owing to his genius in persuading our early engines to keep running, we were able to fly from Eastchurch to Belgium. In 1911 we started the construction of aircraft, first in a shed at Brooklands and then in a disused skating rink at Kingston. Fred Sigrist was largely responsible for the construction of the early types of biplane, one of which, the Tabloid, won the Schneider Trophy in 1914; and from them grew the line of aircraft which played such an important part in the 1914–18 war.[1]

Before the advent of the First World War, T.O.M. Sopwith's designs were being taken up by the nascent Royal Naval Air Service (RNAS) at Eastchurch as the service sought to equip itself with adequate and reliable aircraft with which to experiment in a naval context. One almost gets the feeling that, while it was not certain just how this new discipline might be of use to the Senior Service, it had better get some aircraft and discover just what they could do for the navy.

What they could do was allow the Royal Navy, and its aerial element the RNAS, to project its power over greater distances by virtue of the aeroplane's ability to assist with reconnaissance and gunnery spotting. Soon, to this ability, was added the delivery of rudimentary bombs on the enemy, an early success being a raid against the German airship sheds at Dusseldorf in 1914 by an RNAS Sopwith Tabloid which successfully destroyed Zeppelin LZ.25 in its shed using primitive bombs. As the war settled into a stalemate that stretched on for years, Sopwith Aviation – and the aeroplane – matured into potent entities, a succession of designs from the Kingston company supplying the Royal Navy with the most up-to-date aircraft of the day. At the end of the war, as with most other aviation concerns, the immediate cancellation of aircraft orders saw the company wound up.

Almost immediately, a successor company was formed in 1920 from the ashes of Sopwith Aviation – the HG Hawker Engineering Co. Ltd – with much the same board of directors, staff and premises. The name of the company reflected the prominent position that Harry Hawker, an Australian engineer, had acquired during the period he served as a test pilot and engineer for the company. Although meeting his death in a flying accident in 1921, his name was immortalised in the company's title for the next fifty-seven years. Given the paucity of military contracts available to aviation companies in the early 1920s, Hawker was lucky to remain in business, at first by refurbishing earlier aircraft models for the RAF, but, as the decade matured, HG Hawker Engineering reached a more secure foundation, in large part due to another lucky chance (Sopwith's life appears to feature several such encounters) with the employment of a young draughtsman and designer in the person of Sydney Camm. Camm, who joined the company in 1923 as a senior designer/ draughtsman, would dominate the design of Hawker products for the next forty-three years. Camm was described by many as difficult and complex. Harold Penrose, a test pilot for Westland Aircraft, noted that: 'I can't imagine why his men put up with him. He was a genius – but quite often impossible.'[2]

Throughout the 1920s and early 1930s, Camm and his team produced a series of excellent biplane designs that saw service with both the RAF and the Royal Navy, including the Hart and Fury, both very successful designs that sold widely. With the genesis of Camm's monoplane fighter design in 1935, the Hurricane was available just in time to have equipped the RAF squadrons with significant numbers of aircraft to form the bulk of the fighter defence of the UK during the Battle of Britain and indeed during the Battle of the Atlantic. This would be followed by the Typhoon, Tempest and Fury monoplanes, leading to the Sea Fury in time for the Korean War of the early 1950s. As the last of Hawker's piston-engined aircraft, the Fury was used as the early vehicle for Hawker's first jet engine design which matured into the Sea Hawk. Envisaged as an RAF fighter, the Air Ministry declined to show any but academic interest, being content for now with the Meteor and Vampire then entering service. The Royal Navy, however, in its search for jet-propelled aircraft decided that here was the basis of a worthwhile carrier capable jet and placed an order. Camm's relief was evident in his response, 'Thank heaven for the Navy.'

The Sea Hawk would be the last Hawker aircraft to go to sea until the advent of the Sea Harrier, though it was not for want of trying! In the interim, the Hawker Hunter served ashore at FAA bases as a weapons and tactics trainer, in turn keeping the good qualities of Hawker products before their Lordships at the Admiralty to remind them of the company's record, before the Harrier – after an exhausting campaign – became the fighter of choice for the Royal Navy and introduced V/STOL operation into the Senior Service. And just in time. In April 1982, Argentina invaded the Falkland Islands Dependency, thereby initiating a military response from the UK Government in the form of Operation CORPORATE, a seaborne operation that had at its core the Royal Navy's last two aircraft carriers with embarked squadrons of Sea Harriers with which to prosecute a retaking of the territory, achieved in June 1982 after fierce and bloody fighting, the successful outcome only being possible thanks to the presence of the Sea Harrier squadrons.

Finally, after years of dilatory and often dismissive comment regarding the capabilities of the Harrier, this action put paid to the negative aura with which it had been regarded for years. Yet for all its success, the Sea Harrier did not see the bumper export orders that the company had hoped it would generate; its unique abilities just did not feature in the requirements of many air arms around the world. Perhaps the greatest accolade for the company and its Harrier was the adoption of the design by the United States Navy and its subsequent decision to make the USMC an entirely V/STOL force with the AV-8A and AV-8B aircraft. If this was not sufficient justification for faith in Kingston's Harrier, the next generation fighter to be designed in the United States, and which looks set to equip most of the air arms of the west, includes a STOVL design – the JSF – F.35B Lightning II.

Though the Hawker company and its latter-day replacement British Aerospace (now BAE Systems) no longer inhabits Kingston upon Thames and its outstation at Dunsfold, there can surely be no better obituary than to see its last successful design incorporated into that of the world's leading air power.

Most of the aircraft examined in this work emanated from the design team headed by Sydney – latterly Sir Sydney – Camm. His design philosophy, if he had one, was of attention to detail. In an uncharacteristic appearance, he gave a broadcast via the BBC, entitled 'I am an Aircraft Designer', in April 1942. In this talk, he expressed himself lucky to have been able to convert his boyhood hobby into his profession. From leading the Windsor Model Aeroplane Club, he had progressed to real aircraft via an apprenticeship with Martinsyde of Woking, an aircraft manufacturer supplying machines during the First World War. He later moved to work with George Handasyde on design in the drawing office around 1921 before this business folded, thereafter moving to HG Hawker Engineering in 1923. Camm's way of working when designing a new military aircraft was to start with the engine and armament and the weight of fuel to be carried. Around these fundamentals of the fighter, he would then design the smallest and lightest machine possible, though of adequate strength to resist the forces it would meet in action. While this sounds straightforward, it was often just these elements that were the great unknowns of the design process; engines were often new and untried, armament would constantly evolve and change and the airframe design had to change to meet them.

In March 1949, Camm wrote an article for the *Hawker Siddeley Review* entitled 'Naval Fighter Development' wherein he sought to illustrate his and the Hawker company's approach to designing a naval aircraft. He pointed out that the naval fighter 'must of course embody all the desirable features of the land fighter plus special requirements associated with its work with the Fleet'.

He went on to look at the implications of these additional requirements which cumulatively amounted to increased weight. 'It will be fairly obvious therefore that the one outstanding problem in the naval fighter design is to keep weight to the irreducible minimum, to which must now be added the difficulty of providing sufficient volume in the aeroplane to house the various loads without adding drag.' In considering how this should be approached, he touched on secret trials that had been in progress at RAE Farnborough which entailed the development of aircraft without an undercarriage, the machine landing on a cushioned deck; these trials, perhaps inevitably, resulted in the decision that it was a dead end, not because the procedure did not work but because of the difficulties of manhandling a multi-ton aircraft with no undercarriage on a heaving deck. Camm's words to summarise this were perhaps prescient when he said 'thus we are forced to examine the possibilities of radical changes in future design of the single-seat naval fighter aircraft'. While Camm was discussing the Sea Hawk era, he might just as well have been referring to the V/STOL Harrier, which so greatly simplified the relationship between aircraft and carrier that few changes were needed to allow for Harrier's use from ships at sea: no catapults, no arrestor gear, no blast shields, no wing folding; truly a revolution in naval air development that, unfortunately, was less than welcome during the febrile political atmosphere of the 1960s and 70s.[3]

It will be evident that I have included the Hawker Horsley in the types produced by HG Hawker Engineering. Although not a fighter, it did give the Royal Navy an effective strike capability during the early post-First War years with its ability to carry a torpedo or bombs. It was also Hawker's largest aircraft to date.

It should be noted here that where aircraft totals are given, as, for example in examples of each type manufactured and taken into service, there exists much confusion as to numbers, particularly for the years up to the Armistice of 1918. This situation was not helped by the practice of transferring aircraft between the RNAS and RFC, often without renumbering individual aircraft, and also returning to service many aircraft previously noted as damaged, wrecked or deleted, often with a new serial number. Furthermore, towards the end of the First World War, many aircraft already ordered were cancelled, some having already been built! Where possible therefore, reliance has been placed on the work of Ray Sturtivant and Gordon Page for Air Britain, which offered the most accurate information at time of writing.[4] Information on aircraft carriers has in the main been drawn from *British Aircraft Carriers* by W.G.D. Blundell, 1969. Though long out of print, it is a useful round-up of carrier design from 1911 to 1969.

Chapter 1

The Birth of Naval Aviation

One day in November 1910 a lecture was delivered to interested members of the Royal Navy at its Sheerness naval sub-depot regarding the new (to the military) and fascinating interest in heavier-than-air flight. It was this meeting which, more than anything else, marked the beginnings of the Royal Naval Air Service. Earlier interest in aerial pursuits had revolved around lighter-than-air craft – balloons and kites – and indeed the Royal Navy had commissioned its own dirigible in 1909 for £35,000. Officially named HMA.1 *Hermione*, it was nicknamed 'Mayfly' (it didn't); the craft had come to grief in September 1911 on its first outing at Barrow-in-Furness as it was removed from its shed, effectively ending for the moment Royal Navy interest in lighter-than-air craft, though later, in the First World War, airships were used around the coast on anti-submarine duties, staffed by the RNAS. The lecture concluded with a call for volunteers to be trained in the new discipline and, from 500 names, four were chosen to proceed. The first four chosen – Lieutenants Arthur Longmore (later Air Chief Marshal), Charles Rumney Samson (later Air Commodore), R. Gregory RN, and Lieutenant E.L. Gerrard RM – began their training at Eastchurch on the Isle of Sheppey in Kent, the aircraft concerned being two Short biplanes (Short Brothers had moved their aircraft works to Leysdown on the island earlier in the year), with instruction provided by G.B. Cockburn via the Royal Aero Club. This somewhat haphazard arrangement nevertheless provided the four intrepid sailors with sufficient training that, after six months, they were considered sufficiently qualified to begin the task of instructing the next batch of naval recruits.

Such then were the beginnings of naval aviation in the United Kingdom and these efforts rapidly expanded as more efficient aircraft became available. Already, thoughts had turned to the use of aircraft in an offensive capacity, ideas being formulated for their use as bombers or even torpedo-carriers, though not yet as fighters. By the start of the 1914–18 war, the naval force was sufficient to tackle operations in support of the fleet and prove that it was not a mere flash in the pan. In the opening stages of the war, aircraft use was considered primarily to be for reconnaissance and spotting the fall of shot for the fleet. Added to this would be the responsibility for home defence, the protection of the shores of the UK against intrusions by enemy balloons and, particularly, the feared Zeppelins.

However, to be of any significant use to the Royal Navy, some means had to be achieved of actually taking the aircraft to sea with the fleet and it was to this end that experiments led to the first launch of an aircraft from an RN ship, Lieutenant Samson taking off from a primitive decking erected above the forward gun turret of HMS *Africa* off Chatham in a Short S.27 biplane fitted with air bags on 10 January 1912 while the ship was stopped. On 2 May he bettered this feat by launching from HMS *Hibernia* while it was underway

HMS *Ark Royal* c.1918, showing aircraft on the foredeck and the derricks required to lift them in and out of the water. First laid down as a collier, the ship was taken over by the Admiralty and commissioned as an aircraft carrier in December 1914.

at about 15 knots in a Short S.38. Both these experiments took place from a jury-rigged platform on the foredeck, there being no way for the aircraft to land back aboard. By now, the pace of aeronautical advance was increasing. On 13 April that same year, the Royal Flying Corps was formed and, on 1 July, a Naval Wing was formed within the former organisation – the Royal Naval Air Service – under the command of Charles Samson. It was under this title that the Royal Navy would go to war in the air.[1]

In Monte Carlo in March 1912 a meeting was held to exhibit the progress made with so-called 'hydro-aeroplanes' (not very much); it was evident that use from anything but sheltered water would be impractical at this stage. In any event, the first practical means of taking aircraft to sea was by fitting them with floats, thus allowing them to be lowered from the deck into the sea for take-off and craning them back aboard on completion of the sortie (always assuming that the pilot could find his ship again).

Early experiments with floatplanes for the Royal Navy began when Lieutenant Oliver Schwann RN fitted a privately-purchased aircraft with floats and gas bags and managed to take off from water in November 1911. Lieutenant Longmore also achieved this feat on 1 December, the Short S.27 being fitted with airbags. However, this was not an ideal solution; often the fragile floats would be broken by wave action and even a moderate swell could make the difference between a successful take-off and landing or an ignominious recovery of the aircraft to the deck. But, for now, this was the only alternative if aircraft were to carry out sorties at sea out of range of the shore (though experiments with marine-hulled aircraft – flying boats – were also undertaken). HMS *Hermes* was the first Royal Navy ship to be formally converted as an aircraft carrier, or more accurately, a seaplane tender, having previously been a light cruiser of the Highflyer and class. She had first been commissioned in 1898 and was recommissioned in May 1913 for trials work

HMS *Furious*, c.1918, showing the flying-off deck over the bows. The aft alighting deck appears to be in place by this time. Laid down as a light cruiser, she was completed as a carrier, initially in 1916 and heavily modified in 1918.

associated with the carriage of seaplanes. For this work launching rails were mounted on the foredeck, backed by a canvas hangar and derricks for handling the aircraft on and off the ship. Brought out of reserve at the outbreak of war for ferrying aircraft to France, she was sunk by *U-27* in October 1914.

A further conversion was HMS *Ark Royal*. Laid down as a collier in late 1913 but taken over by the Admiralty and completed as a seaplane carrier, she was commissioned in December 1914. Before heading for the Mediterranean, she embarked her aircraft complement – two Sopwith Tabloids, three Sopwith Seaplanes, two Wrights and a Short. With these she would take part in the ill-fated Dardanelles campaign, the aircraft being used for reconnaissance and gun spotting for the capital ships with mixed results.

The fragile and uncertain condition of aircraft of those early days can perhaps be illustrated by a flight made in June 1911 by the four intrepid sailors. Not long qualified as pilots, it was decided that a momentous journey of over fifty miles should be made from Eastchurch to Brooklands in Surrey where early aviation experiments were progressing on the famous motor-racing track laid out by Hugh Locke King. Two aircraft would be used with Samson and Gregory flying there and Longmore and Gerrard flying back. Samson got away but Gregory's aircraft failed to start, Samson not getting too far before a forced landing resulted in a broken rigging wire. The other aviators, following in a motor car, were able to repair the damage and see Samson back into the air after which they followed on by road and reached Brooklands with no sign of Samson, who had missed Brooklands and carried on. Samson finally reaching Brooklands the next day, the four spent a pleasant time watching the motor sport and noticing that the Brooklands-based pilots were flying in rather stronger winds than they had yet attempted. On the return journey to Eastchurch, Longmore, now piloting the aircraft, had to force land on Walton Heath golf links due to engine woes before finally arriving back at base for a late breakfast.

With continuing development of aircraft, it became possible for Arthur Longmore (now Squadron Commander) to lift off from Calshot on 28 July 1914 carrying a torpedo beneath his Short Folder seaplane and successfully launch it at sea. This seemingly quantum leap in offensive capability was however a one-off, Longmore admitting that, 'It all worked well but, of course, it was a "stunt".' Notwithstanding such 'stunts', a Naval

HMS *Furious*, with flying-off and alighting decks in place. Note the naval airship on the after deck – an SSZ (Submarine Scout Zero) type, probably SSZ-59.

Allocation List of January 1914 noted a total of 120 aircraft, almost certainly a mistake or overcounting since another assessment in July showed the RNAS to have on strength fifty-two seaplanes and flying boats: thirty-nine landplanes and six airships available for operations, a more realistic figure.[2]

In April 1912 the Royal Flying Corps had been established, comprising the aircraft of the Royal Navy and the Army, such as then existed (becoming official in May 1912). However, the RFC came under the control of the War Office, the Army's department of state, the Admiralty not having a controlling presence, clearly not a situation that would sit well with the Senior Service. The RFC then comprised a Military Wing, a Naval Wing and a joint-service Central Flying School at Upavon, Wiltshire. Largely at the prompting of Captain Murray Sueter, first Inspecting Captain of Naval Aviation, Director Air Department, by July 1914 the Admiralty and Royal Navy had largely regained control of their air assets, the Royal Naval Air Service (RNAS) being considered as confirmed on 1 July 1914.

By 1913 naval air stations had been established at Dundee, Calshot at Southampton, Isle of Grain, Felixstowe, Fort George and Great Yarmouth and a flying school at Eastchurch on the Isle of Sheppey and a complement of 828 officers and other ranks. Through 1913 and the early months of 1914, work continued to make the naval aeroplane a more trustworthy

HMS *Furious* c.1918 with Sopwith 2F.1 Camels on deck. Note that the roundels have been painted over as an aid to low visibility.

and useful piece of equipment, trials including torpedo and gun carriage, aerial telegraphy and headlights for night flying, good results being achieved with the Sopwith Bat Boat.

On 4 August 1914, the United Kingdom found itself at war with Germany and its allies. The RNAS quickly mobilised, firstly by delivering aircraft to east coast air stations for use in patrolling the North Sea and the Channel and, secondly, by preparing to decamp to the continent to begin building up a base at Dunkirk under Wing Commander Samson with aircraft and armoured cars. As the first squadrons began arriving, they were directed to Ostend on the 27th of the month, followed by naval units deploying to Antwerp on 3 October. At sea, HMS *Hermes* and *Ark Royal*, the RNAS's seaplane tenders, were quickly supplemented by further carriers converted from coastal shipping. The cross-channel steamers *Engadine*, *Riviera* and *Empress* were taken up by the Admiralty in 1914 and converted at Chatham, also becoming seaplane carriers with a useful turn of speed. Once their use had been assessed, further cross-channel shipping was taken up – *Ben-My-Chree*, *Manxman* and *Vindex* – which were fitted with a flying-off platform in the bows.

The purpose of the RNAS depot at Dunkirk was summarised by Wing Commander Longmore as follows:

1) To endeavour to prevent Zeppelins and aeroplanes operating from bases in Belgium for raids on England.
2) To attack enemy submarines using Ostend and Zeebrugge.
3) To co-operate with monitors (i.e. gunships), both in spotting for their bombardments and protecting them from aerial attacks.
4) To obtain information by coastal reconnaissance, as to movement of ships at Ostend and Zeebrugge.
5) To develop aerial photography and wireless communication from aircraft under active service conditions.

Clearly Dunkirk would be an important base for the RNAS. On 6 June 1915, with three German airships up and heading for England, a detachment of RNAS No.1 Squadron pilots was sent aloft to counter them. Lieutenant Warneford in a Morane caught sight of LZ.37 near Bruges and managed to climb above it before dropping 20lb bombs and destroying it; the destruction of a Zeppelin in the air brought Warneford a well-deserved VC. Other pilots – Wilson and Mills in Henri Farmans – found LZ.38 in its hangar and were able to destroy that one as well.[3]

At this stage of the war most RNAS squadron aircraft would operate from land bases in concert with the military wing of the RFC, though occasional sorties would be made from sea by aircraft flying from the two aircraft carrier/seaplane tenders *Hermes* and *Ark Royal*. As noted earlier, the Royal Navy, as the traditional protector of UK shores, had undertaken to provide what protection it could from aerial attack from Zeppelins and, later, aircraft. However, the Zeppelins were notoriously difficult craft to engage, being able to quickly rise above the ceiling of the early defending aircraft. It was therefore decided that attack on the dirigibles on the ground offered a rather more sporting chance

Squadron Commander Edwin Dunning attempting to land his Sopwith Pup on the foredeck of HMS *Furious*. After an initial success, his subsequent attempt resulted in his aircraft crashing into the sea, Dunning being killed. The handling loops, added to enable the ground crew a purchase on the alighting aircraft, can be seen under the wing and fuselage.

of destroying them. As early as 8 October 1914, an RNAS Sopwith Tabloid destroyed Zeppelin LZ.25 in its shed at Dusseldorf using primitive bombs, quickly followed by a less successful attack at Friedrichshafen on 21 October by Avro 504s. These land-based sorties were then followed on 25 December by a seaborne attack from the seaplane tenders *Engadine*, *Riviera* and *Empress* on the airship sheds at Cuxhaven. Seven Short Folders took part in the raid which, although only partially successful, demonstrated the potential for sea-launched attacks against the enemy.

Taken up in 1914 from the threat of scrappage, the old Cunard liner *Campania* was rapidly converted to a seaplane carrier and, following commissioning in 1915, was capable of flying off seaplanes (on trollies) from her forward ramp. To allow more room for this

HMS *Argus* c.1918. Built from the partially complete hull of the Italian liner *Conte Rosso*. Launched in 1918, it featured a completely unobstructed flightdeck.

ramp, the forward funnel was split and replaced by two smaller funnels with the ramp passing between them to give a longer take-off run. With the poor performance of the seaplane, both on the water and in the air, her seaplanes were replaced by wheeled aircraft fitted with flotation equipment to enable a landing back – of sorts – adjacent to the ship.

The evolution of the aircraft carrier from converted collier capable of carrying aircraft but not deck launching them, to the flat-topped ships that are recognised today as aircraft carriers occurred fairly quickly, driven by the exigencies of the First World War. HMS *Furious* was used extensively as a trials ship. Beginning life as a Courageous-class battlecruiser design, she was converted during construction by the removal of her forward turret and replacement by a flight deck, thus allowing aircraft to take off but not to land. In an effort to overcome this, Squadron Commander Edwin Dunning used a Sopwith Pup to demonstrate the feasibility of landing on this forward deck, though the requirement to jink around the superstructure before lining up for a landing made it a hazardous enterprise. Indeed, after an initial successful attempt or two (sources differ) his next saw the aircraft go over the side and Dunning was killed.

Later on, a further experiment was trialled by the removal of the rear turret to construct a landing deck over the stern but problems with turbulence from funnel gasses and superstructure led to further work which included a round down at the stern. After the war, work in the 1920s saw the complete removal of the superstructure, allowing a three-quarter-length flight deck to be constructed. The original flying-off deck was retained, the new deck terminating short of, and above, this. Under the new deck were constructed two hangars, an upper and lower, the upper hangar opening on to the forward deck, thus allowing aircraft to be removed from the hangar and take off without impinging on landing operations on the deck above. HMS *Furious* would have a long life, seeing action in the Second World War and finally being scrapped in 1948. Her service period had allowed the detail of just what an aircraft carrier should consist of to be worked out prior to this being applied to new designs.

HMS *Vindictive*, commissioned in 1917, was another attempt to create the best platform for aircraft to take off and land aboard. She followed the then state of play displayed in HMS *Furious* with separate flying-off and landing-on decks but, as noted above, this was found to be a cul-de-sac. HMS *Argus*, converted from the Italian liner *Conte Rosso* while still under construction, took the need for a clear deck to the extreme, having no superstructure whatever, but was only commissioned just prior to the Armistice and therefore, in concert with two further aircraft carriers building – *Eagle* and a new *Hermes* – did not see action in the First World War. However, *Argus* did stage a trial with Sopwith Cuckoo torpedo bombers.

Sopwith 1½ Strutter being loaded aboard the US Navy battleship USS *Oklahoma* from the ship's motor launch, in Guantanamo Bay, Cuba, circa 1921. A similar cumbersome process was followed on RN ships. (*USNHHC*)

Probably the same Sopwith 1½ Strutter being loaded onto the USS *Oklahoma*. This image gives a good view of the flying-off platform attached to the turret in the foreground. This allowed aircraft to be launched into wind more easily. (*USNHHC*)

HMS *Eagle*, which began life as the Chilean battleship *Almirante Cochrane*, was bought by the Admiralty at the start of the war with a view to conversion to an aircraft carrier. By the time that reconstruction of this design began in 1917, the time was ripe for the aircraft carrier to mature into the form that would endure through to the end of the Second World War. With a length of 661 feet and beam of 105 feet, displacing 22,790 tons, she had a useful maximum speed of 24 knots and could accommodate up to thirty aircraft. The flight deck offered uninterrupted take-off and landing with the ability to go round again after a wave-off. Her superstructure and twin funnels were grouped in a compact island well to starboard midships and two lifts gave access to hangar space below the flight deck. Completed in 1924, she served mainly on the Mediterranean station and would, following various refits, be active in the Second World War, being eventually sunk in 1942.

By 1918, aircraft were also being carried on the Navy's capital ships, many super dreadnoughts being equipped with flying-off platforms on B and X turrets to enable launch of, typically a float-equipped Sopwith 1½ Strutter or Pup for scouting purposes, this being accepted as a positive enhancement. Many cruisers would also come to sport an aircraft or two mounted for catapult launch, into the 1920s. As an alternative, some other battleships were modified to accept kite balloons, again for reconnaissance purposes, though of less utility than an aircraft able to range ahead of the fleet.

Thus, then, at the end of the Great War, the Royal Navy had progressed from no carriers to twelve, in various stages of evolution, from basic seaplane tender to fully-fledged aircraft carrier. The Armistice and peace would see most of these ships either returned to trade,

Sopwith Camels on the USS *Texas*, 1919, one each on a forward and aft turret, this being a typical arrangement also in the Royal Navy. (*USNHHC*)

laid up or scrapped. The opposition would not come from the German navy but from Whitehall and the newly-fledged Royal Air Force. While the successes of the RNAS in the First World War were undoubted, this did not prevent the service being swallowed again by the RFC when, on 1 April 1918, it was announced that the Naval and Military Wings of the RFC were to be subsumed into a new Royal Air Force. While the RAF would fight for its very existence over the next decade, the naval element would fare poorly in relation to the land element, being reliant on the RAF for funding for aircraft, funding that was always less than desired and which meant that performance of naval aircraft ranked second to land-based designs for many years.

With the signing of the Armistice on 11 November 1918, the fighting on the continental battlefields more or less ceased, save for isolated pockets of friction. UK forces began a demobilisation of servicemen in all three services and, as time went by, the myth that the recent conflict had been the 'War to End all Wars' gained credence with the public at large who saw no further need for expensive armaments. In the Royal Navy, the aircraft carriers became early casualties and were fairly quickly decommissioned. On the battlefields of Belgium, large scrapheaps of tanks were left to rust and, in the air, the Royal Air Force, just a year old, saw vast reductions in its strength. At the formation of the RAF in April 1918, the RNAS had on charge some 2,900 aircraft and a staff of 55,000 officers and

T.O.M. Sopwith seated in his Howard Wright biplane at Brooklands in Surrey. c.1912. The fragility of the airframe is readily apparent. (*BL*)

Sopwith's Bat Boat on the water about to take off, c.1913; this was the first (and only) flying-boat design from Sopwith. (*BL*)

The prototype Sopwith Type St.B at Brooklands with T.O.M. Sopwith and his pilot Harry Hawker, c.1913. The first aircraft was a twin-seater, production versions were single-seat and styled Sopwith SS, more popularly known as the Tabloid. (*BL*)

men, these being taken into the expanded service such that, at the Armistice, the RAF comprised 200 squadrons, 22,500 aircraft, 103 airships and 290,000 officers and men. Within two years, the service numbered 26,000 men and just a few squadrons of aircraft. For the RAF, this period was a fight for life, one plan being to dismantle the service and return the remaining aircraft and men to the Army and Royal Navy. Trenchard, as Chief of the Air Staff, was left fighting for its very existence.

Such then were the beginnings of the Royal Navy's aerial conflict in the First World War. Quickly, aircraft use led to specialised designs tailored to the mission, be it bombing, reconnaissance or what was termed 'scouting'. These early scouts were the first fighters, their role being to literally scout ahead of the Army and take on any enemy aircraft met in combat and best them. It was in the scouting role that Sopwith aircraft would predominate, this early specialisation becoming the hallmark of the Sopwith and Hawker designs which are discussed in the following chapters.

Chapter 2

Sopwith Aircraft

Thomas Octave Murdoch Sopwith was the only son of Thomas Sopwith, a successful civil engineer. On the death of his father in tragic circumstances (young Sopwith shot him dead while on a boating excursion), TOM inherited and thus, at a young age, was able to indulge his youthful passions to the full. From balloons to fast cars and boats to aeroplanes, he was to be found wherever thrills and spills were to be had. In an interview with *Flight* magazine in 1979, he noted:

> Charles Rolls and I used to balloon together before either of us flew, in 1906 …. He was a very keen motorist …. Lord Brabazon was a friend of mine at the same time when we were all ballooning before we got into powered flight. I started ballooning in 1906. I stuck to it for only a couple of years, then gradually drifted into powered flying.

When T.O.M. Sopwith made the fateful decision to begin the manufacture of aircraft for sale, his nautical interests no doubt played a part in the subsequent support obtained for the nascent company from the Royal Navy. Being something of a young man about town and with a sizeable income to support him, Sopwith had been drawn to the new and exciting possibilities opened up, firstly by the craze for ballooning (he co-owned his own) and, when this palled, by the even more exciting opportunities offered by motor vehicles – motorcycles and cars – the faster the better. Sailing was his next adventure, speedboats and yachting offering new thrills and the purchase of the sloop *Neva* with Bill Eyre in which to further explore his quest for aquatic speed. This ownership would have brought him into social contact with members of the Royal Navy, contacts that would later pay dividends.

Having sampled the very early aeroplanes at Brooklands in Surrey, the motor-racing track laid out on his land by Hugh Locke King, Sopwith quickly taught himself to fly, being awarded his pilot's certificate (Royal Aero Club Certificate No.31). With the aid of his yacht engineer, Fred Sigrist, he began successfully to compete for cash prizes in the UK before deciding to travel to the USA to display his new craft and hopefully win some of the competitions being staged there. In this he was successful and, on his return to the UK, he set up a flying school at Brooklands in late 1911 offering tuition in one of four aircraft: an American Burgess-Wright biplane, a Howard Wright biplane, a Blériot-type monoplane or Howard Wright monoplane, before moving into the modification of existing aircraft and the construction of new machines. With Sigrist now a constant presence at Brooklands, the flying school, one of several at the site, set about teaching all-comers ('Boom' Trenchard was one) the technicalities of flight, repairing the aircraft after the inevitable crashes and modifying them to better suit the school's use. One of those taught to fly by Sopwith was Harry Hawker, a young Australian who had obtained employment with him in June and who proved to be a natural pilot with innate ability. As the school aircraft became less and less original due to the frequent alterations made to them, the decision was taken to offer them for sale, at first as modified types; entirely new designs were later sold. Sopwith's and Sigrist's first efforts were lavished on the Burgess-Wright biplane, purchased in the USA and subsequently used for training at the school. (Burgess built Wright designs under licence in the USA.) The pair modified this design by replacing the Gnome engine with a 40hp ABC engine and adding an offset fabric-covered nacelle to offer some protection to the pilot. The aircraft was then used by Harry Hawker to win the October 1912 British Empire Michelin Cup No.1 and £500, with a flight of 8 hours 23 minutes, a new duration record.

Pleased with this success, their next effort was more adventurous and comprised a tractor biplane using the 70 hp Gnome engine from Sopwith's Bleriot and the wings from the Burgess-Wright coupled to a new fuselage based on the Burgess-Wright. First flown by Sopwith and then by Hawker, the Hybrid, as it was known, was sufficiently successful to attract the interest of Commander Oliver Schwann (later Swan) of the Naval Wing of the RFC who arranged for it to be purchased by the Admiralty for £900 – Sopwith's first sale. Sopwith remembered that, 'In due course the tractor was taken to Eastchurch, where its most useful purpose was flying regularly to Whitstable to fetch oysters for the Naval Mess.' Having suffered the rigours of life as a naval aircraft, by May 1913 the machine

The Sopwith D1 three-seater tractor was one of Sopwith's first new designs. Displayed at the 1913 Olympia Aero Exhibition, it was purchased by the Admiralty. The aircraft, powered by an 80hp Gnome rotary engine, featured wing warping, twin tailskids and clear-view panels for observation. (*BL*)

was suitable only for taxiing practice and was returned to the Sopwith works in June 1913 for conversion to a D.1 three-seater before returning to Eastchurch, being finally struck off in May 1914.[1]

With the preponderance of flying schools now in operation, both at Brooklands and Larkhill, Sopwith turned his attention to fulltime manufacture of aircraft. The new Sopwith Aviation Company, created on 15 December 1913 as a private limited liability company with a nominal capital of £26,000, obtained premises in nearby Kingston upon Thames, the former roller-skating rink in Canbury Park Road, which provided suitable accommodation for the company's activities. The first designs produced by the new Sopwith Aviation Company, a three-seat tractor biplane and a flying boat, were displayed on the Sopwith stand at the Olympia Aero Exhibition of February 1913 and created something of a sensation due to their advanced structure and immaculate finish. The three-seater, officially the 'Sopwith Tractor Aeroplane' Three-Seater Biplane, drawn by R.J. Ashfield in January 1913, had two bay wings while the fuselage included clear-view windows for the passengers and was powered by a Gnome Monosoupape engine of 80hp, giving a good turn of speed of 73.6mph (though the brochure only claimed 40–70 mph). The flying boat, more properly the 'Sopwith Hydro Biplane', also known as the 'Bat Boat', began as a two-seat tractor biplane that featured a hull designed and built by boat-builders Saunders of Cowes and was initially (1912) powered by a 70hp Gnome rotary engine mounted on the centre-section struts. The requirement for hydrodynamic shaping of the hull was poorly understood with the result that the planing bottom was likely to be ineffective. The aircraft appears not to have flown.

Sopwith Bat Boat modified for the Mortimer Singer competition by the addition of a retractable undercarriage. This version sported twin rudders and won the competition. (*BL*)

However, the concept was revived and as Bat Boat BB1, now in a pusher configuration, appears to have been the first Sopwith machine constructed in the newly acquired Kingston Skating Rink in January 1913 and the first aircraft for which proper drawings were issued, these being numbered D.0001. This machine was designed as a pusher powered by a 90hp Austro-Daimler water-cooled engine and was one of the two aircraft exhibited by Sopwith on their stand at the Olympia Show of February 1913 where it was purchased by the Admiralty for £1,500. However, such was the urge to get the machine to the Olympia Show that testing only started after it had closed, where the machine showed a studied reluctance to leave the water. Sopwith managed to climb a few feet but then stalled and damaged the aircraft as a result, this being exacerbated by rough weather during the night, the Sopwith order book commenting that it had been 'smashed in trials'. Sopwith instructed the works to begin construction of a new Bat Boat (BB2) to fulfil the Admiralty order, together with a further machine (BB3) for company use, this being possibly a rebuild of BB1.

Bat Boat BB2 was assembled at Salterns Yard in Hamble though built by Sopwith at Kingston, including the hull, and delivered to the Admiralty in June 1913. This again featured the 90hp Austro-Daimler engine but various modifications were included to the rudder and wings to improve the machine aerodynamically. BB3 was constructed for company use with the intention of entering it for the Mortimer Singer prize for an all-British aircraft that could 'rise from and alight on land and water', for which a wheeled undercarriage and an all British engine were required. A Green 100hp in-line water-cooled engine was chosen for this attempt, which was successful, the aircraft being flown by Harry Hawker to win the £500 prize in July 1913 with a speed of around 65mph. This aircraft was then sold to the Admiralty with the 90hp engine fitted. It appears that a total of four Bat Boats were taken up by the Admiralty and numbered 38, 118, 127 and 879.[2] In the Sopwith brochure, which accompanied the Olympia Exhibition, it was noted that the company motto 'Strength through Efficiency' applied to all of its products and it was the intention that:

> the Company will specialise in two types of machines – the Bat Boat Hydro-Aeroplane and the Tractor Biplane, but they are at the same time prepared to construct any type of Hydro-Aeroplane, Biplane or Monoplane as may be required by their customers, and quotations will readily be given for any of these types.

Quite how soon this requirement would come to fruition was probably absent from Sopwith's thoughts at the time. Both types, the D1 tractor and the Bat Boat pusher, were purchased in small numbers by the Admiralty (thirteen D1s and four Bat Boats) but it was a new design, also produced in 1913, that would revolutionise aircraft design.[3]

The new aircraft, the Type St.B, later known as the Tabloid, featured a layout that would predominate until the arrival of cantilever monoplanes in the mid-1930s. It had originated in the fertile imagination of Harry Hawker, who was proposing to return to Australia to visit his parents and who had persuaded Sopwith that it might pay dividends to make it also a Sopwith sales tour. To that end, Hawker, with Sopwith and Sigrist, had schemed a diminutive aeroplane to take with him, lofting it on the skating-rink floor, its small size and simplicity of design ensuring a minimum of problems in the Antipodes. Harold Penrose recalled T.O.M. Sopwith's comment that:

> Design was rather a family affair, but I would give most credit to Harry Hawker. Hawker had a crack at it, Fred Sigrist had a crack at it, I had, and so had all the boys in the shop – but Harry Hawker was the chief instigator.

A two-seat tractor biplane powered by a 80hp Gnome rotary engine, the prototype Tabloid offered comparatively sleek styling, compact form and a closely-cowled engine, the first flight from Brooklands taking place in November 1913. At a subsequent test later that month at Farnborough, the Tabloid achieved 92mph with full fuel *and* a passenger, as good as the Royal Aircraft Factory's latest offering, the BS.1/SE.2, but with heavier load and smaller engine. Such was the confidence in the Tabloid design that Sopwith decided to enter a floatplane version in the 1914 Schneider Trophy competition in Monaco. Flown by Howard Pixton (Hawker was by then in Australia with the prototype) on 20 April, Pixton won at an average speed of 87mph. R. Dallas Brett, a contemporary writer, said of the result:

> It is difficult to convey the atmosphere of astonishment created by Pixton's flight. Hitherto, the English pilots had been regarded with mild amusement whenever they dared to compete with the French experts, and English aircraft were frankly ridiculed in France. The French had been taken by surprise but it was not as if some English machine had snatched a lucky victory through the misfortunes of the other competitors. On the contrary it was abundantly clear that the combination of Harold Pixton and the Sopwith Tabloid was immeasurably superior to any other combination of pilot and seaplane on the continent of Europe.

On the basis of these results, both the Military and Naval Wings of the RFC placed orders just prior to and in the early months of the war, the RNAS ordering eighteen machines and the Military Wing another four, these being single-seat aircraft officially styled the Sopwith SS. C.G. Grey, the irascible editor of the *Aeroplane*, said of the Tabloid:

> A real sensation has been created by the appearance of the new Sopwith biplane 80hp Gnome which is the Sopwith company's first attempt at building a really fast machine. There is no doubt the machine will astonish those who have been led to believe, thanks to the British authorities and the British Press, that we have no manufacturers worthy of consideration in the country.[4]

As the war began, a number of seaplane types had been or were in the process of being produced in small numbers for the RNAS, although none were particularly successful.

They included the HT Seaplane, closely based on the D1, which did not fare at all well, being considered unsuitable in France. This was followed by the Type 137, a large tractor seaplane theoretically capable of torpedo carriage although trials were uninspiring. Also produced, again in small numbers, were the Type S Hydro-Aeroplane, the Gunbus Seaplane, the Type 806 Gunbus and the Type 880 Seaplane. Around the same time, the Type 807, initially finished as a single-seat seaplane and powered by a 100hp Gnome Monosoupape rotary engine offering around 80mph, was constructed. Based on the Circuit of Britain design, it was also known as the Sopwith Folder, employing as it did the Short patented wing-fold mechanism for ship stowage, some twelve being delivered and used in the Aegean during the First World War with limited success. Next came the Type 860 seaplane, which was an altogether larger two-seat machine powered by a 225hp Sunbeam engine, which appears to have sported two different wing forms. One had a three-bay biplane arrangement and the other a two-bay with unequal span wings, at least twenty-two being ordered, although it was not met with anything approaching praise on arrival at the squadrons. Thus, by 1914, a number of designs had been completed but few were considered successful.

At the opening of the conflict that later generations would remember as the Great War and, after 1945, the First World War, Sopwith Aviation had been able to sell forty-eight aircraft to the RNAS, comprising some eleven different designs, well within the small handwork facilities that comprised the Sopwith works. However, as the war progressed, this would not be sustainable and many, indeed most, Sopwith orders would be fulfilled using sub-contract companies.

With regard to the Royal Navy's responsibility for protection on the Home Front, the constant thorn in their Lordships' flesh was the seeming impunity with which the German Zeppelin airships could cruise over the UK in reconnaissance and bombing raids. They were also used as forward reconnaissance assets whenever the High Seas Fleet sought to sally out into the North Sea. The destruction of the airships thus became central to Home Front defence policy as ways and means to counter the threat were considered. A two-pronged offensive policy was evolved that centred on the use of aircraft, firstly to attack directly the Zeppelin in the air and, secondly, to attack the Zeppelin bases. It was hoped that such attacks might have the providential benefit of stinging the High Seas Fleet into action in the North Sea, where it could be attacked by the Grand Fleet and seriously mauled. What was needed as far as aircraft were concerned were, it was decided, fast agile single-seat fighters (floatplanes obviously) with which to tangle with the high flying Zeppelins – enter the Sopwith Schneider.

Schneider/Baby

Based on the winning entry in the 1914 Schneider Trophy contest at Monaco, itself based on the Sopwith Tabloid of 1913, the Schneider was hopefully just what the RNAS needed, a fast (relatively) lightweight single-seat floatplane powered by a 100hp Gnome Monosoupape rotary capable of launch at sea and theoretically capable of reaching the

Float-equipped Sopwith Baby 8172 (one of a batch of 100) at Turks Albany Boat House on the Thames at Lower Ham Road, a conveniently short distance from the Sopwith factory. (*BL*)

Zeppelins in flight. Entering service in 1915 the Schneider – and its development into the Baby – gave the RNAS a worthwhile single-seat scout. Initially configured for carriage of light bombs (the Zeppelin was to be attacked from above), it later featured a Lewis gun mounted on the top wing to allow more realistic attack from below. Orders for the aircraft for the RNAS were the first really large batches that Sopwith had received, some 136 Schneiders and modified Schneiders being ordered in 1915. The plan for these aircraft was to launch them in the North Sea from seaplane carriers to enable them to target the airships as they flew towards the UK coast, a plan that met with singular failure. Other activities saw the RNAS aircraft involved in the Dardanelles campaign, flying from HMS *Ark Royal* on reconnaissance duties, but they did not particularly distinguish themselves. In particular, it was found that the floats of the Schneider frequently broke off while attempting to take-off or land in anything other than flat calm conditions and numbers of aircraft were lost in this way, much to the displeasure of the Royal Navy. The developed Schneider, the Baby, was rather more successful, being widely built in the UK (287 built), sub-contracted to various companies, to clear space for Sopwith's Kingston works to concentrate on later designs, the Blackburn Aeroplane Company, Fairey Aviation and Parnall & Sons building considerable numbers. The Baby featured aileron control rather than wing warping and also a larger tailplane and was powered by the more powerful 110hp Clerget 9Z.

The problem of the unreliability and fragility of these floatplanes was exemplified by an attempted raid on the Tondern Zeppelin sheds with which it was hoped to lure the High Seas Fleet out of their anchorages on 4 May 1916. HMS *Vindex* and *Engadine* approached the coast with the intention of launching their eleven Sopwith Babies for the attack. During attempts to get the aircraft into the air, four of them broke their propellers, three suffered engine failure and one capsized in the wash of an accompanying destroyer. Three Babies successfully became airborne, of which one fouled the wireless aerial of the destroyer *Goshawk* and immediately crashed, the second returned with engine problems and only one actually reached Tondern, where its two bombs missed the target. After the various versions of the Baby, Sopwith machines increasingly, and understandably, dispensed with float undercarriage, becoming essentially land planes.[5]

1½ Strutter

In early June 1915 T.O.M. Sopwith, acting on information received from the battlefield that all was not well with his aircraft, requested permission to travel to France to discuss the situation with the pilots themselves and ask what they wanted from their aircraft. Touring the various aerodromes and talking to the pilots gave Sopwith a much clearer understanding of the problems and the solutions desired by the pilots. The result was three new designs which proceeded almost simultaneously in the Drawing Office at Kingston – the 1½ Strutter, the Pup and the Triplane.

Sopwith 1½ Strutter Type 9700 single-seat bomber version N5504. The aircraft survived the war to become G-EAVB. (*BL*)

Sopwith 1½ Strutter Type 9400 fighter N5093 seen at Brooklands in suitably aggressive pose. (*Author*)

Sopwith 1½ Strutter Type 9400. This aircraft – A1924 – was part of an order of 30 for the RNAS, transferred to the RFC. It appears to be about to undergo an engine check, given the 'erks' holding the tailskid down.

Considered by some to be the first true fighter, the Sopwith LCT, better known as the 1½ Strutter, first flew in December 1915. It was a twin-seat, rotary-engined design (110hp Clerget) giving a speed of around 96mph with single-bay wings. The cleanliness of the design produced a high landing speed for which, as compensation, primitive air brakes were fitted at the wing root trailing edge of the lower wings. The aircraft entered service with the RNAS in 1916 with just a single Lewis gun on a swivelling mount for the observer but this was later supplemented by a single fixed Vickers gun for the pilot, thereby becoming the first Allied machine capable of firing through the propeller arc, thanks to its gun synchronisation gear (a version developed by Sopwith and Harry Kauper). Large quantities of the type were sent to No.5 Wing RNAS at Dunkirk for use in the battle over the trenches. Later deliveries saw the fuselage framing restructured to incorporate a bomb-bay (with the loss of the observer's cockpit) and the transfer of a quantity of the machines to the RFC to assist in the Somme offensive, some sixty machines being transferred. It appears that most 1½ Strutters destined for the RNAS were transferred to the Military Wing of the RFC, either after service with the RNAS or directly from the factory. Of some 1,365 produced, 459 were ordered directly by the RNAS, which also received transfers from RFC orders, seventy machines being specifically issued as Ship's Strutters.

Typical of the actions of the 1½ Strutters based at Dunkirk with No.5 Wing RNAS was a raid on 9 August 1916 when two aircraft flew up the coast to attack the Zeppelin sheds at Brussels. The first pilot, having found the shed at Berchem St Agathe to be empty, attacked another shed at nearby Evere with bombs, resulting in great clouds of

French-built Sopwith 1½ Strutter Type 9400, known to the French as the Sop 1-A2; over 4,500 Strutters were produced in France.

Sopwith 1½ Strutter being launched from the beam turret of the battlecruiser HMAS *Australia* c.1918. The other beam turret was equipped with a Sopwith Pup.

black smoke emanating from the doors and holed roof. The second pilot flew direct to Evere and also dropped some bombs but then turned to the shed at Berchem St Agathe and bombed this as well with inconclusive results. Both pilots survived heavy anti-aircraft fire to return safely to base. Previously, on 7 June 1915, Zeppelin LZ.38 had been attacked and destroyed at Evere by RNAS aircraft.

By 1918 most battleships, especially the super dreadnoughts, were fitted with flying-off platforms on their B and X turrets to allow aircraft to be carried. The usual complement was a 1½ Strutter for reconnaissance and a Pup for Zeppelin attack. Throughout the war, the Zeppelin continued to loom large in the concerns of the British public due to their ability to scout over the mainland, seemingly bombing indiscriminately with complete invulnerability. As the service charged with homeland protection, the Royal Navy was always on the lookout for opportunities to tackle these slippery customers, the Pup having the ability, lacking in the Strutter, successfully to tackle airships. While the responsibility for home defence passed from the Royal Navy to the RFC after 1916, the Zeppelin remained a serious concern for the Royal Navy because the Admiralty believed that they gave the High Seas Fleet the ability always to know where the Grand Fleet, or elements of it, were located, thus denying the British the element of surprise. While this concern was based more on poor understanding of the limitations of the ability of the airship to reconnoitre, rather than the actuality of this ability, it meant that for the duration of the war the airship remained the *bête noire* of the Royal Navy, to be attacked at every opportunity.

Pup

In 1915 a small biplane, designed for Harry Hawker as a runabout, was developed into the Sopwith SLTBP, officially the Sopwith Scout, more commonly known as the Pup. Fitted with an 80hp Le Rhone 9C rotary engine, the Pup could attain 104mph and a ceiling of 20,000 feet. Cecil Lewis in his 1964 book *Farewell to Wings* said that, 'Of all the aeroplanes of the First World War, by far the prettiest to look at and sweetest on the controls, was the Sopwith Pup.'

Quickly ordered by the RNAS, it entered service in July 1916 and was sent to No.1 Wing at St Pol, France, and then to No.3 Wing RNAS. Designed primarily as an agile anti-airship aircraft, the top wing carried an upward-firing Lewis gun for attack from below and it could also carry Le Prieur rockets mounted on the interplane struts; it was also used extensively in the Somme battles with impressive results. Further work was undertaken to allow the Pup to be used at sea as a land plane rather than a seaplane. To this end, a report by the Grand Fleet Aircraft Committee recommended that Sopwith Babies on HMS *Campania* be replaced with Pups, provision of flying-off platforms be made to some light cruisers to allow the carriage and operation of Pups and, most significantly, the conversion of HMS *Furious* to an aircraft carrier. HMS *Furious* would become a remarkably long-

Sopwith Pup. Factory fresh example of the Pup, probably at Brooklands c.1916. (*BL*)

Sopwith Pup B1707 was built by the Standard Motor Co., part of an order for 150. The company supplied most of the Pups for the RFC.

Sopwith Pup N6438, seen fitted with experimental skids during experiments to develop suitable arrester gear. The aircraft skids were fitted with hooks designed to engage fore and aft restraining cables: culminating in a ramp to further slow the aircraft. It was not a success. (*Author*)

lived ship and would form the basis of experiments in carrier design that would culminate in the 'flat-topper' familiar today. Pup production was around 1,796, of which some 226 were RNAS machines, plus a further thirty modified as Ships Pups for use aboard ship. In the winter of 2021, in *Prop-Swing*, the house magazine of the Shuttleworth Trust at Old Warden, Scott Butler described his time learning to fly the Pup. This machine had started life as a Sopwith Dove but had been purchased by Richard Shuttleworth in 1937 and converted to a Pup. It was therefore a genuine Sopwith machine, if rather different to its birth. After a take-off run of about 100 yards, the aircraft was up and away, Butler settling the speed at 60mph, and gentle turns were initiated with no disagreeable characteristics. The stall was found to be around 40mph and was benign. Landing was made at around 50mph and needed to be into wind and a three-pointer if uncontrollable swing was to be avoided. Butler's experiences in displaying the Pup confirmed what contemporary pilots reported – that the Pup was the sweetest of aircraft in which to fly.

Triplane

Closely allied to the Pup was Sopwith's next fighter, the Triplane. Sopwith's design was the first triplane design to enter operational service; its compact structure (shorter but heavier than the Pup) and narrow chord triplane layout, coupled with 110hp Clerget 9Z rotary engine (or 130hp Clerget 9B) gave the Triplane a quite remarkable rate of climb and a top speed of 120mph; the narrow chord wings allowed the pilot exceptional visibility above and below. (Alliott V. Roe had produced an earlier design in 1910 but, with a maximum speed of just 25mph, it had not entered production.) The first complete design for Sopwith Aviation by Herbert Smith started on 18 April 1916 and was completed ready for flight by 30 May. It was immediately taken up by the RNAS with such speed that the first prototype machine, N500, was reportedly in action over France on the day of its delivery. At first the Triplane swept all before it in combat, its climb, manoeuvrability and speed making it a formidable adversary when used by the naval squadrons to whom it was issued; however, in the constant evolution of combat aircraft in the war zone, losses inevitably slowly mounted and the Triplane became obsolescent within a year. By 1917 the Camel was becoming available and the Triplane quickly disappeared from the order of battle as the new fighter supplanted it. All Triplane production went to the RNAS, total production being 199 plus a further two fitted with the Hispano-Suiza engine, some of these being produced in France.

Manfred von Richthofen, the so-called Red Baron, commented that the Sopwith Triplane was the best plane that the Allies possessed due to its superior rate of climb, manoeuvrability, ability to hold altitude in a bank, speed and ability to dive straight down. Anthony Fokker had quickly laid his hands upon a damaged example and turned his attention to producing his own version, initially with cantilevered wings, on which his company was working, but these were later connected with interplane struts after a number of wing failures had cast doubt on the integrity of the design. In the hands of Baron von Richthofen, the triplane became a feared weapon but, following his demise, like the Sopwith original, it fell out of favour.

Sopwith Triplane. Pictured at Brooklands, this Clerget-powered aircraft has yet to be allocated to a RNAS squadron. (*BL*)

Clerget-powered Sopwith Triplane being serviced. Compare the stubby lines of the front fuselage with the Hispano version.

The Hispano-Suiza-powered Sopwith Triplane, of which only two were built, seen here at Brooklands. The in-line engine resulted in rather different lines to the fuselage compared to the Clerget-powered version. (*BL*)

Hispano-Suiza-powered Sopwith Triplane, probably at Brooklands. The change to the frontal area is shown well with the large circular radiator prominent. (*BL*)

Camel

Of all the scout designs produced during the 1914–18 war, it was the Sopwith Camel that was widely considered the most successful fighter although, ironically, perhaps also the most infamous. A design emanating from the trio of Sopwith, Hawker and Sigrist, as were most of the early designs, it was first flown in December 1916. It appeared at a time when the almost traditional single forward-firing machine gun was being replaced on enemy aircraft with a twin-gun arrangement. Instantly outgunned, the Allied aircraft quickly began to fall victim to their opponents' firepower. The Camel would correct that imbalance by entering service with a forward-firing twin Vickers gun armament. However, it was not just the armament that made the Camel the outstanding fighter of the war. Similar in size although with a larger wingspan than the Pup, the Camel was extremely compact, almost squat, with the major masses of engine, armament, fuel and pilot all concentrated together. Initially powered by a 130hp Clerget 9B and later by a 110hp Le Rhone, top speed was around 105mph for the Clerget and 118mph for the Le Rhone while the ceiling was between 19,000 feet and 24,000 feet, depending on engine type. The result of this concentration of masses behind the powerful engine was a legendary turning ability that would not be bettered during the conflict, due to the gyroscopic forces imparted by the engine. Added to this arrangement, the tailplane and fin areas were reduced when compared to the 1½ Strutter and Pup, thus adding manoeuvrability to an extremely agile design.

Quickly ordered by the RNAS (fifty machines), as well as the RFC, the first aircraft reached squadrons in France in May 1917. The Camel was also quickly brought into operational service with the RNAS home defence squadrons. To the Zeppelin menace

Sopwith 2F.1 Camel for the RNAS. Armament was amended to feature a single Vickers gun on the upper cowling and a Lewis gun on the centre section. (*BL*)

Seen at Brooklands in May 1917, this early 1F.1 Camel, N6332, was allocated to the RFC rather than RNAS.

had now been added the long-range Gotha bombers of the Central Powers, intent on causing mayhem to English towns and cities. The Camels operated from Manston and Eastchurch and had some success in countering the Gothas until the enemy changed to night bombing, which made the already difficult task of interception that much more difficult, although some successes were recorded. Totals for the F1 Camel in RNAS service were 102, and for the 2F1 shipboard version, 661.

As well as populating the RNAS French and home defence squadrons, the Camel was widely used from ships of the fleet. While superficially similar to the land-based F1 Camel, the Ship's Camel was a new design and numbered 2F1 to reflect this. Armament on the 2F1 included a Lewis gun mounted above the centre section and a single Vickers firing through the propeller arc. The engine used was normally a 150hp Bentley BR1 or 130hp Clerget, giving a useful speed of around 122mph with the former and 114mph the latter. The ceiling with the BR1 was the better of the two – 17,300 feet as against 12,000 feet for the Clerget.

First delivered in October 1917, these aircraft were operated from light cruisers and battleships, usually from ramps built over one of the gun turrets, some twenty-two cruisers and twenty-five battleships being so equipped. Also used at this time for the carriage and launch of the Camel were lighters towed behind destroyers, the destroyer's best speed being sufficient to allow the aircraft to take off successfully. In perhaps the Ship's Camel's most successful sea-launched strike, aircraft were carried aboard HMS *Furious*, at that time equipped with a forward flying-off deck. Seven Camels were launched on 19 July 1918, their target being the airship sheds at Tondern, which the Camels, fitted with bomb racks, attacked and destroyed two Zeppelins. Clearly the aircraft would be unable to land

Sopwith Camel F1 H508. This aircraft appears to be a late Sopwith Camel manufactured by Boulton Paul, although the serial was actually issued as part of an order for Snipes that was later cancelled. Acquired post-war, the airframe passed through multiple hands until finding its way to the RAF Museum where it is displayed carrying serial F6314. (*BL*)

back aboard and so three Camels force landed in Sweden, two made their way back to the fleet and ditched and another was lost, presumed killed.

In the first flight of replica Camel G-BZSC by 'Dodge' Bailey at Old Warden on 18 May 2017, Bailey was already aware of the Camel's legendary flying propensities, exacerbated by the close concentration of the aircraft's masses and the smaller than usual tail surfaces. As it was a rotary-engine aircraft, the gyroscopic precession of the engine/propeller resulted in cross-coupling of yaw rate to pitch rate, the result being that pitch-up caused a right yaw and vice-versa and was proportional to engine RPM. Yawing would therefore give either a lightning fast or a sluggish turn, coupled with either pitch-up or a dive. Bailey's initial flight was without incident, take-off being performed with due regard to the likelihood of swing as the tail came up which was easily controlled and, once airborne, it was noted that directional stability was not straightforward, it being difficult to keep the aircraft in balance although reduction in power made this easier. Pitch sensitivity was also noticeable but this had been expected. Stall was found to be benign and occurred between 35 and 40mph indicated. Landing was found to be without difficulty, at approximately 60mph, using the blip switch to slow down and a smooth touchdown achieved.[6]

Thus far, the various Sopwith machines had been purely scouts or fighters but, after contact with Commodore Murray Sueter in October 1916, the company set about designing an aircraft suitable for air-launching a torpedo. First flown in June 1917, the Cuckoo was a two-bay biplane with split undercarriage to allow for torpedo carriage. Power came from a 200hp Sunbeam Arab, a 200hp Wolseley Viper or a 275hp Rolls-Royce Falcon III. Maximum speed ranged from 93 to 116mph, depending on the engine fitted. Due to prolonged problems with the sub-contracted manufacturing companies (Sopwith were busy with scout design and manufacture), the Cuckoo did not become available to the RNAS until after May 1918 and not until November was the aircraft ready for operations. Its debut was therefore stillborn, seeing no action. But the type was retained post-war for several years, some 350 being built by sub-contract, Sopwith producing the first example only.

Periodically, the RNAS produced lists of the disposition of aircraft at its many bases. One such, dated 24 February 1917, reveals that Sopwith machines were ubiquitous throughout the service with, at the time, the Baby, Schneider and Pup, mainly with Clerget engines, representing Sopwith aircraft at UK bases. On the continent, Dunkirk held many Sopwith types at St Pol, Petite Synthe and Coudekerke, including 1½ Strutters, both 9400 scouts and 9700 bombers; 9901 Pups and Triplanes. At Luxeuil, No.3 Wing overwhelmingly favoured Sopwith aircraft with 1½ Strutters, both single- and two-seat types, all Clerget-powered, representing most of the machines on charge. At Mudros and at bases in the Aegean, No.2 Wing had a variety of aircraft on charge, including both types of 1½ Strutter in some numbers. The UK experimental establishments also held Sopwith machines for various trials; Eastchurch had a couple of 1½ Strutters for performance checks while, at Grain, a number of Babies were held for type and performance checks, including deck trials.[7]

The Great War saw Sopwith aircraft being built by an unprecedented variety of sub-contractors, many with no previous aviation experience. By 1917 these included W. Beardmore, Blackburn, Boulton & Paul, Clayton & Shuttleworth, Nieuport & General, Ruston Proctor, Mann Egerton and Vickers, together with a host of smaller concerns making detail fittings for the larger concerns. Each new design was the best that Sopwith could produce at that time. Performance was largely driven, firstly, by engine power/weight ratio, an important concern when the aircraft is of modest weight and, secondly, the integrity of the construction and its ability to withstand aerodynamic forces with the minimum of weight gain. Each design also represented a constant need to respond to advances in opposition aircraft design which, of course, was constantly evolving and therefore new design followed hard on the heels of the previous design at remarkable speed. The Tabloid/Schneider had seen its first flight in 1913; the Baby first flew in September 1915, the 1½ Strutter flew three months later. Then followed the Pup in February 1916 and the Triplane in May and the Camel in December 1916. So, in the space of three years, Sopwith had produced six successful naval aircraft, and, in the process, seen the speed and ceiling of its product rise from 87mph and 7,000 feet for the Schneider, to 122mph and 17,300 feet for the 2F1 Camel.

Aircraft production in the vast Ham works at Kingston in December 1918. Aircraft visible are mainly Salamanders and Snipes. (*BL*)

The rise of the Sopwith concern was primarily due to two factors: the first was the high quality of the workmanship that Sopwith insisted on for his aircraft and the second the outbreak of the Great War. It has been estimated that at the start of the war Sopwith Aviation comprised eighty employees occupying some 1,700 square yards of floor space at the skating rink. By the time of the Armistice in November 1918, the Sopwith concern comprised some 3,412 employees occupying over 13 acres in Kingston and Ham. Together, according to Air Ministry statistics, they had produced 10,400 aircraft and 837 seaplanes.[8]

The evolutionary development of Sopwith aircraft produced for the fighting services over the period of the war was mirrored largely by a similar process in France and Germany. Just prior to the outbreak of hostilities, various German companies had been producing a monoplane called the Taube (Dove) originally developed by Igo Etrich. This bird-like design, a complex maze of rigging wires which held the thing together, was used by many fledgling companies to begin their own journeys into aircraft design and construction. As a reconnaissance aircraft, it was of its time – frail and not particularly reliable, but did provide a good basis for new designs to emerge. Soon a variety of German companies were producing effective designs, often monoplanes, unlike in the UK where these were frowned upon, and quickly produced formidable opposition to the early UK aircraft. Companies such as Aviatik, Halberstadt, Junkers, Albatros and Roland were instrumental in providing excellent fighting scouts with which to counter advances in the UK.

The Sopwith Schneider and its development, the Baby, were normally used in a marine environment, hence their float undercarriage, and therefore seldom tangled with the early aircraft of the Central Powers. It was the land-based naval squadrons that came up against determined opposition over France and Belgium. The 1½ Strutters of 1916, particularly when used as bomber escorts, were typically matched against Halberstadt and Albatros D.II and V scouts. As pure scouts, it would have fallen to the crews of the 1½ Strutters to take on the Fokker Eindecker E.1, its synchronised machine gun now countered by that fitted to the Strutter, using a patented Sopwith-Kauper interrupter gear. The Sopwith Triplane, introduced to the naval squadrons in mid-1916, was similarly pitted against the Albatros D.III and V, at first very successfully. Finally, the Camel, that most ubiquitous of British fighters, was busy countering the Fokker Triplane and also the redoubtable Albatros variants.

Of the German aircraft companies, perhaps the most successful was Fokker Fluzeugwerke founded by the Dutchman Anthony Fokker. An early success was his Eindecker E.I, E.II and E.III monoplanes which featured the first interrupter gear (designed by Franz Schneider) which allowed the machine gun to fire through the propeller arc. This simple arrangement caught the Allies on the hop, the rapidly rising toll of British and French aircraft being shot out of the sky being dubbed the 'Fokker Scourge'. However, Fokker was perhaps best known as the producer of the Fokker Dr.1 Triplane as flown by Baron von Richthofen, the so-called 'Red Baron'. Just as the Fokker Eindecker had swept all before it in 1915, in 1917 it had been the turn of Sopwith's Triplane to shock the Central Powers with its remarkable climb and manoeuvrability. As seen above, the Sopwith Triplane was soon in the hands of Fokker and a triplane variant was produced that brought great success to Manfred von Richthofen before his death in April 1918.

The growth and evolution of European air arms involved in the conflict that was the First World War show just how fast was the scramble to maximise the potential of the aerial domain in wartime. In terms of naval aviation, the UK opened the First World War with around ninety-four aircraft and 727 personnel. By the last year of the war, these figures had increased to 2,900 aircraft and 55,066 personnel. Similarly in France, which had seen the outbreak of war with just eight operational type aircraft and 208 personnel, this had increased to 1,264 aircraft and 11,059 personnel while Germany fielded twenty-four aircraft and around 200 personnel at the outbreak of war, increasing to 1,478 aircraft and 16,122 personnel at the Armistice. The lower figures for French and German naval air arms are understandable when it is remembered that these were continental powers with their main military strength in the army rather than the navy. Great Britain on the other hand, as a maritime nation, had always looked to the Royal Navy as its primary military force; it was a deliberate policy to retain but a small army which could be rapidly expanded when need arose.[9]

In sum, Sopwith saw twenty-six of its products enter service officially with the RNAS in the period up to August 1914, out of 200 aircraft officially taken on charge by the service, these being the first allocation of serial numbers to the RNAS (ie. Serials 1–200). The next 799 serials representing the second naval allocation (i.e. 801–1600), running from 1914 to 1915, included 124 Sopwith products, subsequent orders seeing previously unheard of quantities of aircraft in the hundreds being obtained.

The armistice of 11 November 1918 saw aircraft orders for Sopwith and indeed all other aviation concerns either drastically reduced or cancelled outright. Between 1914 and 1918 Sopwith production had been on a truly vast scale, the company estimating that some 11,237 Sopwith aircraft had been constructed by the company and by sub-contractors in Great Britain with another 5,000 produced in France.[10] In that time the aircraft had evolved at a prodigious rate from uncertain beginnings to scientifically-designed craft capable of speed, manoeuvrability and the ability to carry sizeable loads. The knowledge and experience thus gained would soon be transferred to a new concern as Sopwith Aviation (trading as The Sopwith Aviation and Engineering Company Ltd) was voluntarily liquidated at a board meeting of 6 October 1920 and a new company established shortly thereafter with much the same personnel and premises.

As T.O.M. Sopwith remarked in an interview with Robert Parke in his later years:

We started the war building aircraft in a shed at Brooklands in Kingston and ended with an output of 90 ships a week at Kingston alone. Overnight it ended, so we had to liquidate the business and the Sopwith company. I wanted to stay in aviation and couldn't very well start a company with the same name. So we simply called the new swindle the Hawker Company, and the name stuck. We had capital of £20,000. We did quite well.[11]

On 15 November 1920, papers had been submitted registering the formation of the 'HG Hawker Engineering Co. Ltd' with capital of £20,000 in £1 shares. Its articles of association described the proposed activities of the new company as 'the manufacture of motor cycles, and to carry on the business of manufacturers of and dealers in cycles of all kinds, internal combustion engines and steam engines, motor cars, aircraft etc.' The first directors were announced as Frederick Ibbotson Bennett, engineer; Harry George Hawker, aeroplane pilot; Thomas Octave Murdoch Sopwith, engineer; Frederick Sigrist, engineer; V.W. Eyre, engineer. What would follow would be a series of superlative designs that would furnish the Royal Navy and the Royal Air Force with aircraft for the next eighty years.[12] While the new company would no longer bear his name, T.O.M. Sopwith would remain the backbone and driving force for the successor companies until his retirement. On 18 May 1933 the first of a number of changes occurred when the name of the company was changed from HG Hawker Engineering Co. Ltd to Hawker Aircraft Ltd with Sopwith as chairman and a share capital of £800,000. In 1934 Hawker Aircraft Ltd purchased Gloster Aircraft Ltd and, in 1935, with the purchase of the J.D. Siddeley group of companies, Sopwith was instrumental in the launch of a new company – Hawker Siddeley Aircraft Co. This concern would act as a holding company within which his other concerns – Hawker Aircraft, Gloster Aircraft, Sir W.G. Armstrong Whitworth Aircraft, A.V. Roe & Co. and Air Service Training – would continue to trade under their own names until 1963 and the launch of two new companies – Hawker Siddeley Aviation and Hawker Siddeley Dynamics – which would see the old company names subsumed into the new concerns. Also joining the parent company at this time were Blackburn Aircraft, de Havilland Aircraft and Folland Aircraft. Thus the majority of the UK's aircraft companies came under the auspices of Hawker Siddeley Aviation. Retiring in 1980, Sopwith had singlehandedly supported and, in some cases, saved, the UK's aviation industry for over fifty years, not a bad legacy for the onetime young playboy.

Chapter 3

The Inter-War Years

As seen in the first chapter, the Royal Navy lost control of its air component with the formation of the Royal Air Force. While theoretically the military and naval components were equal, the Royal Navy consistently lost out when aircraft were being specified and ordered. The fleet found itself in the invidious position whereby, although it had responsibility for aircraft embarked in capital ships, those embarked on its carriers fell under RAF control when ashore. Even aboard the carriers, 30 per cent of the flying personnel and 100 per cent of the maintenance personnel were supplied by the RAF, the two services' crews working well together. But it did result in a proportion of crew on the carriers being ignorant of the ways of the sea and the minutiae of seaborne life which, in a wartime situation, where, for example, accurate ship recognition was required, could mean the difference between life and death.

The crew complement of the carriers was also marked by the fact that while aircrew and maintainers were RAF personnel the remaining ratings and officers were Royal Navy. Consistent campaigning within the Admiralty resulted in limited recognition of naval desires by the formation of the Fleet Air Arm in 1924 as an organisational component of the RAF. Campaigning would continue throughout the inter-war years in an effort to restore full control of naval air assets to the Admiralty, ultimately successfully when it was agreed in 1937, in what became known as the Inskip Award, that this was the right course, the decision taking full effect in early 1939.

The Armistice of November 1918 saw the immediate slashing of the defence budget and, with it, most new aircraft orders. Aviation companies were quickly reduced to fighting over what scraps could be found, some turning to manufacture of items as diverse as motor cars and motorbikes to household utensils. As seen earlier, Sopwith Aviation could not long endure such a situation and had entered liquidation in 1920, having met all of its debt and tax liabilities. Out of this was founded HG Hawker Engineering Co. Ltd, having retrenched into the old Canbury Park premises and given up its main location at the vast Ham factory.

Early board meeting minutes give a flavour of the disparate work being undertaken by the fledgling company, very different to the intensive aircraft production of the recent war. The first board meeting on 29 November 1920, with T.O.M. Sopwith, Harry Hawker, Frederick Bennett present and Fred Sigrist taking the chairman's role, saw a resolution adopted for Sopwith and Hawker to conclude a contract with A.C. Motors for the manufacture of 'sporting two-seater bodies' for their chassis. On 1 February 1921, the Hawker board minutes noted 'an agreement between the company and FI Bennett appointed him Works Manager and giving him a royalty on the bicycles, was read and approved'; this would have been motor, rather than pedal cycles. By September 1921, motorcycles were still on the agenda, it being agreed that a motorcycle with a Blackburn 2¾hp engine be built as a one-off. With the appointment of Captain Thomson as aircraft designer, discussed at the 3 January 1922 meeting, plans to concentrate on aircraft manufacture were coming to the fore; the meeting of the following month including 'a lengthy debate was entered into on the subject of production and delivery of aircraft and it was resolved to push delivery as far as possible'.

While initial designs were attempted, the small workforce was kept in work by obtaining contracts for the refurbishment of Sopwith Snipes. It should be noted that T.O.M. Sopwith's personal contacts within the Royal Navy would not be sufficient for the new Hawker company to match the success of the Sopwith designs within the RNAS. The new austere atmosphere meant that each design would have to fight for orders on its merits alone. At this time, Air Ministry orders were, perhaps understandably, thin on the ground; after all, what nation would any new aircraft be required to fight? Since the Central Powers, Germany, Turkey and Austro-Hungary, had been defeated and were rigorously constrained by the Treaty of Versailles, it was difficult to find any country that might threaten the UK's peace, though its recent ally France was always a possibility. Thus it was that, for a time at least, the RAF and its Naval component would continue to rely on the aircraft that had been current at the end of the conflict, which for the Royal Navy meant reconditioned 2F1 Camels and for the RAF others, including Sopwith Snipes.

Another reason for the paucity of thought and finance directed at the fighter from an RAF/Air Ministry point of view was the development of the so-called Trenchard Doctrine in the late 1920s and 1930s, wherein Lord Trenchard, Marshal of the Royal Air Force, in common with many others, believed that defence against aerial attack by enemy bombers was almost impossible to counter, the only recourse being the deterrent value of a large bomber force with which to threaten to devastate the enemy heartlands and destroy not their ability to make war, but their will to make war. Thus from this came the notion of the 'knock-out blow' which would see a massive RAF bomber force attacking the enemy to deliver a definitive defeat which would destroy its will to make war. In this scenario, the defensive fighter was simply not required; defence would come from attack by bombers. This belief was not finally overturned until the advent of the various re-armament bills passed through Parliament from 1935 onwards.

With regard to the aircraft carrier, the post-war fleet possessed just a few ships with which to continue the ability to launch and recover wheeled aircraft aboard. Firstly, HMS *Furious* and *Argus*, both representing but a stage in the evolution of the carrier and both being converted from other designs, presented less than ideal operating bases. The next carrier to be built was also a conversion, this time from a former Chilean battleship order that had stalled during the recent war. Purchased from Chile in 1917 as the *Almirante Cochrane*, construction was completed in 1924 and featured a single island on the starboard side and a full-length flight-deck of 652 feet with a hangar deck 400 feet long. HMS *Eagle,* as she was commissioned, was approaching the final form of carrier design that we would recognise today, a design that would broadly remain unchanged until the 1950s. At the time, she was the world's largest carrier, displacing 22,600 tons and could carry twenty-four aircraft in four flights. The next carrier, commissioned as HMS *Hermes*, was just half the size of *Eagle* at 10,850 tons but was constructed from the keel up as a carrier. Laid down in 1918, she was completed in 1924, thus, with *Eagle*, doubling the Royal Navy's effective carrier fleet.

During the period 1920–1939, the inter-war years, the aircraft carrier continued to evolve although that evolution was at a slow pace given the paucity of defence funding and the anti-war political stance of government and much of the populace. However, with *Hermes*, a consensus had been reached as to just what an aircraft carrier should comprise.

In 1925 the first of two further modern carriers was commissioned; HMS *Courageous* had started life as a shallow-draught battlecruiser designed for a specific role in 1907. Serving through the Great War along with her sister ship HMS *Glorious*, she was seen as something of a 'white elephant', not fitting easily into fleet operations, and the pair spent most of the war in reserve. Converted after the war along the lines of HMS *Furious* in her then configuration, *Courageous* emerged in 1925 as a fully-fledged aircraft carrier of 22,500 tons, a length of 786 feet and beam of 81 feet and capable of 31 knots. HMS *Glorious* was commissioned two years later along very similar lines although with a slightly longer flight-deck. Both ships spent the inter-war years with the Mediterranean Fleet, *Courageous* also being used in the Atlantic. Both ships were fitted with a pair of accelerators (i.e. hydraulic catapults) in the bow, the first of the carriers to sport this innovation. Sadly, just a fortnight into the Second World War, *Courageous*, ironically on anti-submarine duties, was sunk by German torpedo from *U-29*.

Before examining the new Hawker enterprise's designs, a few words regarding the personality whose name was immortalised in that of the new company. Harry George Hawker was an Australian, born at Moorabbin, Victoria, on 22 January 1899 where his father had a blacksmith and wheelwright business. With little interest in academic work, Harry ignored school and started working for a motor company to pursue his ambition to be an engineer. In this he succeeded and progressed with several companies until, chancing upon a flying display by none other than Houdini, was enthralled by the magic of aeroplanes. In 1911, in company with Harry Kauper and Harry Busteed, he arrived in England, all three being intent on an aviation career. Hawker obtained a position with T.O.M. Sopwith in July 1912 and arranged for flying lessons, quickly becoming proficient and gaining his licence in October, adding the testing and display of Sopwith's aircraft to his mechanical knowledge. A series of competition wins quickly marked Hawker out as an exceptional pilot, becoming an integral part of the small Sopwith design team. Through the First World War, the team of Sopwith, Sigrist and Hawker consistently produced winning military designs for the armed forces that saw the company become one of the leading lights in aeronautical production. After the war, Hawker remained with Sopwith and Sigrist, the new company being named after him. It should be noted that Hawker had a number of serious crashes in various aircraft but always appeared to recover well and continue his work. However, all was not well: bouts of unexplained illness attended by back pain, while minimised by Hawker, pointed to a serious health problem. However, this did not prevent Hawker from venturing upon a perilous decision to become the first man to fly the Atlantic and claim the *Daily Mail* prize of £10,000.

In the company of Kenneth Mackenzie Grieve, he arrived in Newfoundland in March 1919 with the specially designed Sopwith machine, dubbed the 'Atlantic' and prepared to become airborne before any competitors could beat him to the prize. Fred Raynham, who had flown for Sopwith, was also present with a Martinsyde design. With inclement weather delaying any attempts, it was not until 18 May that Hawker and Mackenzie Grieve chanced a take-off and disappeared into the murk. Before too long, the engine began seriously to overheat and, eventually, Hawker brought the aircraft down to ditch close to a passing ship that had been spotted. Luckily, the pair were rescued but, since the vessel had no wireless, they could not signal their survival and were given up for lost. A week later, however, on approach to the south coast, they were able to alert the country to their survival and returned to a heroes' welcome.

With the war now over, Hawker supplemented his time with the new company by assisting on display of various other company's designs. On 12 July 1921, while flying a Nieuport Goshawk from Hendon, the engine caught fire and, in an attempted landing, Hawker was killed, the subsequent inquest identifying the source of the mysterious back pain that had plagued him: death was considered to be due to haemorrhage due to spinal tuberculosis as well as the effects of the fire. Thus did the Hawker company begin its journey without its namesake.

The HG Hawker Engineering Company's first new designs, submitted in answer to Air Ministry specifications, were for the Duiker, a parasol observation aircraft that failed to impress anybody, and the Woodcock, a two-bay biplane with an Armstrong Siddeley Jaguar radial engine, both the work of Captain 'Tommy' Thomson, Hawker's first chief designer.

Woodcock

The Woodcock was conceived as a 'day and night interceptor', the design being submitted in 1922 and rewarded with an order for a single prototype. This aircraft, J6987, evaluated at A&AEE Martlesham Heath in August 1923, was not a success. Handling was described as 'rotten', and the rigging wires soon became slack. The failure of both Thomson's designs to achieve any recognition may have been instrumental in his departure and his replacement with W.G. 'George' Carter, Sopwith's former chief draughtsman. The Woodcock was extensively modified, the wings becoming single-bay and the Jaguar II engine giving way to a Bristol Jupiter IV radial, the changes warranting a new mark number: Hawker Woodcock II.

The second aircraft, the revised Woodcock Mk.II, J6988, arrived at Martlesham in July 1924. Performance was slightly improved. The first production machine, J7512, arrived at Martlesham in May 1925; one pilot found it 'nicer than the original'. The production aircraft was of wooden construction with fabric covering; wingspan was 32 feet 6 inches and length 26 feet 2 inches. Empty weight was 2,083lb and loaded 3,023lb. Armament was two synchronised Vickers machine guns mounted on the side of the nose. Martlesham noted that the Bristol Jupiter IV engine delivered 402hp driving a two-bladed wooden propeller with a maximum speed of 141mph at 6,500 feet with a service ceiling of 22,500 feet.

The developed Woodcock Mk.II at Brooklands. Although much improved over the original two-bay design, the Mk II was still a somewhat ungainly beast, even with the cylinder cowls giving some semblance of streamlining. (*BAE/BL*)

One of a batch of Woodcocks completed for the Danish Navy and termed Danecock. This example seen at Hawker's Canbury Park premises is nearly ready for skinning. (*BAE/BL*)

After further modification, the aircraft received a modest order for ten aircraft from the RAF, featuring twin Vickers guns and night-flying equipment. There is some evidence that the Woodcock was trialled by the Royal Navy but it did not enter operation with that service, the ten aircraft going to the RAF, which received further batches totalling sixty-seven. However, an export version of the Woodcock, the Danecock, an Armstrong Siddeley Jaguar-powered aircraft for Denmark, saw three going to the Royal Danish Naval Air Service while a further twelve aircraft were licence-produced at the Royal Danish Navy Dockyard, those aircraft retiring only in 1937. Thus did the HG Hawker Engineering Co. Ltd enter the business of aircraft construction.

It was around this time, in fact in November 1923, that a new member of the drawing office arrived in the person of one Sydney Camm, employed as a senior draughtsman. Camm brought with him much needed experience in the fighter field, having been employed by HP Martin and George Handasyde in their aviation company, Martinsyde, on various successful designs employed in the Great War. With their factory at Woking and flight sheds at Brooklands, Camm would have been familiar with the Sopwith/Hawker designs being produced in the locality, an advantage while making his presence felt at Hawker. With the departure of George Carter to join Gloster Aircraft in 1925, Camm, clearly already identified as a designer of note, was appointed Chief Designer over several longer-serving members of the team. From that point on, Camm's influence over Hawker designs would dominate for the next forty years until his death in 1966. In that time he would be responsible for some of the UK's and the world's great fighters, several of which would see service with the Royal Navy. His philosophy was quite simple really: 'I'm only interested in designing fighters; there's no finesse in anything else.'

Hedgehog

The first dedicated Hawker design for the Royal Navy was the Hedgehog, a three-seat fleet reconnaissance biplane of 1923 with single-bay folding wings featuring flaps on both sets of wings and drooping ailerons, and a Bristol Jupiter IV engine delivering 398hp, giving a maximum speed of 116mph and a service ceiling of 13,500 feet. Designed to meet Air Ministry Specification 37/22, the crew of three were seated in tandem, pilot, observer and gunner, and, on its assessment at Martlesham in September 1924, it drew unstinting praise for the design, being purchased by the Air Ministry and receiving the serial N187. Although described as 'a nice kite', performance was not much better than the Blackburn it was intended to replace.

Unfortunately, by the time that trials had been completed, the order was cancelled due to performance not being sufficiently in advance of existing designs. While it may seem that, thus far, the Hawker company was not faring particularly well in the aircraft manufacturing business, it must be remembered that retrenchment of the RAF and even debate about its very existence meant that finance for new types was extremely thinly spread. Relying on government orders left Hawker little option but to persevere with the refinement of their designs and hope that an order would come their way.

The single Hedgehog, a three-seat fleet reconnaissance aircraft bearing more than a passing resemblance to the Woodcock. No order was forthcoming for this design since it failed to offer any meaningful improvement over existing designs. (*BAE/BL*)

Hawker Hedgehog being worked on at Brooklands. It appears to carry no serial number. (*Author*)

Horsley

That order came in 1926 in answer to Air Ministry Specification 26/23 of 1923 for a two-seat day bomber. Although not a fighter, it did allow Hawker to rekindle contacts with the Royal Navy, and to restart quantity production of aircraft. The Horsley gave the Navy the opportunity to develop its aerial torpedo delivery practices, work that would come to fruition in the Second World War. A large wooden biplane, the Horsley was originally designed by Sydney Camm under the tutelage of Carter, featured biplane wings of two bays and was powered by a Rolls-Royce Condor III engine of 673hp. First flown in late 1924 and named the Kingston, following revised specifications, 23/25 and 24/25, the Horsley design was modified and pleased the ministry with its ample load-carrying ability. Although described by one Martlesham pilot as 'a sloppy old cow', it may be that it was the least bad of the entries since an order was placed in 1926 for thirty machines. The other contestants were the Handley Page Handcross, the Bristol Berkeley and the Westland Yeovil. Although the order was principally for the RAF, implicit in the later specifications was the ability to carry a torpedo, which interested the Royal Navy, although, because the

Horsley Mk.Is under construction at Canbury Road, Kingston, in 1926; there are ten machines in this line-up. (*BAE/BL*)

Hawker Horsley S1452 at Brooklands. (*BAE/BL*)

specification had attempted to combine the bomb-carrying requirement of the RAF and the torpedo-carrying requirement of the Royal Navy, it was found to be too cumbersome for RN carrier operation and too heavy to carry adequate fuel for the RAF requirement![1]

In 1926 Hawker had modified a Horsley Mk.II, J8006, to take a torpedo weighing 2,069lb and transferred it to the Torpedo Development Flight at Gosport for trials and, in March 1927, to Martlesham. An order for twelve torpedo-bomber variants was later received, powered by the RR Condor IIIA engine. This was later followed by an order in 1929 for eighteen aircraft with a further eighteen in 1931. Camm was able to redesign the aircraft as a metal structure instead of the wood used for the first two prototypes and thus allow a much more substantial fuel load to be carried, resulting in a happy RAF while the RN carrier operation requirement was dropped, the torpedo-delivery role being performed from land.

The production version was assessed at Martlesham in the summer of 1928 in the guise of the first production machine, S1236. Although the ceiling was 1,750 feet lower than the bomber variant, testing continued, including replacement of the Condor III with a Leopard III engine and also a Rolls-Royce H engine. As tested, the engine variants performed thus: Condor IIIA – 701hp giving 126mph and ceiling of 17,000 feet; Leopard III – 873hp giving 128mph and ceiling of 17,750 feet; Rolls-Royce H – 812hp giving 126mph and ceiling of 19,000 feet. Although not a fighter, the Horsley had allowed the Royal Navy to refine its development work on airborne torpedo delivery, work that would pay dividends in the next war. Also received was an order from the Greek Naval

Hawker Horsley J8932 seen here at Brooklands fitted with a dummy torpedo. This aircraft was the prototype for the all-metal airframe. While flown by Flt Lt Waghorn (the 1929 Schneider Trophy winner) at Farnborough on 4 May 1931 , the aircraft crashed, killing the pilot. (*BAE/BL*)

Hawker Horsley S1247 in the Brooklands flight sheds fitted with float undercarriage c.1927. (*BAE/BL*)

Hawker Horsley J8006, fitted with Rolls-Royce Condor IIIB engine and sporting a torpedo, is flown in typically boisterous fashion by 'George' Bulman. (*BAE/BL*)

An example of the Danish Horsley, known as the Dantorp, built for the Danish Navy. This is number 202 of this version of the Horsley, seen fitted with floats in 1932. (*BAE/BL*)

Air Service for the torpedo-bomber variant, six aircraft being supplied. Also supplied were two aircraft under the name Dantorp, for the Royal Danish Naval Air Service, again in the torpedo-bomber variant, these aircraft powered by the 805hp Armstrong Siddeley Leopard IIIA.

Squadron service for the Horsley was with the Coast Defence Torpedo Flight based at Donibristle, in 1928, later renamed No.36 Torpedo Bomber Squadron. Transferring to Singapore in 1930, the aircraft remained in service until 1935.

The Horsley also featured in plans for the RAF to attempt to set new long-distance endurance records in 1927. Accordingly, a Horsley was modified to carry a much increased fuel load and, on 20 May, set off from Cranwell heading for India, some 5,000 miles away. The crew were next heard from following a ditching in the Persian Gulf after a flight of some 3,420 miles which, while a new record, was quickly beaten by Charles Lindbergh's epic Atlantic flight of 3,590 miles from New York to Paris. Further flights using the Horsley failed to beat the first flight record and the idea was quietly dropped.

Hoopoe

Also received in 1926 was specification F.9/26 for a single-seat interceptor fighter to replace the AW Siskin and Gloster Gamecock fighters in the RAF. Although the specification was for an RAF aircraft, Hawker's submission, the Hawfinch, was ready for service trials before other contenders and the opportunity was therefore taken to submit the aircraft for deck-landing trials aboard HMS *Furious*, at which the aircraft behaved admirably and allowed the experience gained to influence Sydney Camm's early thoughts on a fleet fighter, to specification N.21/26. Assessment at Martlesham was enthusiastic, the Hawfinch being described as 'exceptionally pleasant with no vices'.

Camm's response to specification N.21/26 was the Hawker Hoopoe, construction of which began at Kingston in 1927 as N237 and which was submitted for service trials in 1928; this was one of eleven submissions to the specification. As would become common practice for Camm from this period onwards, his design did not slavishly follow the specification precisely, Camm delivering not what the customer thought they wanted, but what Camm believed they should have. The first Hoopoe was a single-seat, two-bay biplane powered by an uncowled Mercury II of 450hp, which Martlesham pilots found to be 'comfortable, handled well at mid-speeds but needed lots of rudder at high speed and lots of elevator at low speed'. Oh, and the brakes were harsh. Despite this, the aircraft was felt to have sufficient promise that it was sent for its deck-landing trials.[2]

Following trials in 1929 at Felixstowe with float undercarriage, the aircraft was found to be underpowered, the engine being changed for a more powerful Mercury VI of 520hp. Around 1930, for the second phase of the competition, with the Hoopoe and Gloster Gnatsnapper now attracting official funding, the Hoopoe was re-engined, with the Jaguar VIII with Townend ring returning a lower horsepower of 405hp. Following return to Kingston for replacement of the wings with single-bay units in 1930, the aircraft found favour with the Martlesham assessors and, once again at Kingston, the engine was

Hawker Hoopoe N237 at Brooklands. Built to Air Ministry 21/26, this was the only example. (*BAE/BL*)

changed, this time to an Armstrong Siddeley Panther III radial offering 500hp. With this engine, maximum speed was increased to 188mph and ceiling to 30,600 feet. Although the Hoopoe consistently performed well, it was now being overshadowed by its successor to specification N.21/26, as noted below, and therefore never entered service.

Nimrod

This development, the Nimrod Fleet Fighter, appeared to owe much of its design to the Hart family of aircraft but, in fact, had an entirely separate evolution although the use of an in-line engine, the Rolls-Royce Kestrel, allowed close cowling of the engine installation, giving a distinctly Hart-like appearance. The use of the Kestrel by Hawker in their Hart and Fury family of aircraft allowed a far cleaner profile than was achievable with the bulky radial engines of the day with their many protuberances. Working from the experience gained at Kingston with the Hawfinch and Hoopoe designs, Camm had already drafted the outline of his fleet fighter and, in 1930, a specification, 16/30, was written around the design. At first known, at least within Hawker, as the Norn (possibly a contraction of Naval Hornet) or HN.1, the prototype was first flown in early 1930 and this and a second machine were taken on charge by the Air Ministry. The aircraft featured what by now were considered typical Hawker lines, much attention to detail being applied to ensure a clean design. Wings were single-bay with pronounced stagger and the engine a Rolls-Royce F.XIMS as the Kestrel was first known. This in-line engine resulted in very clean fuselage lines and was water-cooled with the radiator under the cockpit. Flotation

Hawker Nimrod Mk.I serial S1580, part of a batch of twelve. (*BAE/BL*)

bags were fitted in the top wing structure and in the rear fuselage with provision made for either wheel or float undercarriage.

The Nimrod arrived at Martlesham in 1930 and quickly showed its superior qualities. The subsequent report noted that the aircraft 'is considered a splendid aircraft to handle and should be very easy to land on deck'.[3]

Hawker Nimrod aloft. (*BAE/BL*)

Hawker Nimrod displays its sprightly performance during take-off from its carrier. (*BAE/BL*)

The Rolls-Royce FX.IS gave 480hp, conferring a max speed of 200mph at 13,000 feet and a ceiling of 27,500 feet. The Nimrod won the 1930 Fleet Fighter competition following deck-landing and catapult trials. Following the Martlesham assessment, an order was raised for forty-two machines, the first flying in 1931. Production machine S1577 returned to Martlesham in late 1935 for further trials, including the fitting of a metal Fairey Reed propeller. Performance was superb although fitting the arrestor hook and other equipment would push the CG aft. To remedy this, the wings were swept back and the tailplane enlarged, the aircraft being designated Nimrod (Intermediate); thirty-six of this type were ordered. Later Nimrods (designated Mark II) were fitted with the Kestrel IIS engine, giving 477hp and 195mph for a ceiling of 26,900 feet, and a Kestrel VFP of 608hp giving 192mph and a service ceiling of 28,800 feet. A total of eighty-seven Nimrods eventually entered service. Following further shipboard trials conducted aboard HMS *Eagle*, service clearance was achieved in June 1932 with first squadron aircraft allotted to No.408 Flight aboard HMS *Glorious*, replacing ageing Fairey Flycatchers. Nimrods were fitted with an arrestor hook from K2823 onwards, together with a headrest to absorb the force of catapult launches.

A Nimrod fitted with floats was assessed by the Marine Aircraft Experimental Establishment (MAEE) at Felixstowe between October 1934 and May 1935 as part of

Hawker Nimrod S1578, the second aircraft built, equipped here with floats, is moved to the water by its naval handling crew, probably at Felixstowe. (*BAE/BL*)

a series of trials to assess the spinning characteristics of seaplanes. It was found that spin recovery was possible after two turns and a loss of height of 1,000 feet. Unfortunately, there were no comparable tests on the landplane version to date and therefore the assessment was of limited value. An earlier test in 1934 had assessed the ability of the Nimrod landplane and seaplane to recover from inverted flight. The conclusion reached was that the seaplane version tended to stall when inverted and recovery was difficult, resulting in a loss of some 4,000 feet in height before the aircraft was again under control. The landplane (called a ship-plane in the report) however, while unstable inverted, was easy to recover with a height loss of less than 2,000 feet. In July 1935 A&AEE Martlesham Heath carried out trials on Nimrod K2823 to ascertain the performance difference between an aircraft fitted with the Kestrel IIS engine (K2824) and one with the Kestrel V. Conclusions were that maximum speed increase was of the order of 15mph at 20,000 feet and reduced the time to climb to 20,000 feet by three-and-a-half minutes.[4]

The Nimrod was one of the early examples of British enterprise to grace foreign trade exhibitions, being displayed at the El Palomar event at Buenos Aires in 1931 and in Japan in 1932. The aircraft served with Naval Air Squadrons No.800 aboard HMS *Courageous*, No.801 aboard HMS *Furious* and No.802 aboard HMS *Glorious*. The Nimrod performed very well and remained in service until 1939, when it was replaced by the Gloster Sea Gladiator, some eighteen aircraft remaining in the inventory at the beginning of the Second World War. Small export orders saw two delivered to Denmark, fitted with Kestrel IIIS engines, as a lead-in to licence production but this does not appear to have happened. A single Nimrod was exported to Japan in 1934 following its display at the 1932 Exhibition and a further example went to Portugal for evaluation.

Hawker Nimrod Mk.I serial K2840 was later converted to a Mk.II. (*BAE/BL*)

A number of Nimrods survived into the Second World War, eighteen aircraft being held at Eastleigh and Worthy Down, mostly fitted with 525hp Kestrel IS or 640hp Kestrel V radials. All had been struck off charge by 1942.

As the then latest fighter possessed by the Fleet Air Arm, what was the Nimrod like to fly? Peter Holloway, writing in the 2016 edition of the Shuttleworth Trust's house

A line up of Danish Nimrods c.1933. (*Danish National Archives*)

magazine *Prop-Swing*, described a flight made in the Nimrod II held by the Trust starting with his attempts to actually start it.

> The Nimrod is blessed with an ingenious air-start system. This sequentially fires charges of compressed air and fuel into the cylinders. An instant start is assured, that is, until I got involved. After several attempts, all we got was a concentrated blast of flame and smoke from the rear, left cylinder.

Nonetheless, his next attempt was rather more successful. Having started the Kestrel V engine:

> I line up on the westerly runway, open the throttle slowly through the gate (a restriction in the throttle quadrant to prevent over-boosting), checking that we have a reassuring 2,400rpm and 6lb of boost. As I climb away I reduced power and quickly scan the instruments, again aided here by my time honoured habit of marking the faces of the instruments with red Chinagraph.
>
> The rate of climb is astonishing for an 80-year-old machine and I find myself shouting 'wow!' more than once … . At high speed the controls feel quite heavy but at the same time nicely harmonised and without excessive yaw. The Nimrod uses up far more sky than I'm used to and this encourages me to bank quite steeply in the turns and perform dynamic wing-overs. Utterly glorious!
>
> All too soon it is time to land … . As I set up a gentle curve onto final and close the throttle … the Kestrel fires off a series of crackles, pops and loud bangs … I straighten up into the flare and … wheel the machine on, allowing the tail to finally settle. What a machine![5]

Osprey

The Hawker Osprey was another design that appeared to owe much to the extremely successful Hart series and did in fact have a closer relationship to the Hart than the Nimrod had (it was known as Hart O.22/26 until the end of 1929). Specification O.22/26 called for a two-seat fleet fighter/reconnaissance aircraft, having a performance similar to the Hart, and the Hart prototype, J9052, having completed its initial flight trials, was converted to reflect the O.22/26 requirements. Folding wings were introduced and the structure strengthened to allow for catapult launching; later, a float undercarriage was installed together with alterations to the fin and rudder, allowing these to be tested prior to detailed design commencing for the Osprey. First flown in summer 1930, the Martlesham trials revealed one serious shortcoming, a great reluctance to recover from a spin. Suspicion fell upon the swept wings and lack of authority of the fin. Remedial work resulted in an enlarged fin and rudder which allowed a normal spin response to be reported.

Following the success of the Hart prototype trials with Osprey modifications, contract cover was provided against revised Specification 19/30, and manufacture commenced on the small batch at Kingston in 1932. Further batches were produced, the aircraft designated

Hawker Osprey at Brooklands. (*BAE/BL*)

Osprey Mk.III (with Kestrel IIMS5 of 575hp) and Osprey Mk.IV (with Kestrel V of 607hp). Maximum speed of the Osprey Mk.III was 167mph with a service ceiling of 18,500 feet and of the Osprey Mk.IV, 175mph and a ceiling of 25,400 feet. While at Martlesham, test aircraft S1700 suffered a serious incident whilst undergoing terminal velocity dive tests. The speed (240mph) was sufficient to operate the hydrostatic valve of

Float-equipped Hawker Osprey Mk.III K3629 on its catapult aboard a cruiser.

Hawker Osprey Mk.I, serial S1681, overflies HMS *Eagle*. (*BAE/BL*)

the dinghy stowed in the top wing, causing it to inflate, tear loose and wrap itself around the tailplane. The aircraft was landed safely.

In common with the Nimrod, the Osprey was selected for production in stainless steel in an attempt to reduce the saltwater corrosion of the primary structure, particularly the aluminium components. Only three Nimrods and six Ospreys were thus built for extended trials at sea. Trials at Felixstowe using an Osprey saw the aircraft fitted with a variety of single central floats for trial purposes but which were not extended to squadron aircraft, these using the more conventional twin float arrangement when required.

In Royal Navy service the fighter role predominated, the aircraft entering service in 1932, replacing Fairey Flycatchers aboard the carriers *Eagle* and *Courageous* and the cruisers *York*, *Dorsetshire* and *Exeter*. Operated by Naval Air Squadrons No.800, No.801 and No.802 in company with the Nimrod, the aircraft remained in service until superseded by the Fairey Skua in 1939. In 1933 the Swedish Navy placed an order for four Ospreys to be carried aboard the cruiser *Gotland*, due for launch in 1934 (aircraft delivered 1935), further aircraft being built under a licence agreement. Portugal also ordered the aircraft, initially two examples, and a further example was purchased by Spain. The Hart/Osprey prototype, J9052, was later one of several aircraft shipped to the trade exhibition in Buenos Aires aboard HMS *Eagle*. The Osprey continued in Royal Navy service until withdrawal in 1938, replaced in many cases by the Fairey Fox, but thirty were still in service in September 1939.

By the start of the war in 1939, a number of Ospreys were still in the naval inventory, fitted with either the 630hp Kestrel IIMS or 640hp Kestrel V, mainly grouped at Eastleigh and Worthy Down, thirty airframes being extant at that time out of a total of 132 constructed. Most of those had been struck off charge by 1941 although K5750 survived until 1942, being based at Porton Down on chemical warfare trials. The last Osprey appears to have been K5757, allocated to Worthy Down and not struck off charge until April 1944.

Hawker Osprey Mk.III K3615 sporting wheeled undercarriage. (*BAE/BL*)

We have seen then that, post-war, the air component of the Royal Navy fared poorly. It has been said that, in 1919, the complete naval aircraft component comprised one spotter-reconnaissance squadron, one fighter flight and half a torpedo squadron, plus a seaplane and flying-boat flight![6] As can be seen from squadron allocations above, in the 1920s, squadron name-plates were sparse indeed, the operational squadrons, those likely to be ship-borne, 800, 801, 802 and 803 Squadrons, not being stood up till 1933, by the simple amalgamation of former flights. The 700 series squadrons were mainly formed in 1936 or later, again often formed out of former flights. While squadron strength in the Royal Navy was certainly growing throughout the 1930s, it was with aircraft that were or would soon be obsolete when faced by fast monoplane fighters and bombers. While passably acceptable on the high seas, they would offer poor protection when in range of land airfields.

Several other Hawker designs were used by the Fleet Air Arm in the 1930s, usually in training or communications roles. Seven Hawker Hart trainers were acquired from ex-RAF stocks, based at Eastleigh and Lee-on-Solent in the early war years together with four Hawker Audaxes, also refugees from the RAF. Lastly, seven Hawker Henleys, the Hurricane's stablemate, designed as a two-seat light bomber but relegated to target-towing roles, were used by the Naval Co-operation Unit at Hatston in Orkney.

These then were the Hawker aircraft that served the Royal Navy during the inter-war years. Seen by many to be the golden age of the biplane, their reign was swiftly drawing to a close, thanks to work being carried out by Hawker's Chief Designer, Sydney Camm.

Hawker Osprey Mk.III K4322 launched from its cruiser. The catapult cradle can be seen clearly in this view. (*BAE/BL*)

It had become clear to many in the services and in aviation design that the limits of what could be achieved in terms of speed and armament had been reached with the biplane design. Equally clearly, it was the monoplane that would provide the pattern for future development. The problem lay in the ability to design a wing sufficiently robust to defy the stresses that would come with greater speed without deforming or failing entirely and without the rigging wires that so cluttered the biplane design. What was required then was a cantilever wing able to support its own weight on the ground and the weight of the aircraft in the air. It would be this puzzle to which Sydney Camm now turned his attention.

Chapter 4

The Sea Hurricane

In times of war small events can have disproportionate consequences. It has been suggested that events during the retreat from Narvik in Norway, following the abortive landing of Allied forces to counter the German invasion in 1940, may have influenced the later decision to select the Hawker Hurricane for use aboard Royal Navy carriers. On 7 June 1940 the position of the British forces at Narvik had become untenable and No.46 Squadron was ordered to destroy their Hurricanes and head for the harbour to be evacuated. Squadron Leader Kenneth Cross argued hard for permission to land his squadron's Hurricanes aboard the carrier HMS *Glorious*, from which they had flown several days earlier, although none of his pilots had ever landed on a carrier previously. With permission granted for the attempt, Cross and his fellow pilots were able to land all ten aircraft aboard the carrier, which then departed with two destroyers for British waters. Unfortunately, the ships were spotted by the German battleships *Scharnhorst* and *Gneisenau* and in the subsequent attack, HMS *Glorious* was sunk and 1,515 men lost. However, the successful take off of massed Hurricanes, and the subsequent landing of this force, had shown the potential of Hurricane operation from an aircraft carrier. This potential would become reality in short order.

Development

The aircraft that came to be called the Hurricane had begun its gestation in 1930 with the issuing of specification F.7/30, which sought an interceptor to replace the existing designs (Bristol Bulldog and Hawker Hornet, soon to be renamed Fury and about to enter service) with one of significantly greater speed (up to 250mph) and armament (four machine guns). While the promise of a large production contract attracted many manufacturers with innovative schemes, Sydney Camm believed that, with suitable development, the new Fury interceptor could be made to conform to the requirements of F.7/30 and thereby save a great deal of expense for the company. Sadly for Camm, but also to his and the country's great advantage, Hawker's Fury development, the P.V.3, failed to win the confidence of the Directorate of Technical Development (DTD), F.7/30 failing to bring forth any radical new design. The eventual winner, the Gloster Gladiator, would be obsolete even as it entered service in 1937, although it did meet the speed and armament requirements of the specification. The reason for that obsolescence would be the Hurricane and Spitfire, both flying by that date.

In August 1933, discussions between Camm and Major Buchanan, Director DTD, had resulted in proposals for an interceptor monoplane, again based on Camm's wonderful

Interior of Hawker's assembly building at Brooklands. Hurricanes are being fitted with the wooden formers that will give shape to the fuselage. At the far end of the shop can be seen the last biplanes being erected. (*BAE/BL*)

Fury biplane and at first known as the 'Fury Monoplane', to include the evaporative cooled Goshawk engine from Rolls-Royce, dropped the following year and replaced by the PV.12 Merlin. The initial proposal included a retractable undercarriage and enclosed cockpit. The proposals achieved partial compliance with specification F.5/34 but were then given official form by the issue of F.36/34, written around Hawker's design as it then stood in August and discussed in detail with Captain Liptrot at the Air Ministry. This design featured an armament of four Vickers guns, two in the fuselage within reach of the pilot and two (with Brownings as an alternative) in the wings outside the propeller disc. In June 1934 a scale model was constructed for wind tunnel testing and drawings commenced in the Experimental Drawing Office.

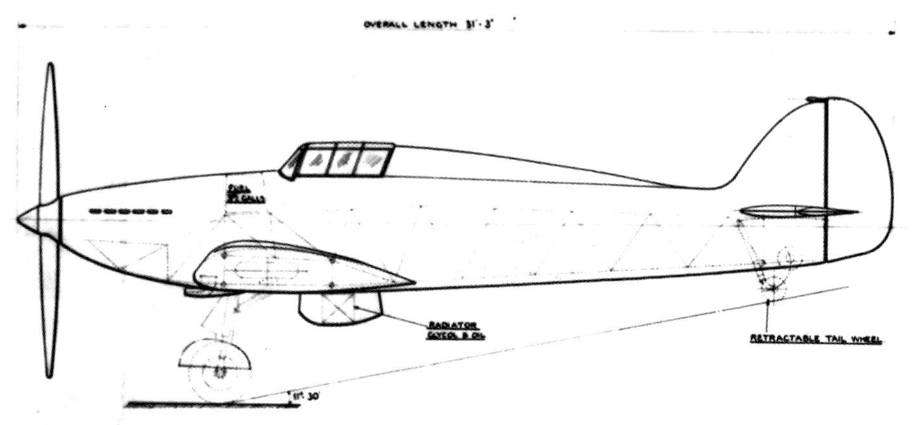

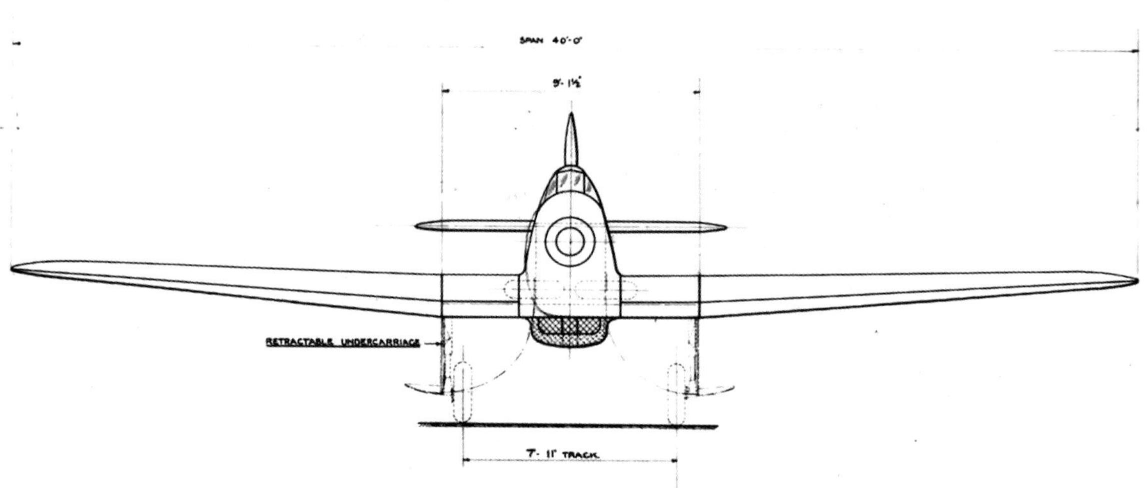

Hawker High Speed Interceptor Monoplane. Sydney Camm's design for the first Hurricane fitted with a Rolls-Royce Merlin engine. Note that the prototype had a retractable tail wheel, a feature deleted on the production aircraft. (*BAE/BL*)

At this early juncture, the estimated weight of the aircraft was 4,670lb. With an Air Ministry assessment of a mock-up at Kingston in January 1935, the following month a contract was raised for a prototype for one 'F.36/34 Single Seat Fighter – High Speed Monoplane', still with the four-gun armament, and construction of K5083 commenced in the cramped confines of the Experimental Department in Canbury Park Road, Kingston upon Thames.

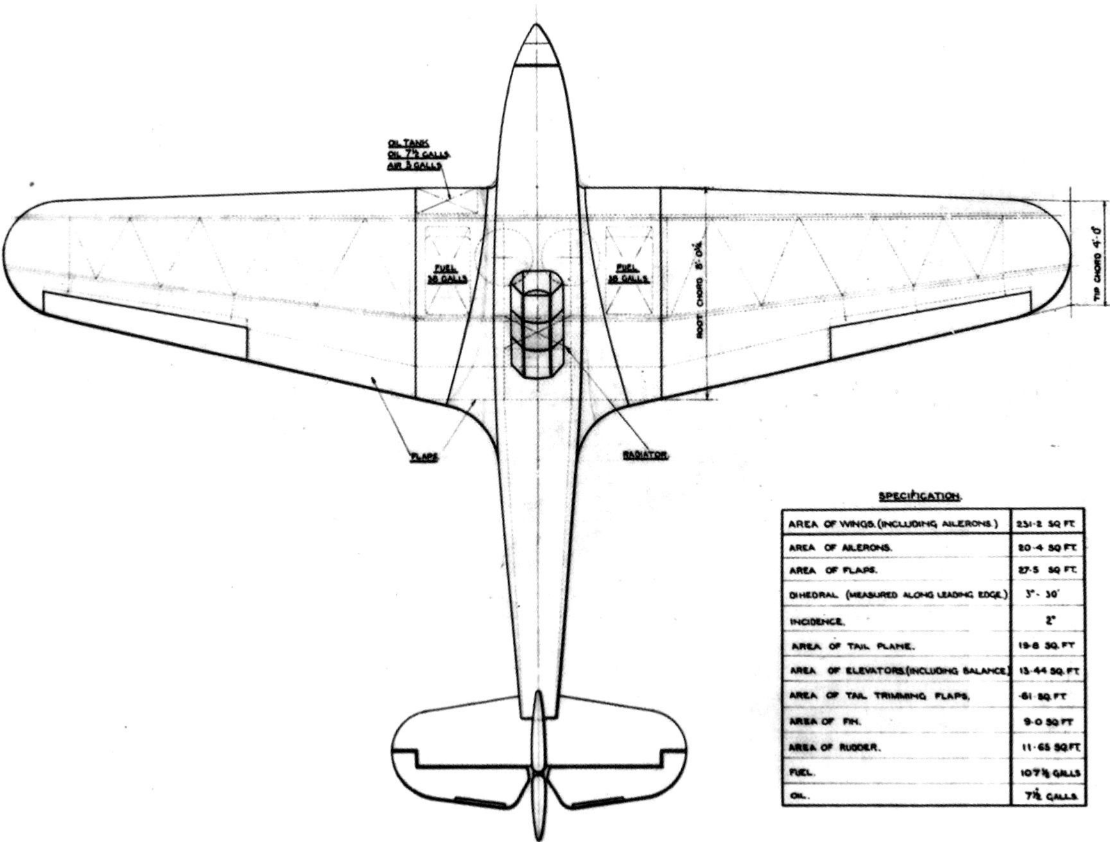

In July the company was asked to investigate the provision of metal stressed-skin wings (to date, the wing was designed to be fabric covered) and to provide for an eight-gun battery of wing-mounted guns; by August, the estimated weight had grown to 5,200lb.

On 23 October 1935, K5083 was transported by road to Brooklands airfield for final assembly and initial flight testing, this aircraft having no provision for guns. Fitted with the Rolls-Royce Merlin C and Watts wooden two-blade propeller, the first flight in the hands of 'George' Bulman occurred on 6 November 1935.

Hurricane construction, probably at the Langley factory. The braced tubular skeleton is readily apparent here. To the left of the female worker is a side former that will give shape to the fuselage. (*BAE/BL*)

This image of the early Rolls-Royce Merlin II shows just how clean a design it was. By the end of production, the engine was rather larger and cluttered with additional equipment. The item bolted to the rear (left) of the engine is the supercharger. (*BAE/BL*)

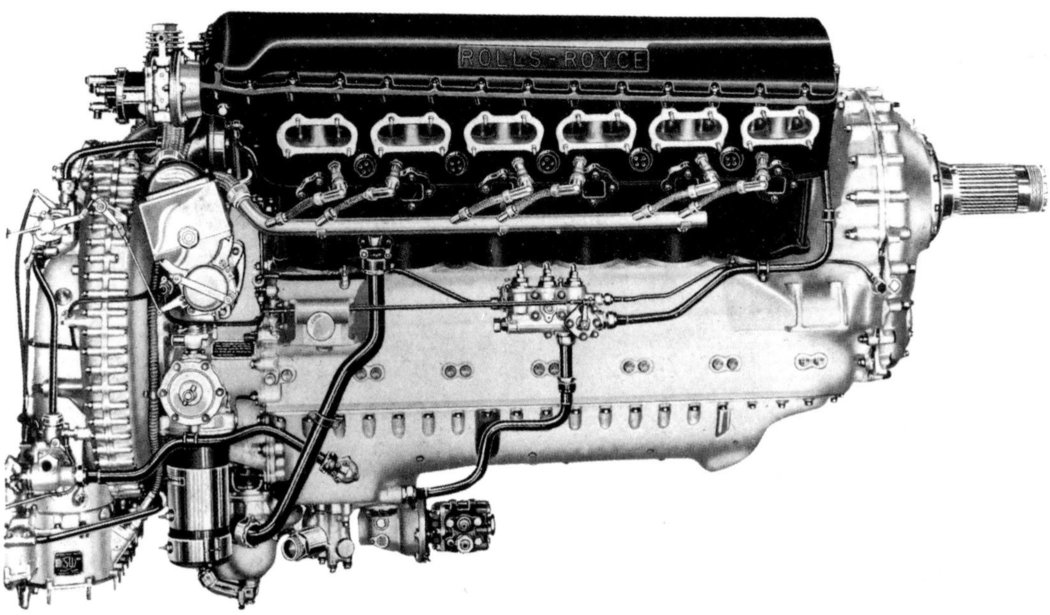

While this dry description makes it all sound easy, it should be remembered that this was Camm's team's first cantilever monoplane construction, Hawker's first design with retractable undercarriage, the first with an enclosed cockpit, the first with full-span flaps, the first with an eight-gun wing-mounted battery and the first with the new Merlin liquid-cooled engine. That most of the sundry problems and vicissitudes were solved in such a short time by the small Hawker team was a great tribute to the men – Sopwith, Camm and Sigrist – responsible for the running of the enterprise. It is important to remember also that Camm's successful design needed to incorporate the same basic design processes that had held sway in the Kingston factory for the past decade, the tubular-steel framing and fabric covering remaining well within the skill-sets available in the factory at that time. At this juncture there was neither the time nor the will to completely rejig the factory with expensive new tooling for stressed-skin construction (as per the Spitfire) to be introduced. Cost was always an important consideration at Hawker. That all-important cantilever wing design achieved the desired strength and torsional stiffness requirements by employing Hawker's tried and tested dumb-bell spar design, featuring polygonal steel-spar booms connected at top and bottom to a steel web, making for an extremely resilient construction, with the front and rear spars joined together by a Warren girder-like arrangement of diagonal members overlain by lightweight ribs for the first fabric-covered wings. The later metal wings used a more conventional arrangement of light alloy extrusion spar booms linked with light alloy plate webs together with lightweight chordwise ribs, the whole then plated to form a stressed skin.

While considering the wing design, since Hawker had no wind tunnel of their own, they had relied on the National Physical Laboratory at Teddington for advice. That their recommendation resulted in a thick wing of some 19 per cent t/c (the Spitfire was 13 per cent at the root), was always a regret for Camm since it restricted the top speed and altitude of his fighter. Not realised at the time was the fact that turbulence within the compressed air tunnel at NPL was distorting the results, a problem that would also affect the forthcoming Typhoon.

A further problem had the Hawker design team burning the midnight oil: how to calculate the load factors that would be imposed on the wing and therefore adequately to stress the design. A cantilever structure was outside Hawker's then current experience but eventually the problem was picked up by Dr Percy Walker, at that time working for Hawker. He was able to resolve the stress requirements into a series of complex equations which he then attempted to solve using a spiral slide-rule. When this failed, he turned for advice to an old colleague who put him on to a set of five-figure logarithmic tables which went some way to resolving the issue. Finally, sufficient work could be completed that allowed a fair degree of confidence to be placed in the final calculations and this, together with additional strengthening of the spars, produced a wing that would eventually carry twice the load of the original design, initially 4,800lb and latterly 9,061lb for the Mk IIC with drop tanks.

Flight testing at Brooklands soon showed that the prototype was capable of at least 300mph, was entirely controllable in flight and virtually viceless, Bulman admitting that he

The prototype F.36/34 Hurricane, K5083, seen here at Brooklands 1935. Changes to the production version included the deletion of the lower wheel covers and the tailplane struts together with a strengthened canopy and fitting of armament. (*BAE/BL*)

had taken the aircraft to around 300mph in a gentle dive and investigated the stall which occurred at around 80mph with flaps retracted. Almost the only fly in the ointment was the Merlin C engine, delivering approximately 950hp, which continually gave trouble and which would later lead to a requirement to change the contours of the aircraft's nose to accommodate the redesigned engine. Despatched to Martlesham Heath on 5 March 1936, the aircraft received a detailed assessment by the technical officers of the establishment.

Initial reactions to the new aircraft here were positive. Dives were completed to 310mph, elevators were light and responsive, although the ailerons and rudder were considered too heavy at high speeds. Trials of the eight-gun armament led to the discovery that the gun bays were being excessively cooled, hot air from the engine being used to heat the bays. Later trials revealed a reluctance to come out of the spin, a small ventral fin and longer rudder curing this admirably. Production Hurricane L1562 was trialled with a three-blade, two-pitch propeller in August 1938 and taken to 319mph at 18,000 feet and dived to a maximum of 380mph with no discernible problems.

Meanwhile, back at Kingston, on 3 June 1936, the long-awaited contract, for 600 machines, officially named Hurricane on 27 June, was received and, on 20 July, the full specification, F.15/36, for the production standard aircraft was received. However, production of the new fighter was now delayed whilst Rolls-Royce worked feverishly to get the Merlin engine operating reliably. The early Merlin was beset by many and varied problems, resulting in constant delays in flight testing, both at Brooklands and at Martlesham Heath.[1]

The Merlin was a step change in Rolls-Royce engines at this date. Promising previously unattainable horsepower coupled to a slim frontal area, it promised much but, in the beginning, delivered little. Rolls-Royce's first production model, the Merlin F (or Merlin I), at first showed promise but only by derating the performance of the engine. This was, however, superseded by the Merlin G or Merlin II (delivering approximately 1,030hp) which promised a far better reliability and it was agreed that this mark would be used for both the first Hurricanes and the first Spitfires. While the new engine was good news, it came at a price. The Merlin II had a different profile which necessitated a halt to production of the Hurricane until new contours could be designed and drafted for the front end of the aircraft and it was therefore not until 12 October 1937 that the first production aircraft, L1547, was flown by Philip Lucas. Thereafter, production aircraft began to appear at an ever increasing rate at Brooklands and, later, at Hawker's new factory and airfield at Langley near Slough.

The first Hurricane Mk.1s were allocated to No.111 Squadron at Northolt, where the increased tempo of flying allowed the aircraft to be wrung out and problems reported back to Hawker at Kingston. The early Hurricanes still featured the wooden two-blade Watts propeller used on the prototype and lacked the ventral fin, added to improve the aircraft's spinning characteristics. Also deleted were the tailplane struts (Chapman had them removed while Camm was in hospital); they were a belt-and-braces fit anyway; the tailplane had been designed from the start as a full cantilever assembly. Also deleted were the D-flap wheel doors, which caused problems on rough ground. The cockpit canopy was also strengthened after Bulman lost his trilby when the initial canopy on K5083 had parted company with the aircraft, much to his annoyance! Prior to the start of the war in 1939, the Hurricanes began receiving three-blade propellers, initially as two-pitch and later as fully-variable pitch constant-speed units, which did much to improve the Hurricane's performance but some front-line units entered the war still flying the old Watts propeller aircraft.

When war was declared on 1 September 1939, the UK had sixteen notionally operational Hurricane squadrons totalling 280 aircraft out of a total of 572 aircraft delivered to date. Nearly all the first 600 aircraft of this first contract were fitted with the fabric wing, most of them being replaced with the metal wings during subsequent service at MUs. (By the time of the Battle of Britain, almost all Hurricanes had the metal wing.) However, whatever the production modification state of those first Hurricanes, they were a marked improvement on anything previously featured in the RAF inventory and filled the pilots with confidence that they would meet the enemy on equal terms. It must be said that the first months of the war were ones of confusion and ill-considered actions that failed to provide the country with the victories that would inspire confidence in the fighting forces. One such episode was the Norwegian campaign with which this chapter opened whereby hesitancy and political half measures coupled with dubious (or complete lack of) Naval and Army planning led to ignominious outcomes for the British forces engaged in the actions.

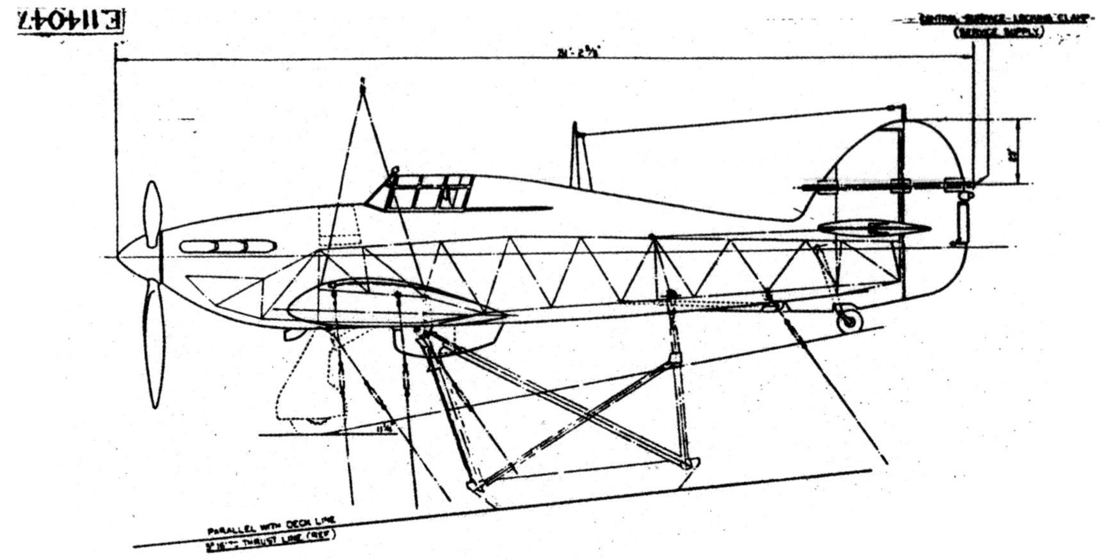

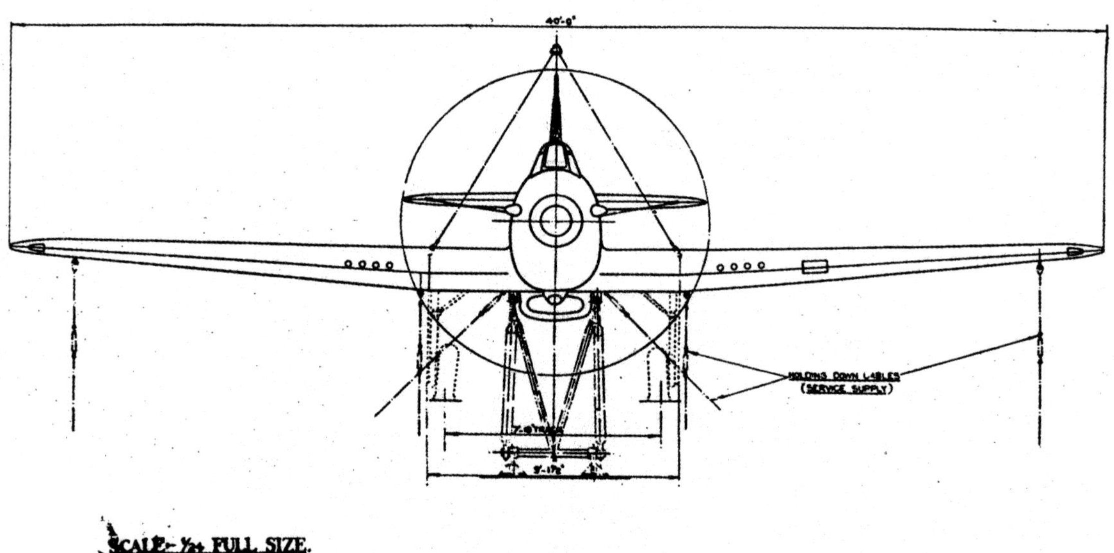

This GA drawing shows how the Hurricane Mk.IB was located on the catapult carried by the Fighter Catapult Ships (FCS). Although the Hurricane Mk.IB carried an arrestor hook, any launch from an FCS catapult was a one-way affair, there being no provision for landing back aboard. (*BAE/BL*)

It was, of course, a different matter when the RAF, the only British force that had taken to heart modern fighting tactics, was called upon to defend the country from heavy and prolonged air assault by the German Luftwaffe. The Battle of Britain has rightly become an enduring memory of those months when Britain stood within a whisker of invasion and inevitable defeat. It was the fighters of the RAF, and predominantly the Hawker

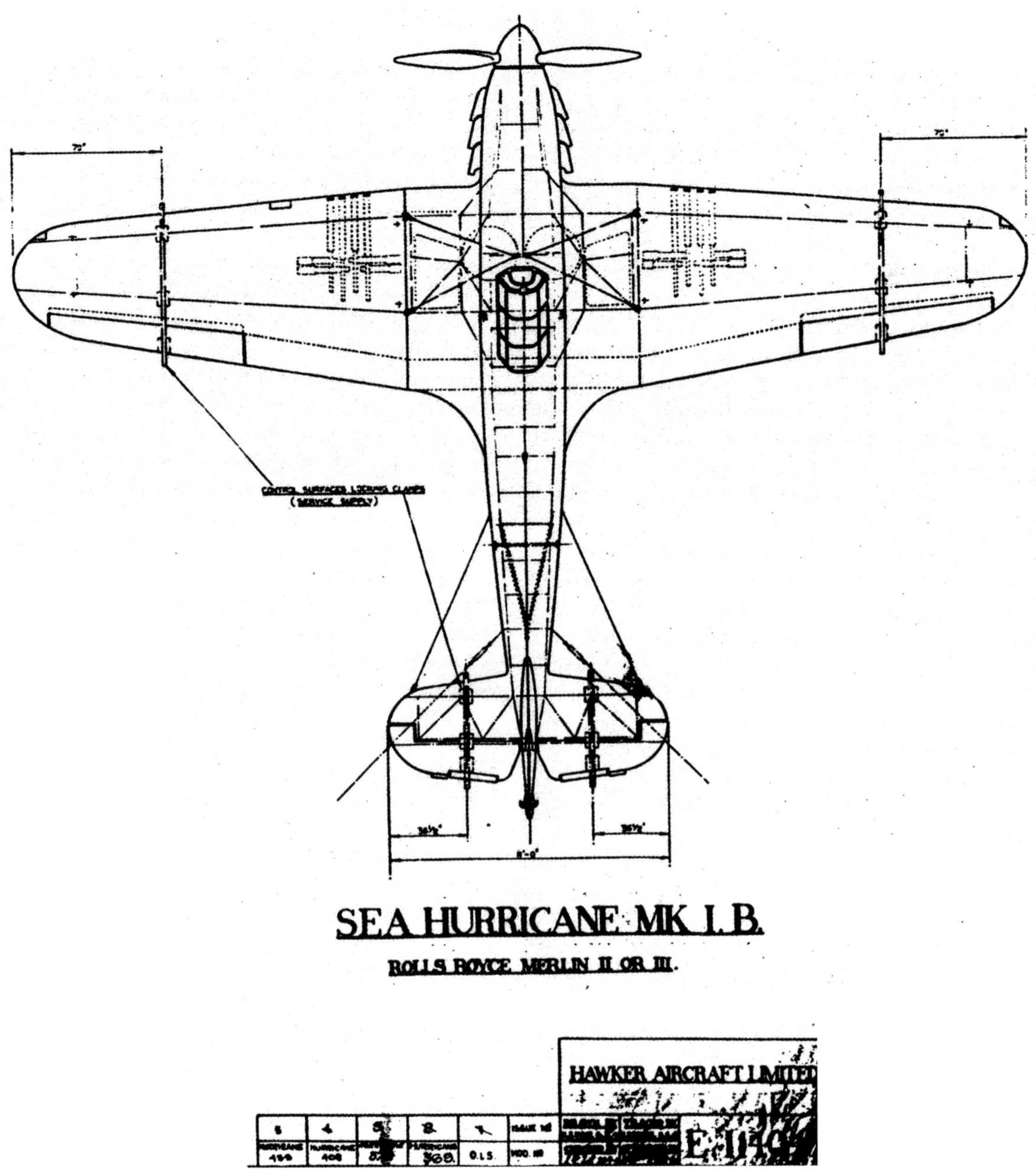

Hurricane (it achieved more 'kills' than all other defences combined, including those of the Spitfire), that turned the tide. However, this is a story, not of the aircraft in RAF service but within the ranks of the Royal and Merchant Navies.

That Sydney Camm and his team had not turned their thoughts to a naval version of the Hurricane in its early days seems most likely as they had their hands full producing the production version of the aircraft and plotting its subsequent evolution into a faster, harder-hitting fighter for the RAF. That said, an earlier requirement for a naval fighter/

bomber, 0.27/34, had achieved a response from Hawker Aircraft Ltd. This was for a biplane fitted with a RR Pegasus PE.5S radial engine, sharply staggered wings and spatted fixed undercarriage, already looking obsolete when compared to the prototype Hurricane which flew just a year later. In the event, this led to the Blackburn Skua, designed to meet the 1934 requirement for a fighter and dive-bomber. Entering service in 1938, it was principally a dive-bomber rather than a fighter although it offered the Royal Navy a faster, more heavily-armed aircraft than the biplanes with which it had until then been saddled and a chance to deploy their first cantilever monoplane with folding wings and retractable undercarriage. The four Browning guns in the leading edge plus a free Lewis gun for the observer gave the aircraft a useful capability but its speed, 225mph, was sadly less than enthralling.

Slightly later, the search for a dedicated fighter for the Royal Navy led to the Fairey Fulmar. Originally designed as the P.4/34, a fast light day bomber, developed from the company's Battle light bomber (to which Hawker tendered the Henley), when Requirement 0.8/38 was issued for a two-seat naval fighter, it was decided that the Fairey P.4/34 could, with minimal changes, answer the need. With an instruction to proceed in May 1938, the aircraft that emerged offered a slim two-seat monoplane with folding wings and retractable undercarriage suitably stressed for catapult launch, although this was not required, and an arrestor hook. Power was derived from a Rolls-Royce Merlin VIII giving 1,080hp and a top speed of 280mph. Armament was supplied by an eight-gun battery in the wings. Entering service in 1940, finally the Fleet Air Arm was getting more modern fighter aircraft with which to ply its trade.

Operational Use

Having entered the war with seven carriers – *Furious* (1917), *Argus* (1918), *Eagle* (1920), *Hermes* (1923), *Courageous* (1925), *Glorious* (1927) and *Ark Royal* (1937) – by 1940 the Royal Navy was down to just five, following the loss of *Courageous* in 1939 and *Glorious* in 1940. When merchant shipping carrying vital imports to the UK came under increasing attack by shore-based bombers and German U-boats operating in concert with reconnaissance Focke-Wulf Fw.200 Condors, aerial protection for the convoys was simply not available. At this critical juncture, the Admiralty decided to fit certain merchantmen with a catapult from which an 'expendable' fighter could be despatched to oppose the bombers and Condors and hopefully destroy the enemy or at least drive them off. For the hapless pilot, this would be a one-way flight. Unless he was in range of suitable land, a ditching in the vicinity of the convoy and a wet return to the ship was the best that could be offered. Initially, five ships were selected for the modifications – the former ocean boarding vessels *Ariguani, Maplin, Patia* (sunk before coming into active service) and *Springbank* and the merchantman *Michael E* – these becoming Fighter Catapult Ships (FCS) and No.804 Naval Squadron was selected for the operation. Training commenced on Hurricanes and Fulmars at Yeovilton.

Thus would the Hurricane go to sea. That it was never designed for shipboard operation is a truism but its sturdy construction did mean that, as an urgent expedient, minimal change would be required to fit the aircraft for such a life. However, these would not be new aircraft; the Hurricanes were modifications of existing aircraft, most being old Mk.Is that had survived the Battle of Britain. Those first Hurricanes were modified simply by the addition of catapult spools, located either side of the radiator bath, thirty-five aircraft being supplied initially and identified as Sea Hurricane 1As. Each ship would carry two Hurricanes and three pilots and be operated by Royal Navy crews. The first operational use of the FCS saw the Fulmar rather than the Hurricane deployed but none of the Fulmar operational flights resulted in the destruction of the Condor target. Indeed the Fulmars failed to even catch up with the enemy. From these early episodes, the Hurricane was exclusively selected for future operations. In addition, other merchant vessels would be provided with a rudimentary deck from which a fighter could be launched, these becoming Catapult Armed Merchantman (or Catapult Aircraft Merchant Ship – CAM). Those would sail under the Red Ensign, crewed by merchant seamen and still carrying cargo, while the aircraft would be operated by RAF ground and aircrews.

The Hawker board minutes of 2 September 1942 noted:

It was further reported that 35 Hurricane aircraft were to be converted to Sea Hurricane type by September 15th for special purpose work, and the necessary priority requirements have been granted by MAP. The General Manager expressed confidence that delivery would be effected in accordance with requirements.

It would perhaps be pertinent here to clarify just how many Sea Hurricanes were produced, by whom and exactly what each mark constituted. Indeed, what exactly was a Sea Hurricane? The confusion arises mainly because almost no new-build Sea Hurricanes were built; all were modified 'land' Hurricanes of various marks, some modified on the Langley production line. The only new-build contract appears to have covered a batch of sixty Sea Hurricane Mk.IICs in the serial range NF668-NF703 and NF716-NF739. Secondly, Hawker only produced a few modified Hurricanes, the bulk being produced by sub-contract companies, some by Gloster Aircraft, but mainly by General Aircraft at Hanwell; Canadian Car and Foundry in Canada also produced numbers of Sea Hurricanes.[2]

So, what exactly *was* a Sea Hurricane? Frank Mason, for many years operating within the Hawker Project Office at Kingston, in his book *The Hawker Hurricane* (Aston 1987), concluded thus:

Conversion of some low-hour Sea Hurricane IAs and Hurricane Is of all vintages started in May 1941, and by October about 120 Mark IBs had been completed; unfortunately for administrative tidiness, this designation also covered a small number of early Hurricane IIAs and IIBs as well as some Canadian (Sea) Hurricane Xs, XIs and XIIs with eight or twelve gun wings. There have been many attempts to exactly define what a Sea Hurricane 1B was and the nearest that can be suggested was 'any Hurricane which possessed an arrestor hook and whose gun armament did not protrude forward of the wing leading edge', but even this was later complicated by some 'hooked Hurricane IIs'.

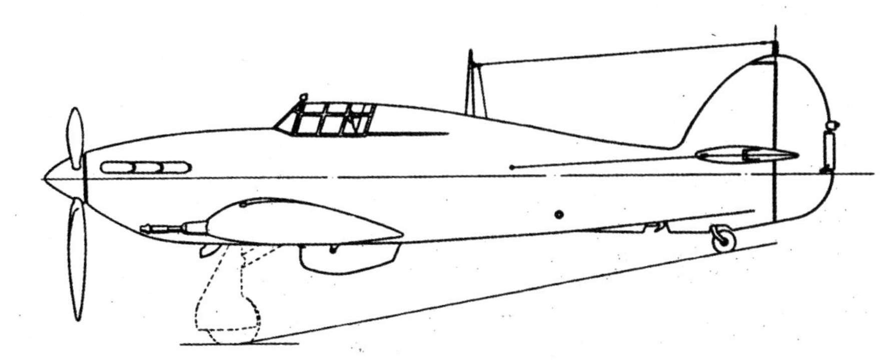

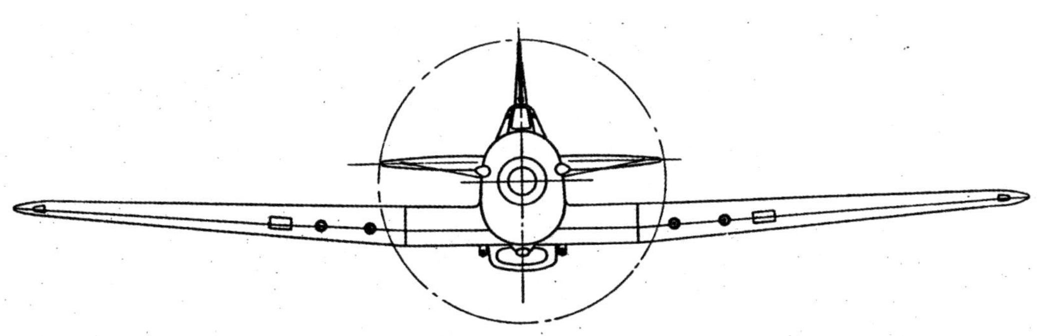

This GA shows the Hurricane Mk.IC, the cannon-equipped version used on escort carriers. Note the arrestor hook and catapult spools adjacent to the radiator bath. (*BAE/BL*)

Regarding the various marks, generally speaking, and based on Hawker's own definitions, the fitting of catapult spools and attendant local airframe strengthening resulted in the designation Sea Hurricane IA. The addition of an arrestor hook and the rather more extensive strengthening required, plus catapult spools (though not always), usually a naval radio in place of the RAF version, and an eight-gun wing, produced a Sea Hurricane Mk.IB. The fitting of the naval equipment to the standard Hurricane I with the Merlin III engine, eight-gun wing, hook, but no catapult spools produced the Sea Hurricane Mk.IC (this mark was also fitted with the cannon-armed wing). The Sea Hurricane Mk.IIB consisted of a Merlin XX powerplant, no catapult spools, a hook, provision for overload tanks and bombs, while a 'Hooked Hurricane' Mk.IIB had the Merlin XX and hook but no provision for tanks or bombs and was for land-based deck-landing practice. Lastly, the standard Hurricane with naval equipment but without catapult spools plus a Rolls-Royce Merlin XX engine and four-cannon 'universal wing' was designated Sea Hurricane Mk.IIC. Though not always! There were also standard Hurricane IIAs and IIBs that were simply issued with a hook and remained designated Mk.IIA or Mk.IIB.[3]

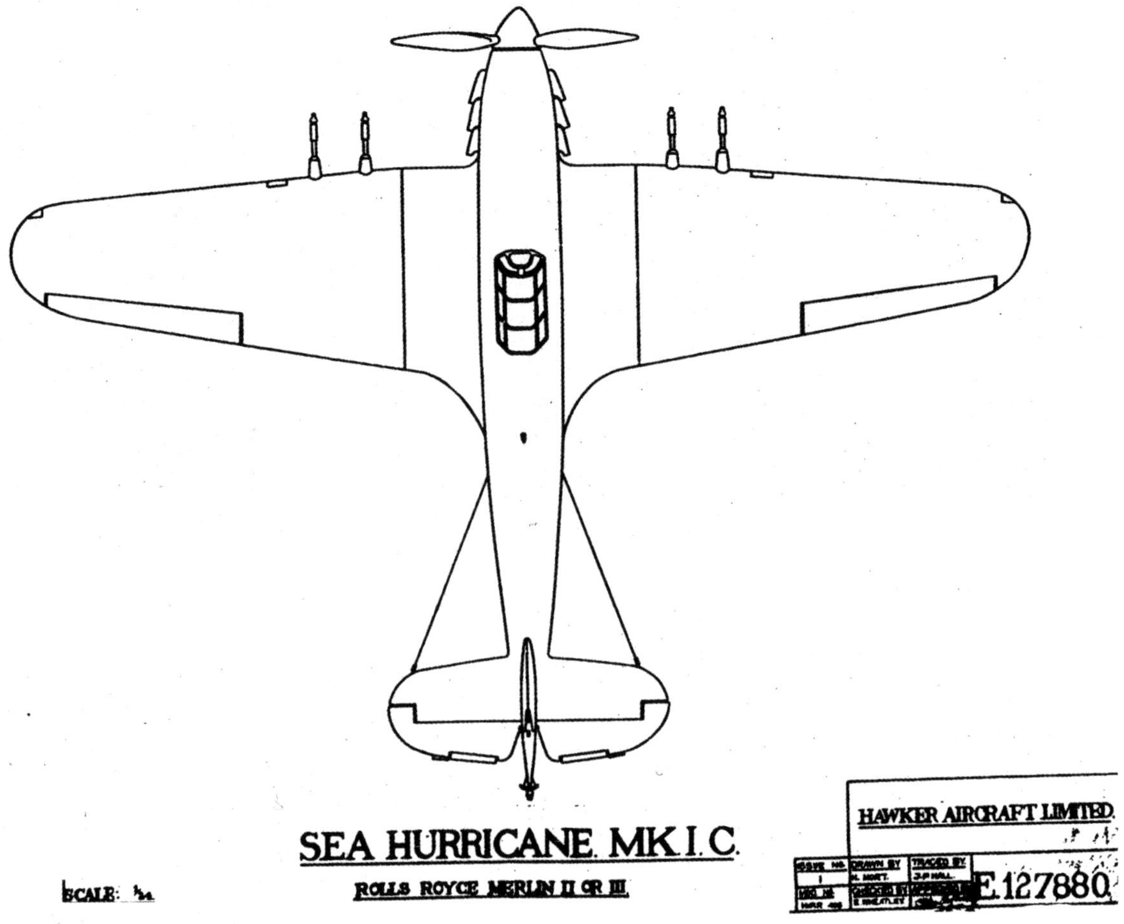

Adrian Stewart in *Hurricane: The War Exploits of the Fighter Aircraft* argues that, because the Sea Hurricane IAs were launched from merchantmen and 'apart from those operating from the Fighter Catapult Ships, they did not operate from vessels of the Royal Navy, nor …were they manned by naval pilots, nor could they return to their ships', it might be said that 'the first true Sea Hurricane was the Mark IB, which was designed specifically to operate from aircraft carriers'.[4]

The fitting of catapult spools to early Mk.1 Hurricanes had been a fairly simple matter, requiring only local strengthening around the centre section. However, the fitting of an arrestor hook required more substantial stressing and it was not until March 1941 that a prototype flew in this configuration and was tested at Boscombe Down.

These stop-gap aircraft carriers were never more than that and success was limited. However, the mere presence of a CAM-ship was sufficient to make the enemy more hesitant in pursuing attacks on the convoys. Arrangements were urgently put in hand to provide the convoys with rather more effective aerial protection in the form of small escort carriers and, as these joined the fleet, the activities of the FCS and CAM ships were run down. As far as the Hurricane was concerned though, its presence at sea would continue from the

Sea Hurricanes aboard an unnamed aircraft carrier. There appear to be eight Sea Hurricanes plus several Grumman Martlets. (*Author*)

new carriers. Those escort carriers would mainly be the product of American shipyards, modified from merchantmen and supplied to the UK via Lend Lease arrangements, but the first UK-built escort carrier was named HMS *Audacity*. *Audacity* had started life as the MV *Hannover*, a banana carrier with a speed of around 15 knots. Modification included cutting her down to boat-deck level and the fitting of an uninterrupted flight-deck of 368 feet and small bridge structure. Unfortunately, there was no room for a hangar and therefore all storage and servicing would have to take place on deck. For the fighter complement, the Admiralty pressed for the Hurricane, a tacit admission that the existing Fleet Air Arm aircraft were just too ponderous in combat.

Since these Hurricanes would be capable of landing on, as well as either a free or catapult assisted take-off, Hawker designed an A-frame type arrestor hook to be fitted just forward of the ventral fin, which was cut away forward of the tail wheel to accommodate the actual hook, and naval radio equipment fitted, these acquiring the designation Hurricane Mk.1B.

It was found that many of the Hurricanes so supplied had numerous defects that delayed the aircraft in service but luckily the Fleet Air Arm at this time also acquired a consignment of Grumman Wildcats (originally for the French) renamed Martlet, ten of which were allocated to *Audacity*. The Wildcat/Martlet had been designed as a naval aircraft from the outset and was therefore a robust design well suited to the tough life aboard a carrier.

Audacity's first convoy protection duties began directly she was commissioned, in September 1941 on the Gibraltar run with Convoy OG74, with six Martlets rather than Hurricanes aboard. Having escorted several convoys on the Mediterranean route, on 21 December 1941 she was torpedoed and, despite her holds being full of empty barrels as a buoyancy expedient in the event of such attack, eventually sank. Unfortunately, her short life did not allow much in the experimental use of these small carriers, which would have to wait for the first of the US-built ships supplied to the UK, HMS *Archer*. Commissioned at Norfolk, Virginia, on 17 November 1941, *Archer*, a Long Island-class carrier, was a considerable improvement on *Audacity*, displacing 9,000 tons with a maximum speed of 17 knots and having a flight deck of 410 feet, 87 feet wide and a 'half hangar' occupying about one third of the length of the ship, a catapult (accelerator) and an elevator (aircraft lift). She could accommodate up to fifteen aircraft.

As the first of the new BAVG escort carriers (BAVG-1), early problems identified had to be rectified and applied to later ships of the class. During her working up, it was found that thick smoke from the diesel engines tended to obscure aircraft trying to land on; the first trial of the catapult ended in disaster with a US Navy Wildcat being prematurely released and crashing over the side. The engines packed up, as did the gyro compass, as well as the steering gear, soon followed by the radar, allowing *Archer* to collide with another vessel, causing a return to the yard for urgent repairs. However, in time, *Archer* did return to active use but not as a first-line vessel, ultimately being used as an aircraft ferry ship.

Meanwhile more BAVG escort carriers were commissioned in the USA and joined the Royal Navy's order of battle as *Avenger*, *Attacker* and later, Ruler-class carriers, *Avenger* and *Biter* and *Dasher* being BAVG-2, -3 and -4 respectively. Too slow for fleet operations, they were used to provide aerial protection for the Atlantic and Mediterranean convoys. Following these Avenger-class carriers, the eleven Attacker-class carriers could accommodate an increased inventory of twenty-four aircraft, as could the twenty-three Ruler-class vessels, the last of which, HMS *Reaper*, was commissioned in February 1944.

This digression into the carrier component of convoy protection is necessary since upon them fell the less glamorous job of deterrence and on which the Sea Hurricane served principally, the main convoy routes being the Atlantic run between the USA or Canada and the UK; the Mediterranean run between the UK and Malta/Gibraltar as well as North Africa; and the Russian run to Archangel in the White Sea and back. The North American convoys' greatest threat was from the U-boat packs, sometimes guided by Fw.200 Condor reconnaissance aircraft, which caused devastation to shipping in the earlier years of the war before a combination of long-range aircraft, ASDIC, radar countermeasures and Ultra intelligence allowed the Allies to target the packs and move to the offensive. For the Mediterranean voyages, the principal threat came from shore-based aircraft of the

With everything down, and sufficient wind over deck, the Hurricane's landing speed was benign, always supposing that the flaps and undercarriage had not been damaged in combat of course. (*BAE/BL*)

German Luftwaffe and Italian *Regia Aeronautica* flying from western France, Sardinia, Sicily and North Africa. The Russian convoys had to run the gauntlet of land-based aircraft in Norway as well as submarines throughout the voyage. It was principally the aerial threat that the Sea Hurricane would have to battle.

It was widely considered at the time that the Russian convoys were the most trying: the weather was usually foul, the summer nights in the northern latitudes were so brief as to provide little respite from observing shadowers and submarines and the chances of survival in the event of a sinking were minimal. After the disaster of convoy PQ17, which had been almost wiped out after an ill-considered order to scatter, PQ18 sailed in early September accompanied by HMS *Avenger* carrying her own twelve Sea Hurricanes, six Sea Hurricanes of No.802 Squadron, six Hurricanes from No.883 Squadron and a further six spare aircraft stowed in the hangar partially dismantled, these being a mixture of Sea Hurricane Mk.1Bs and Mk.IIBs. Also brought aboard were three Fairey Swordfish and crews from No.825 Squadron.

Sailing from Scapa Flow on 3 September 1942, *Avenger* and her destroyer escort reached Seyðisfjörður in Iceland on the 5th, where an attack by a Condor was repelled. Eventually joining the convoy, the entire enterprise set sail for the Barents Sea and Russia. As the voyage progressed, numerous enemy aircraft and submarines were sighted and chased to little effect and two ships were torpedoed. Ju.88s of KG30 swept in and bombed the convoy, causing the Sea Hurricanes to give chase. Unfortunately, this was but a feint to draw off the defenders while He.111s and Ju.88s moved in to bomb and torpedo the ships, hitting eight for the loss of one He.111 to the Hurricanes. As the fighting developed, the Hurricanes' tactics were changed and greater success achieved. With *Avenger* being singled out for special attention, the Sea Hurricanes were certainly not short of targets and their tally began to mount.

Having lost forty-one aircraft to the combined defences of Hurricane and AA fire and had many other attacks thwarted by the Hurricanes, the attacks petered out as the convoy came within reach of land-based Catalina flying boats and HMS *Avenger* was instructed

Hurricane pile-up. The rear Sea Hurricane appears to have missed the wires and come to an abrupt halt thanks to the aircraft in front. (*Author*)

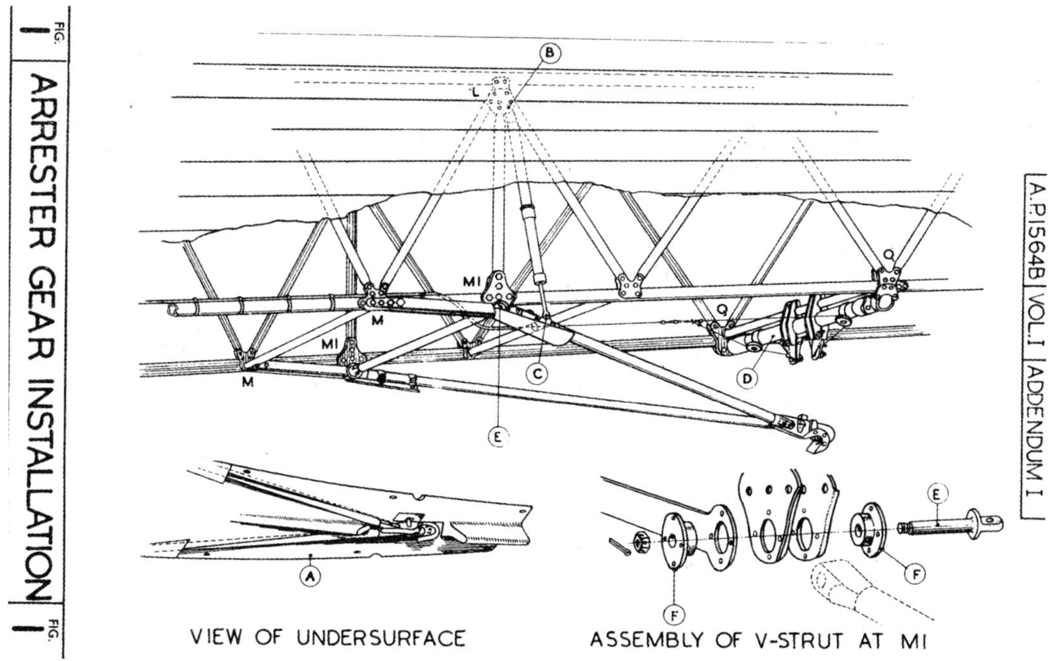

This drawing shows the detail of the arrestor-hook assembly on the rear underside of the Hurricane. The hook is carried on a V-strut attached to the reinforced tubular skeleton of the rear fuselage together with its damping struts and hook retention clip. (*BAE/BL*)

to leave PQ18 and join the homeward-bound QP14 since *Avenger* was required for a forthcoming amphibious landing in North Africa, Operation TORCH. One aspect of the operation was that the 0.303 guns of the early Sea Hurricanes were found to be less than effective against the armoured bombers of the Luftwaffe and requests were made for the 20mm cannon-armed Sea Hurricane Mk.ICs or Mk.IICs for future operations. On HMS *Vindex*, a UK-built escort carrier ploughing the Atlantic convoy routes as part of an anti-submarine task-force, this problem was addressed in typical Fleet Air Arm style. Sporting a mix of Sea Hurricanes and Swordfish bombers, a local modification was introduced whereby the 3-inch unguided rocket projectiles (RPs) in use on the Swordfish were rigged up on a Sea Hurricane and the modification cleared by A&AEE Boscombe Down in April 1944, thus giving the aircraft a much needed heavy hitting capability against the U-boats although it is unclear whether the Hurricane was ever successful in sinking a submarine with RPs. This modification was already in play for land-based Hurricanes, for example those in use in the Mediterranean campaigns: Boscombe Down had tested the carriage of RPs on Hurricane L1780/G on 2 November 1941 and a more prolonged series of tests with Z2320/G and X2457/G on 29 September 1942, Z3092/G on 11 January 1943, KZ189 in June 1944 and LB743 in January 1945. These trials featured a battery of four RPs carried under each wing. Sometimes, the four-cannon armament of the IIC was reduced to two and sometimes omitted completely, or indeed left in situ. Although it appears that this modification was principally considered as an anti-shipping tactic, its existence had clearly not permeated the ranks of the Fleet Air Arm to any degree and its use at sea against submarines had clearly not been considered until now.[5]

Whilst the escort carriers were fully occupied in the northern seas of Europe and the Arctic, the fleet carrier HMS *Indomitable* was, or should have been, fighting a lonely war in the southern waters of the Indian Ocean. Having been delayed in her arrival there by damage incurred during her work-up in the Caribbean, her role was to prove less than glamorous at first. With the Imperial Japanese Army and Navy running riot across the Far East, HMS *Indomitable*, 'Indom', was used as a ferry to deliver urgent aircraft reinforcements to various Empire outposts at risk of destruction. To this end, on New Year's Eve 1941, *Indomitable* had put into Cape Town, South Africa, and then pushed on hurriedly up the east coast of Africa to Port Sudan to collect a consignment of fifty Hurricanes, along with fifty RAF pilots and a hundred RAF ground crew to erect and fly them – somewhere. The Hurricanes, unlike those already in use on the carrier, were broken down for stowage and the carrier set off again with its precious cargo on its peregrinations around the Indian Ocean.

As it became clear that the Hurricanes were destined for Batavia in the Dutch East Indies, where they would stem the tide of Japanese destruction flowing westward, work began to rebuild the Hurricanes. It soon became clear that the groundcrew had never worked on the aircraft before and the task of getting the Hurricanes ready for flight fell to the carrier squadrons who, of course were fully tied up with flying and servicing their own Sea Hurricanes. Eventually the work was complete and the RAF Hurricanes were flown off to Batavia where, within twenty-four hours, every one of them was destroyed by marauding Japanese fighters!

By 1942 Hurricane Mk.IIBs and Mk.IICs began to filter through to the Fleet Air Arm. These later models featured the Rolls-Royce Merlin XX of 1,280hp or Merlin 22 coupled to a constant-speed propeller in place of the earlier Merlin II or III providing 1,030hp. Although the extra power gave an improvement in maximum speed, 336mph against 318mph of the early engine/prop combination, it came at the price of increased weight, up from 4,670lb for the Mk.I empty to 5,800lb for the Mk.IIC. However, climb speed and altitude were improved, a climb to 20,000 feet taking 11.7 minutes in the Mk.1 against 9.1 minutes for the Mk.IIC. Maximum altitude was now 35,600 feet rather than 33,400 feet of the old Mk.I. The IIB Hurricane had its gun armament increased to twelve Brownings while the IIC had these replaced by four Hispano 20mm cannon.

Operation TORCH, conceived in July 1942, was to be an amphibious landing by British and American forces on the coast of North Africa in Morocco and Algeria against Axis and Vichy French forces. D Day would be 8 November and comprised three taskforces arriving at the coast simultaneously at Casablanca in French Morocco, and Oran and Algiers in Algeria. British support would include the carriers HMS *Formidable*, *Victorious*, *Argus* and *Furious*, together with the auxiliary carriers HMS *Avenger*, *Biter* and *Dasher* (*Eagle* had been lost in convoy to Malta and most of her Sea Hurricanes went down with the ship). Losses of Sea Hurricanes were made good with Seafires, giving the force a better interceptor although with a concomitant increase in landing accidents. Thus the

Hurricane being serviced and replenished aboard a carrier; the aircraft is probably a Hurricane Mk.IB since it carries the eight-gun Browning armament. (*PA*)

auxiliary carrier force mix would be: *Avenger* – twelve Sea Hurricanes, *Biter* – fifteen Sea Hurricanes, *Dasher* – twelve Sea Hurricanes plus six spare Seafires. The fleet carriers would carry a mix of Martlets (Wildcats), Seafires, Fulmars and Albacores. The Algiers landings went ahead against moderate opposition, the Sea Hurricanes of HMS *Avenger* flying sixty sorties, and by 10 November, a truce had been arranged. However, in Oran opposition was fiercer, Vichy fighters defending the three airfields, causing some losses amongst the Albacores intent on bombing those fields. However, by 10 November, with Allied fighters operating from the captured airfields, a surrender was accepted. The Sea Hurricane had acquitted itself well and demonstrated its flexibility at sea. With the cannon-armed variants predominant, the Fleet Air Arm was able to obtain improved offensive combat ability from an airframe that was tough enough to withstand the rigours of life at sea. In contrast, the Seafire was considered a better fighter and would become the aircraft of choice for the Fleet Air Arm squadrons but it was not a good deck landing aircraft, many crashes on deck testifying to the fragile narrow track undercarriage being its weak point.

While Operation TORCH had been a great success, unfortunately on her way from Gibraltar to UK escorting convoy MKF1, HMS *Avenger* was torpedoed and blew up, sinking almost immediately with the loss of all but twelve of her crew. For the ship's No.802 Squadron, this was their third sinking of the war, having previously been embarked in *Glorious* and then *Audacity*, both sunk by the enemy.

Hawker Nimrod I S1581 (G-BWWK), built in 1932 and powered by a Rolls-Royce Kestrel V engine, normally based at IWM Duxford with The Fighter Collection. (*AW*)

Hawker Nimrod II K3661 (G-BURZ) is the sole remaining airworthy Nimrod II, built in 1934 and based at IWM Duxford with the Historic Aircraft Collection. (*AW*)

Hawker Nimrod I S1581 and Sea Hurricane Z7015. (*AW*)

Hawker Sea Hurricane Z7015 of the Shuttleworth Trust, based at Old Warden Aerodrome. Manufactured by Canadian Car and Foundry at Fort William and converted to a Sea Hurricane IB in the UK, it is the only airworthy Sea Hurricane in the world. (*AW*)

Hawker Sea Hurricane Z7015 of the Shuttleworth Trust based at Old Warden Aerodrome. Manufactured by Canadian Car and Foundry at Fort William and converted to a Sea Hurricane IB in the UK. It is the only airworthy Sea Hurricane in the world. (*AW*)

Hawker Sea Fury marked up as SR661, the first Sea Fury prototype. Built as an Iraqi Fury and now registered as G-CBEL, it is based at North Weald. (*AW*)

Hawker Sea Fury marked up as SR661, the first Sea Fury prototype. (*AW*)

Hawker Sea Hawk FGA.Mk.6 WV826, built in 1954, based at the Malta Aviation Museum, Ta' Qali Museum, Malta. (*AW*)

Hawker Sea Hawk WV908, built in 1954 as a FGA.Mk.4 and upgraded to FGA.Mk.6, based at RNAS Yeovilton formerly with the Royal Navy Historic Trust and now with Navy Wings. (*Andrew Harker Alamy*)

Hawker Hunter GA.Mk.11 XF301 is now believed to be based in the USA. (*BAE/BL*)

Hawker Hunter GA.11, seen at RNAS Yeovilton while operated by Airwork Services as part of the FRADU operation. (*Author*)

Hawker Hunter T.8M XL602 while used as Sea Harrier systems trainer at Dunsfold in June 1990. The aircraft subsequently donated its rear end to an ongoing project to display a Hunter adjacent to the former Hawker factory at Richmond Road, Kingston upon Thames. (*Author*)

BAe Sea Harrier FRS.Mk.1 from No.899 NAS and Spanish AV-8S 805/01 in formation. (*BAE/BL*)

Sea Harrier FRS.Mk.51 IN617, fitted with ferry tanks, now believed preserved in a park facing the sea at Bandra, India. (*BAE/BL*)

BAe Sea Harrier FRS.2 ZA195, the first FRS.2 development aircraft, carrying a full complement of AMRAAM missiles. (*BAE/BL*)

BAe Sea Harrier F/A.2s XZ495 and ZD615 up from the Sea Harrier OEU, No.899 NAS. (*BL*)

While Malta was defended ferociously by the Allies and never fell to Axis forces, this achievement was won at great price. Re-supply convoys had to fight their way from Gibraltar against sustained attack by U-boats, E-boats and land-based bombers which were responsible for a heavy attrition of convoy vessels and escorting warships. Some 718 aircraft had been delivered in this way between 1940 and 1942, of which 333 were various marks of Hurricane, later replaced by 367 Spitfires. Such was the intense fighting in the attempt to subdue Malta that attrition would quickly erode these figures so that at times the defenders were down to fewer than ten airworthy fighters and the island spent many months on starvation rations as convoys were decimated attempting to break the prolonged siege.

Operation PEDESTAL of August 1942 was perhaps the most vicious and prolonged attack on a convoy. It was also perhaps the Sea Hurricane's swansong. After that, the Seafire was the preferred mount of the Fleet Air Arm, more potent in aerial combat but worryingly fragile on board ship. Fourteen merchant ships comprised the convoy, accompanied by a large and impressive naval protective screen including four carriers, HMS *Eagle*, *Furious*, *Victorious* and *Indomitable*, although *Furious* could not operate her fighters due to being used as a ferry for a contingent of Spitfires for the island; two battleships – HMS *Nelson* and *Rodney*; twenty-four destroyers, eleven submarines and seven cruisers together with many other support ships, comprising in total over fifty ships. This vast armada had but one aim: to ensure the safe passage of the merchant ships to Malta, which was on the verge of starvation. At the end of July 1942, Admiral Weichold, the German Kommandeur

Sea Hurricane Mk.IB Z7015 of the Shuttleworth Trust at Old Warden Aerodrome. Manufactured by Canadian Car and Foundry at Fort William and converted to a Sea Hurricane Mk.IB in the UK, it is the only airworthy Sea Hurricane in the world. (*AW*)

Oberbefehlshaber Mediterranean, received an intelligence report that 'a large-scale Allied operation is about to break into the Mediterranean. Large merchant ships and fleet units are being fetched from far and wide in preparation'. The enemy then had plenty of time in which to prepare his response.[6]

HMS *Victorious* carried five Sea Hurricanes of No.885 Squadron, *Indomitable* had twenty-two Sea Hurricanes of Nos. 800 and 880 Squadrons (eleven each) and on *Eagle* were sixteen Sea Hurricanes of Nos. 801 and 813 Squadrons, making forty-three Hurricanes, plus Grumman Martlets and Fairey Fulmars. (HMS *Argus* was also involved in the early stages but detached to Gibraltar without entering the Mediterranean.)

On 11 August at 13.15 a U-boat – *U-73* – fired torpedoes that hit HMS *Eagle* which quickly sank, losing all but four Sea Hurricanes and 162 crew. Hugh Popham, a pilot aboard HMS *Indomitable*, witnessed the catastrophe from his Hurricane cockpit:

> I was in position on the catapult, engine running. The flight deck engineer waggled the ailerons to draw my attention to something or other, and I looked out over the port side to see what he wanted. And, as I did so, I stared in shocked surprise beyond him to where *Eagle* was steaming level with us, half a mile away. For as I turned smoke and steam suddenly poured from her, she took on a heavy list to port, and the air shook with a series of muffled explosions. Over the sound of the engine, I yelled: '*Eagle*'s been hit'. Listing to port, she swung in a slow, agonised circle, and in seven minutes turned abruptly over.

While the Sea Hurricanes had concentrated on the threat from above, a submarine had closed with the convoy and dealt death and destruction from below.[7]

That evening, the aerial threat finally materialised in the form of massed ranks of Ju.88 bombers, upon which the Sea Hurricanes and Martlets fell and drove them off. Next day, another large force of Ju.88s came in, intent on bombing the convoy but, again, was driven off with the loss of twelve of their number. Throughout the day, raid after raid fell upon the ships of the convoy, Ju.87 Stukas, Ju.88s, He.111s as well as numerous Italian Regia Aeronautica aircraft, including Savoia-Marchetti SM.79 and 84 torpedo bombers. Through several days of intense bombardment and torpedo attack, including an attack on HMS *Indomitable* that damaged her seriously for the loss of twelve personnel and on *Victorious*, the convoy slowly wound its way to Malta, finally arriving on 14 and 15 August with the loss of thirteen vessels and 457 personnel but the island blockade was broken, which allowed it to fight on and take the offensive to the Axis convoys attempting to re-supply their forces in North Africa. Sea Hurricanes and Martlets had flown multiple sorties against the constant waves of Axis bombers, in many cases breaking up their attacks, though they were unable to reach the high-flying Ju.88 reconnaissance aircraft that constantly shadowed the convoy. Losses for the fleet Air Arm consisted of thirteen aircraft on operations and another sixteen Sea Hurricanes when HMS *Eagle* sank but the island fortress was saved to fight another day.

Work had been carried out by Hawker Aircraft Ltd to produce a folding-wing design for the Sea Hurricane to ease handling aboard the small escort carriers but, as seen below, the introduction of the Seafire precluded this work reaching production status. The primary duty allocated to Sea Hurricanes when aboard was the defence of the fleet against bombers and torpedo-bombers such as the ubiquitous Ju.87, Ju.88 and He.111 as well as the Savoia Marchetti SM.79 and 84. This would, if within reach of land bases, include defending against fighters such as the Bf.109, the Reggiane Re.2001, Macchi C.200 and C.202 Italian fighters. Mostly the Sea Hurricane gave a good account of itself but it was no secret that the pilots would have preferred Seafires.

By 1943 the Sea Hurricane was being withdrawn in favour of the Seafire on the escort carriers. It had after all always been but an interim response to a chronic shortage of capable fighters in the Fleet Air Arm. However, it had proved to the doubters at the Admiralty that high-performance fighters could be operated safely at sea and provided the Fleet Air Arm with its most capable fighter at a time of desperate need. In the later stages of the war, most Sea Hurricanes were either relegated to training establishments or were in storage at AHUs although a number continued to serve aboard till the end of the war, mainly from the Hawker new-build batch of Sea Hurricane Mk.IICs. The last Sea Hurricane in service was NF700 of No.835 Squadron which served aboard HMS *Nairana*. Post-war, most of the Sea Hurricanes were scrapped although some found new life with foreign countries. Some fifteen Sea Hurricanes went to the French Aeronavale, mainly IICs and some Canadian XIIs. Most Hurricane exports, such as those to Portugal and Persia, were standard late Mk.IICs.

Finally, how many of these conversions were produced? Stewart (above) thinks 500 to 550 to be a fair estimate. Other estimates based on a 1944 RAF census, suggest 634. However, a search of the serials of Hurricane conversions to Sea Hurricanes in *British Military Aircraft Serials 1912–1966* by Bruce Robertson suggests only 411 official conversions. Perhaps the closest one may approach the question is the work carried out by Ray Sturtivant and Mick Burrow in *Fleet Air Arm Aircraft 1939–1945*. This gives the most likely numbers as: Sea Hurricane conversions, all marks, 345 plus sixty new-build Sea Hurricane Mk.IICs by Hawker at Langley, making 405 in total. However, this number is likely to increase when the sixty-seven unidentified aircraft in their list are considered; most will have been Sea Hurricanes of various marks. Finally, the Fleet Air Arm used numbers of 'standard' Hurricanes when based ashore in the war-zone, e.g. during the protracted battles in the Western Desert, some 195 being used with a further ninety-five Hurricane Mk.IICs from the RAF stocks, although these do not seem to have been used operationally, as well as for training duties at various establishments. So it appears that, in toto, the Fleet Air Arm had in its inventory during the 1939–1945 period some 405 Sea Hurricanes of all marks, plus further un-modified Hurricanes.[8]

What was the Sea Hurricane like to fly and how did it compare with the Mark Mk.IIC? Frank Chapman has much experience of flying the Sea Hurricane owned by the Shuttleworth Trust at Old Warden. In an interview in *Aeroplane* from August 2024, he noted:

The Sea Hurricane is more Mk I standard, with a smaller engine and a smaller radiator. If you talk to some of my colleagues … they will say it's possibly the worst handling Hurricane in the UK! I can understand the comment as, being a Sea Hurricane, the CG is further aft than on any of the others. The Hurricane was always close to neutrally stable longitudinally, and in manoeuvre it was slightly manoeuvre-unstable in that you would pull into a turn and it would have a tendency to wrap itself into the turn. I was warned about this beforehand, so I knew it was coming but that's quite an interesting aspect of the Sea Hurricane handling. Other Hurricanes are more benign. I think, in part, this is why pilots used to like it in the Second World War. Due to these characteristics, it was good for tracking targets in a turn. I can fully understand why, as a gun platform, it was a great machine.[9]

The CG location was different for the Sea Hurricane. Chapman explained it thus:

The addition of the hook and the small engine on the early Hurricanes gave the Sea Hurricane a CG further aft than the rest. I have flown the Mk1 and 2 and they do have better pitch handling characteristics, especially the Mk2 with Merlin 35. Knowledge of whether the Shuttleworth Sea Hurricane is representative of those delivered to the Navy seems to be missing at OW [Old Warden]. It could be that pilots accepted the negative manoeuvre stability as it is certainly something one can adapt to, but is an unusual aspect of the type's handling qualities. Even at slow speed after take-off and during the latter stages of the approach the longitudinal stability is minimal to say the least. With the small radiator on the Sea Hurricane and Mk1s there were always cooling issues and you'll notice we always perform 5–10mins cool down after a display and prior to landing and we are running on far lower boost than during wartime to save the engine.

On a final note, F.H.M. Lloyd, in his 1945 study of the Hurricane, reported:

A year after the delivery of the Last Hurricane, in September 1945, the fifth anniversary of the Battle of Britain was marked in London's Thanksgiving Week with a massed flight over the capital by Fighter Command … Both the event and the occasion served as a tragic reminder of the passing of an old and trusty warrior, for not a single Hurricane was included in the massed formation.[10]

Chapter 5

Sea Fury

If the Hawker Hurricane marked the successful genesis of a distinguished line of monoplane fighters, then the Sea Fury surely marked the zenith of that line. Henceforth, Hawker products would be exclusively jet powered. Design of the Hurricane had begun in 1934 and, by the time it entered service in 1937, Camm and his team were already considering means by which its performance could be enhanced. Henceforth, this development would follow two separate courses, one of which would be improvements to the basic Hurricane exemplified by the Mk I, and the other development of related but improved designs.

With regard to the basic Hurricane, improvements would concentrate on increased performance and increased hitting power of its armament. The early Rolls-Royce Merlin II and III were supplanted in the Mk.II Hurricane by the Merlin XX, increasing horsepower from 1,030hp to 1,280hp or, with the even later Merlin 22, to 1,460hp. Related speed and altitude increased from 324mph and 34,200 feet with the Merlin II or III (and three-blade Rotol propeller) to 336mph and 35,600 feet with the Merlin XX. Armament improvements for the interceptor versions were dealt with by replacing the original eight-gun design with a twelve-gun Browning battery, described by Boscombe Down as 'the worst gun installation seen', and, on the Hurricane Mk.IIC, with four Hispano 20mm cannon. But, whatever finessing was applied to the Hurricane, the one stumbling block for radical improvements was always that thick wing, which saw the Hurricane relegated to ground attack, firstly in the Mediterranean zone and later in the Far East.[1]

In later years, Camm allegedly lamented his acceptance of the data from the National Physical Laboratory compressed-air wind tunnel, upon which he had based the Hurricane wing. It was not realised at the time that turbulence within the new wind tunnel caused by its design (possibly no allowance for boundary layer problems) had skewed the results to suggest that a thickness/chord ratio of less than 20 per cent would not improve drag so Hawker settled on 19 per cent with the promise that this would give the best performance for an interceptor. It may well be that Camm would have instinctively suspected this result but it suited Hawker to accept it, given that designing their first cantilevered wing became easier with a thicker section and made stowage of the undercarriage considerably easier. To design a thinner wing was not an insuperable problem for the Kingston team, and indeed a new wing was designed wherein a thinner section might have been incorporated. The requirement to carry a wide variety of stores in the ground-attack versions led to the design of the so-called universal wing, which allowed convenient carriage of everything from drop tanks to bombs, rocket projectiles and heavy tank-busting cannon. While a thin section could have been included, by this time, the Hurricane was seen almost exclusively as a ground-attack aircraft for which enhanced speed and altitude were secondary requirements at best and the t/c ratio remained at that 19 per cent figure.[2] Work was conducted at RAE with the Hurricane in the 24-foot wind tunnel on drag reduction but this was four years after its first flight and the widespread acceptance of the aircraft into RAF squadron service.[3]

So it was that, with Hurricane development curtailed by design strictures and the requirement to produce as many as possible for the forthcoming showdown with Germany, a parallel course was followed by the Hawker design department on new and improved fighters. One obvious lead would be the use of newly developed engines of much greater potential power than the available Merlins.

The first of those new engines was another product from Rolls-Royce named Vulture. Early versions, i.e. the Vulture II, were developing 1,760hp and the later Vulture V was potentially capable of delivering 1,980hp. This engine featured an innovative X layout with four banks of cylinders (twenty-four cylinders in total) disposed around a common crankshaft. Around the early promise shown by this engine, Hawker designed a tubular and stressed-skin monoplane of 9,250lb with provision for twelve Browning guns or four 20mm Hispano cannon. First flight of this aircraft, the Tornado, came at Langley in October 1939 and was soon followed by a contract for 500 aircraft, most construction to be undertaken by Avro at Manchester, where their Manchester medium bomber would also be produced using the same engine.

The other new engine was being developed by Napier to a design by Major Frank Halford. This, the Sabre, would be a sleeve-valve, rather than a poppet-valve, design which Harry Ricardo had predicted in 1927 would be necessary to increase the efficiency of the reciprocating engine. This would also be a twenty-four-cylinder design potentially capable of producing 2,000hp from a horizontal H-shaped layout whereby the two banks of cylinders on each side were connected to common exhausts. By 1940 the Sabre was delivering 2,200hp and Hawker had already, in 1937, produced a design using the Sabre, which was named Typhoon, with a contract raised for 250 aircraft with a possible further 250 to follow. By 1940 it was clear that all was not well with the Vulture engine, the engines suffering frequent failures due to con-rod fractures and, with Rolls-Royce absolutely committed to Merlin production, Vulture engine production was ceased and the Tornado project abandoned.

So it was that Hawker concentrated on the Napier Sabre-powered Typhoon, flying the first example in February 1940. At the height of the Battle of Britain A&AEE took the unusual route of carrying out testing at Hawker's Langley site, such was the push to get the aircraft into service. The powerful engine resulted in a strong swing to starboard that needed to be quickly countered. Another aspect of the Sabre was its propensity to induce severe vibration in the cockpit to the extent that it impaired pilot vision, a problem never completely cured. Nonetheless, production was quickly underway at Gloster's Hucclecote factory, feeding early aircraft to Boscombe Down and direct to squadron use.

However, no sooner had the Typhoon begun entering service with the RAF than serious problems arose. While the Vulture engine had ultimately been abandoned due to constant failures, the early Napier Sabre was little better, having a nasty habit of quitting quite suddenly. Secondly, fumes from the engine were found to be entering the cockpit, threatening to asphyxiate the pilot. Equally seriously, the entire tail unit would sometimes part company with the rest of the aircraft with almost always fatal results. While these serious problems would slowly be resolved, it did not help the aircraft to gain a reliable reputation, some campaigning for the entire project to be abandoned. Perhaps most concerning, however, was the fact that Hawker's new interceptor was incapable of achieving the manoeuvrability at altitude necessary to intercept anything, particularly the new German fighter, the Fw.190!

A product of the RAE low-speed tunnel in April 1938, the Typhoon wing was again a thick and substantial component that precluded high altitude ability (18 per cent t/c). While the Typhoon would later be tested in RAE's High Speed Wind Tunnel (HST), this was not until 1942 when the aircraft was already in service.[4] However, the Typhoon would find its niche in rocket-equipped ground attack, largely thanks to Roly Beamont's urgings (he had led the Typhoon development flying with Hawker and later the first squadron thus equipped); as a high level interceptor, it was a non-starter. Whilst an evil reputation preceded its entry into wide-scale squadron use, some recognised in its high-speed, hard-hitting qualities something special. 'Jim' Sheddan, a New Zealander who had the job of delivering Spitfires and Typhoons to operational squadrons, thought the world of the beast:

> Typhoons were big. At seven tons they were nearly twice the weight of a Spitfire which, with its Rolls-Royce motor had been around for some time while the Typhoon with its Napier Sabre was a new creation ... Given the opportunity [I] would have flown nothing else.[5]

While the Typhoon would go on to create its own legend in the days after the Allied landings in France in June 1944, it did leave Hawker and MAP with a problem: there was still a need for a new fighter with which to counter the latest German products. In 1941, mindful of the above, Camm had discussions with Director DTD, regarding a Spitfire-type wing fitted to a Typhoon, and again powered by the latest Napier Sabre (it would appear that as early as 1940, a thin wing – 14.5 per cent t/c at the root, down to 10 per cent at the tip – had been schemed in the Hawker Design Office.) The scheme with the revised thin wing was tendered to Air Ministry specification F.10/41 as the Typhoon II and a contract for two prototypes was issued in November 1941.

By 1942 the Typhoon Mk.II had been renamed the Tempest, the various prototypes being tested with a variety of engines, including the new Centaurus radial from Bristol and Rolls-Royce's new liquid-cooled Griffon. In mid-1942, a contract for 400 Tempest Is was issued and, as the Tempest Mk.V, first flew in September 1942 with a Sabre IV engine. The Tempest was designed as a stressed-skinned aircraft throughout and again was a large fighter initially powered by the Napier Sabre IIA, B or C delivering 2,180hp which, entering service in late 1943 as the Tempest Mk.V, gave a maximum speed of 426mph and a ceiling of 36,500 feet. This mark was followed by the Tempest Mk.II, which derived its power from the Bristol Centaurus V or VI 2,520hp radial engine. This combination produced an aircraft capable of a maximum speed of 442mph and an altitude of 37,500 feet. Finally, Hawker had achieved success in producing a high-speed, high-altitude fighter able to outfly anything pitted against it. Ironically, its swansong would be achieved at levels seldom exceeding 2,000 feet as it proved to be one of the few aircraft capable of matching the speed of the V-1 unmanned bombs fired against the South East in the summer of 1944.

Jim Sheddan was impressed with the Tempest:

> Of all the Allied fighters in action during the last twelve months of the war the Hawker Tempest, powered by a Napier Sabre sleeve valve engine, was in a class of its own. In the hands of an experienced pilot it was more than a match for any aircraft flying on either side of the lines.[6]

Development

This digression into Hawker's fighter evolution has been necessary to understand where and how the next naval fighter from the Hawker Aircraft Co., the Sea Fury, came about. As discussed, the Tempest was, for a fighter, a large aircraft. With a span of 41 feet and a loaded weight of 13,250lb, this was a lot of aeroplane. In discussions at Kingston with DTD in November 1942 to consider the desirability of producing a smaller, lighter, more manoeuvrable Tempest, Camm aired his thoughts on reducing the wingspan by deleting

LA610, first flown on 27 November 1944, was one of six Fury prototypes. It is seen here fitted with a Napier Sabre VII for test purposes in early 1945. This was the fastest of the various Fury prototypes. (*BAE/BL*)

the wing centre section and bringing the two remaining wings together, thus reducing the span from 41 feet to 38 feet 4 inches, and coupling this to the Bristol Centaurus radial engine of the Tempest Mk.II. (In the event, the span had to be increased slightly to allow the inboard cannon to clear the propeller disc.)[7] This proposal was drawn in January 1943, broadly complying with specification F.6/42, as the Tempest Light Fighter (Centaurus), a more detailed specification, F.2/43, based on the Hawker proposals following shortly thereafter. At the Hawker board meeting of 4 February 1943, 'It was…unanimously agreed that a new prototype or prototypes based upon the specification F.2/43 and utilising Centaurus and if possible the Griffon engine be put in hand and for completion as soon as possible.'[8]

It was agreed that Hawker would provide two prototypes based on the F.2/43 scheme and built in the experimental shop, to be followed by three pre-production machines six months prior to any production aircraft. Contract cover for these first two aircraft was received on 9 April. They were to be powered by Bristol Centaurus CE.12SM engines.

While this would be a machine suitable for the RAF, in April another specification, N.7/43, was received, this time for a naval fighter, Camm suggesting to DTD on 12 April that the two specifications might be met with the same basic aircraft (having already suggested this to Bristol Engines). With this suggestion falling on receptive ears, Camm further suggested in July that Boulton Paul undertake the design work for the naval variant.

Aerial view of Fury prototype NX802 showing its clean lines and powerful Centaurus radial engine to good effect. (*BAE*)

DTD later agreed that Boulton Paul be responsible for the initial two naval prototypes but with Hawker retaining design responsibility, contract cover being received for these in October 1943. (There were some concerns at Hawker regarding the quality of work emanating from Boulton Paul but presumably, with Hawker retaining design oversight, it was felt to be manageable.) At this point, the decision was made that production naval aircraft would be produced by Hawker, in parallel with the RAF version. On 1 December the board 'agreed that the adaption of the F.2/43 for naval purposes was desirable. Mr Camm was requested to obtain the necessary priority instructions to enable this particular version to proceed ahead of the land version.'[9]

On this basis, six prototypes were agreed in December 1943, the first powered by the Centaurus XII; the second aircraft powered by either Centaurus XXII or, if ready, Rolls-Royce Griffon; the third and fourth machines to be the naval variants powered by Centaurus engine; the fifth to be fitted with either Griffon or Centaurus XXII and the last to also carry the Rolls-Royce Griffon. Detailed work on the naval requirements began in January 1944, entailing visits to RAE Farnborough to view films of arrested landings to better inform the design and stressing process for both arrested landings and assisted take-offs, from which it was decided to use a sting arrestor hook rather than an A-frame type as fitted to the Sea Hurricane.

By early 1944 a more detailed naval specification, N.22/43, was received and contract cover obtained for 200 F.2/43 RAF standard and 200 N.22/43 Royal Navy standard aircraft, half of the latter to be built by Boulton Paul Aircraft Ltd. By June 1944 priorities at the Air Ministry were changing, not helped by concerns regarding the delivery of parts manufactured by Boulton Paul being raised. It was decided that the priority was the naval

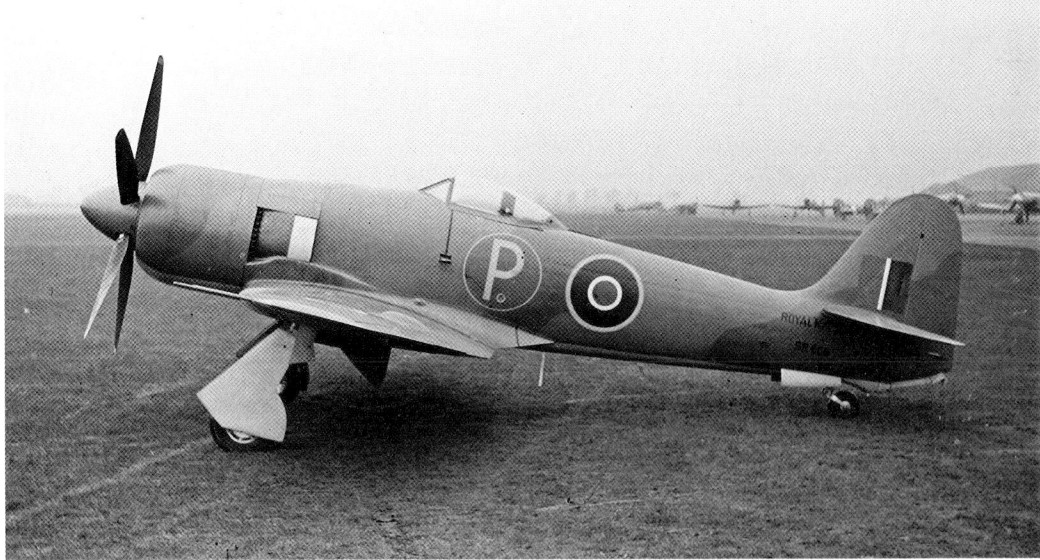

Prototype Sea Fury Mk.X SR666, at Langley. The aircraft is fitted with a four-blade Rotol propeller (later replaced with a five-blade unit) and the original short arrestor hook that was later lengthened following problems during deck-landing trials. (*BAE*)

version and the construction plan to be: a) F.2/43 – two prototypes with Centaurus 12SM engines; two prototypes with Griffon engines. b) N.22/43 – one prototype from Boulton Paul; two prototypes from Hawker. The first prototype, NX798, an F.2/43 completed at Langley in July, was flown by Philip Lucas on 1 September 1944. This aircraft was fitted with the Bristol Centaurus XII with a Rotol four-blade propeller, followed by LA610 powered by a Griffon with six-blade contra-prop on 27 November. At this point, the RAF aircraft was named Fury Mk.I, the naval variant, Sea Fury Mk.X.

However, it was already becoming evident that the end of the war was fast approaching and limited retrenchment in aircraft orders began to be felt. Firstly, the Sea Fury contract was reduced in January 1945 to 100 machines by the simple expedient of cancelling the Boulton Paul order, the incomplete Sea Fury prototype being constructed by the company later being sent to Langley for completion. This would be followed by the eventual cancellation of the RAF Fury order in its entirety. The first Sea Fury prototype, SR661, flew on 21 February 1945 with a Centaurus XII and Rotol four-blade prop. This was not a fully representative naval aircraft, not being fitted with wing fold, although an arrestor hook was fitted. This was followed by a further prototype; SR666 in October 1945 having hydraulic wing fold and powered by a Centaurus XV radial engine and five-blade Rotol propeller.

The Board heard at its 11 July 1945 meeting that:

A change in priority had brought the Sea fury X (production delivery) forward to January 1946 but it was felt that there would be considerable difficulty in meeting this. However, special measures were being introduced such as the use of simpler tools and semi-hand methods and 25 sets of parts were being manufactured on these lines.[10]

The first prototype Sea Fury Mk.X (semi-navalised), SR661, reached Boscombe Down for evaluation in November 1945, fitted with a Centaurus XII driving a Rotol four-blade propeller, followed by the SR666, fully navalised. Handling was generally favourably received other than the absence of an aileron trimmer but the high torque developed by the engine needed caution on take-off. Interestingly, the first prototype Fury Mk.I, NX798, had visited A&AEE in October 1944 for initial assessment. Apart from some praise for being the 'first aircraft with really effective spring tab ailerons and rudder', there were some concerns, namely nose heaviness with increase in speed, a violent wing drop on landing and vibrations. A change to a larger tailplane and elevator and movement of the oil cooler to the port wing cured the nose heaviness and wing drop.[11]

The task of clearing prototype Sea Fury SR661 for carrier operations fell to Captain Eric 'Winkle' Brown at Farnborough in 1945. In initial trials at the aerodrome, he found that the powerful engine, with its inclination to swing the aircraft to starboard, required careful use of the rudder if the pilot was not to over-correct the swing. He also found that the rudder was ineffective on the landing run, so harsh braking was required to keep the aircraft straight on deck and a tailwheel lock was one of the recommendations for service use. This was followed by carrier trials aboard HMS *Ocean* by SR661, confirming

Sea Fury TF898, probably at Langley, fitted with bombs as part of the trials work to clear the Sea Fury as a ground-attack aircraft, the Sea Fury FB.Mk.11. (*BAE/BL*)

Sea Fury Mk.X at Langley, still fitted with the early Rotol four-blade propeller and initial arrestor hook design. (*BAE/BL*)

good control and view for deck landing but requiring more rudder power for take-off, a tail-wheel lock, improved engine starting and larger capacity accumulator. The first fully-navalised Sea Fury, SR666, first flew with a Centaurus XV engine and Rotol five-blade prop, representing the production version of the early aircraft complete with wing fold and extended sting arrestor hook.[12]

Operational Use

Production of the Sea Fury was carried out at Kingston and Langley beginning with contract 3682 for fifty Sea Fury Mk.Xs and fifty Sea Fury FB.Mk.11s dated 7 July 1944, followed by a contract for a further thirty-five in October 1946.[13]

Eventually contracts for FB.Mk.11s totalled 775 aircraft through to November 1951 (plus fifty Mk.Xs). TF898, the third production machine, went to RAE Farnborough before joining HMS *Illustrious* during 1947 for deck trials which were completed successfully although with some concerns regarding the arrestor-hook installation, eventually resulting in a lengthened arrestor hook. Initial release to service saw the Mk.X issued to Nos. 778, 802, 803, 805 and 807 Squadrons for early work up in the interceptor role while, back at Kingston and at Boscombe Down, work had proceeded on the fighter-bomber version. This, the FB.Mk.11, entered service in 1948, replacing the Mk.X Sea Fury in most of the squadrons already allocated the aircraft. The FB.Mk.11 featured the developed Bristol Centaurus 18 radial engine with five-blade Rotol propeller, delivering 2,480hp, offering

Sea Fury Mk.X TF898 aboard HMS *Victorious* 1946/7 during deck trials. It has the later Rotol five-blade prop fitted. (*BAE/BL*)

Sea Fury Mk.X, probably TF898, taking off from HMS *Victorious*. (*BAE/BL*)

a maximum speed of 460mph and service ceiling of 35,600 feet together with a universal wing able to accommodate a wide range of ordnance.

First deliveries of the Sea Fury FB.Mk.11 went to No.802 Squadron in May 1948, followed by Nos. 801, 804, 805 and 807 Squadrons, seeing service aboard the light fleet carriers HMS *Ocean*, *Theseus* and *Glory*, allowing just enough time to work up before the next global crisis erupted with the invasion of South Korea by the communist North Korea with the connivance of the USSR and communist China on 25 June 1950.

Following enquiries from Iraq regarding a training version of the Fury, Hawker schemed a two-seat variant, the T.Mk.20, of which a prototype and eighty-seven further aircraft were produced, various countries taking them in small numbers, including the FAA. The T.Mk.20 was manufactured at Langley, first flight at Langley being in January 1948. Those aircraft were based at shore establishments only, having no catapult spools or tail hooks for carrier use. The aircraft featured a Perspex tunnel connecting the two cockpit canopies over which was a periscopic sight such that the instructor could view the student's sight during bombing exercises. However, given that bomb delivery was in a dive, the last place that a sensible instructor's eyes would be was on the sight!

The light fleet carrier was a design originating in the early 1940s and laid down in 1942 and 1943. The design was based on that of merchant ships with the notion that they could be refurbished after military use and join the merchant fleet, although none did. Two classes were planned – the Glory (or Colossus) class of ten ships and the Majestic-class of six ships – none of the Majestic-class would serve with the Royal Navy. Representing a design midway between the fleet carrier and the escort carrier, the light fleet carrier certainly offered better accommodation for crew and aircraft than the escort carrier and was more economical than the large fleet carriers.

Of the Glory (or Colossus) class, HMS *Colossus* was the first to be completed in December 1944, followed by *Vengeance* (January 1945), *Venerable* (January 1945), *Glory* (April 1945), *Ocean* (June 1945), *Perseus* and *Pioneer* (1945), *Warrior* (January 1946), *Theseus* (January 1946), and *Triumph* (April 1946). Most of the class were similar, displacing 13,300 tons, a length of 695 feet and beam of 80 feet allowing space for around forty aircraft depending on type. Their geared turbines could produce 40,000hp giving a speed of 25 knots. Of the Majestic-class, none were completed during the Second World War and, at war's end, those already in build were significantly delayed as work wound down. All six were eventually built (though *Leviathan* was never commissioned) and later sold to other navies.

The unprovoked invasion of South Korea came as a shock to the United States, which had withdrawn its occupying forces from the south in 1948–9. With the creation of North Korea with the USSR as its sponsor and South Korea under the protection of the US, initial border skirmishes were followed with a full-scale invasion of South Korea by the

Sea Fury Mk.X about to land aboard her carrier. Note the 'Batsman' at right centre and the ten arrestor cables awaiting pick-up by the aircraft's hook, together with the generous flap area available. (*BAE/BL*)

Sea Fury Mk.X up from its carrier. This head-on view shows the aircraft's clean lines and purposeful demeanour. (*BAE/BL*)

North on 25 June 1950 with the encouragement of the USSR. In a series of unpleasant surprises for Stalin, hoping to make mischief in Asia to balance his failing dominance in Europe, the US quickly organised a UN resolution to combat the invasion and, with the support of other UN forces, including the UK and Australia, landed troops to oppose Kim Il-Sung's invasion, from nearby Japan where the US occupation force was conveniently located. For the UK, opposition took the form of Royal Navy resources, initially via the presence of HMS *Triumph*, which had been stationed off Japan, with No.800 Squadron equipped with Seafire FR.Mk.47s and No.827 Squadron equipped with Fairey Fireflies. On station by 3 July, the first strike was launched comprising Fireflies in the ground-attack configuration escorted by the Seafires, also in ground-attack configuration. This would be the pattern for the first strikes before *Triumph* turned for Sasebo in Japan to replenish. At this point it was recognised that a carrier support ship was required for deep maintenance and replacement of aircraft and HMS *Unicorn* was duly despatched to the war zone.

Replacing *Triumph* and *Unicorn* in theatre, HMS *Theseus* and *Warrior* (as support ship) arrived in early October 1950 to take over the offensive role, with the twenty-three

Sea Fury FB.Mk.11 WN485 c.1952. This aircraft has been fitted with rocket projectile (RP) rails and drop tanks under each wing.

Sea Furies of No.807 Squadron for ground attack and fighter cover and twelve Fireflies of No.813 Squadron in the anti-submarine role covering the Yellow Sea area. The Sea Fury FB.Mk.11s were capable of carrying two 500lb bombs and drop tanks but, due to the problems of achieving sufficient wind-over-deck for *Theseus*, the bombs were later replaced with 60lb unguided rockets. Thus began the next phase of the air component of the Royal Navy, ground interdiction being the bulk of the work for the Sea Furies, with additional standing patrols over the fleet in case of any appearance by North Korean aircraft. *Theseus* would suffer recurrent bouts of catapult unserviceability during her time in Korea, resulting in a requirement to use RATOG boosters to get the aircraft airborne, a problem that would not be solved for some time.

Following *Theseus* came HMS *Glory* with the Sea Furies of No.804 Squadron and Fireflies of No.812 Squadron, reaching its station on 26 April 1951. Although at this stage facing no aerial opposition, many of the Sea Furies suffered damage either from anti-aircraft fire or shrapnel from their own weapons as they continued the punishing series of ground-attack missions against enemy forces and infrastructure. As *Glory* prepared to sail from the war zone in late September 1951, she was replaced by the Australian carrier HMAS *Sydney*, also equipped with Sea Furies. She would remain on station until January 1952 with Nos. 805, 808 and 817 Squadrons embarked. Thus the light fleet carriers *Glory*, *Ocean*, *Theseus* together with *Warrior* and *Unicorn* acting as troopship and aircraft transports and

Sea Fury VR943 leaves the carrier HMS *Glory* for another ground-attack sortie during the Korean War, carrying a clutch of 60lb rocket projectiles. (*USNHHC*)

HMAS *Sydney* operated in turns off the west coast of Korea, mainly providing ground-attack assets for the ground war but also at times tangling with North Korean aircraft, including Mikoyan-Gurevich MiG-15 jets flown by Soviet pilots.

The initial success of the invasion of South Korea resulted in South Korean and UN forces being steadily pushed down the peninsula. The government abandoned Seoul and established itself at Pusan in the far south of the country. At this point, a previously planned amphibious landing by US troops at Inchon, behind enemy lines, on 15 September 1950 saw the UN forces once more on the offensive. North Korea's run of victories ceased, Seoul was recaptured and the North Korean forces were pushed north up the peninsula. UN forces fought their way north and approached the Yalu river in October and it became clear to the USSR and Communist China that their 'easy' victory in Korea had turned sour and immediate action would be required if they were not to face the unpleasant prospect of Western forces being stationed on their doorstep. On 25 October, heavy forces of the Chinese Red Army were encountered and rapidly overwhelmed the UN forces in the region, which fell back to the region of the 38th Parallel, from which, during the autumn of 1950, Allied forces were once more pushed south with Seoul lost again. Sustained fighting in the spring of 1951 saw UN forces once more moving north and Seoul was relieved on 14 March. Having reached the 38th Parallel and beyond by May 1951, the UN forces settled down to defending their positions, as did the North Korean and Chinese forces, thus setting in train a stalemate that has broadly endured until today. The Armistice of July 1953 formalised this situation.

When China had agreed to commit ground troops to Korea, the USSR had agreed to provide an air component which comprised sixteen operational air regiments equipped with the MiG-15 jet fighter. The MiG-15 was a shock to western nations, who were unaware that the Soviet Union had achieved such a high-performance jet aircraft in so short a time (courtesy of Nene jet engines thoughtfully sold by Rolls-Royce to Stalin with the agreement of the then Labour administration). First encountered in November 1950, in combat interceptions the MiG-15 pilots would seek to use their superior speed by diving down on the Sea Furies, making a firing pass, before zooming back to altitude. However, the FAA pilots found that, if they could keep the MiGs in view and react to the diving attacks, the superior manoeuvrability of the Sea Fury at low level meant that they could usually best the enemy or at least stay out of harm's way. Indeed, Lieutenant Peter 'Hoagy' Carmichael of No.802 Squadron was credited on 9 August 1952 with the first Sea Fury victory against the MiG and it is believed that there were several other successes. It would seem though that the shoot-down was actually the work of Lieutenant Brian 'Schmoo' Ellis but, as flight leader, Carmichael was credited with the kill. However, this was a one-off occurrence. Eventually, the USAF deployed the F-86 Sabre jet fighter to the region to combat the MiG on a more equal footing.

Following his time as naval pilot at Farnborough, Eric Brown had joined No.802(F) Squadron at Culdrose flying the Sea Fury FB.Mk.11, assigned to HMS *Vengeance* as part of the 15th Carrier Air Group, during which he was tasked with forming an aerobatic team comprising four pilots and aircraft, which proved to be a great attraction wherever they performed. Of his time on the aircraft, Brown concluded:

> Although I enjoyed the delightful handling characteristics of the Sea Fury in aerobatics, the major part of our squadron flying involved combat weapon training and its effectiveness in that role was all-important, especially in the light of the Korean War in which it was to play such a prominent part.[14]

Export Aircraft

The Sea Fury was one of several modern aircraft offered for export after the Second World War and an early customer was the Royal Canadian Navy, which had acquired some thirty-seven Sea Furies of both marks, starting in 1947 when Mk.X TF909 was delivered for evaluation purposes, later aircraft being siphoned from RN contracts. This was followed by twenty-four FB.11 aircraft. Further aircraft, mainly Sea Fury FB.Mk.11s, were supplied from subsequent Royal Navy contracts, presumably as attrition replacements. Those aircraft were used aboard HMCS *Magnificent*, a former Majestic-class carrier, undertaking NATO duties in the Atlantic. Eventually some sixty-four aircraft were supplied to the Royal Canadian Navy. Also supplied from Royal Navy contracts were

Sea Fury FB.Mk.11 (or FB.50) of the Dutch Kon Marine pictured at Valkenburg in September 1948. (*Dutch National Archives*)

Sea Fury FB.Mk.11 (or FB.50) of the Dutch Kon Marine pictured at Hawker's Langley airfield. (*Author*)

Sea Fury FB.Mk.11 WG565 of the Royal Canadian Navy pictured at McCall Field, Calgary, Alberta. (*Lynn Garrison*)

orders for Sea Fury FB.Mk.11s for the Royal Australian Navy, beginning with twenty aircraft supplied in 1949, followed by a further seven in 1951–2. They were embarked on HMAS *Sydney*, the former Majestic-class carrier HMS *Terrible*, and operated in Korean waters during the conflict of 1951–2. Those aircraft were all siphoned off from existing Royal Navy contracts and were therefore presumably financed by MDAP funding. In all some ninety-nine Sea Furies were acquired by the Royal Australian Navy.

Also acquiring Sea Furies was the Royal Netherlands Navy, the Koninklijke Marine or Kon Marine, which purchased ten Sea Fury Mk.50s (i.e. Mk.X) in October 1946 for use on the ex-Royal Navy escort carrier HMS *Nairana*, renamed HNLMS *Karel Doorman*, and later on the ex-light fleet carrier HMS *Venerable*, also renamed *Karel Doorman*, under the aegis of the Netherlands Naval Aviation Service, the Marineluchtvaartdienst. They were delivered in 1948 and later upgraded to FB standard, becoming FB.50s. In 1950 a further twelve FB.Mk.11 aircraft were purchased as FB.50 Sea Furies. The Netherlands also undertook the licence production of Sea Furies from 1948 numbering a further twenty-five FB.50s. Service appears to have alternated between embarked deployments within the NATO environment and shore basing at Valkenburg.

Iraq was another country to acquire this most modern of fighters, expressing interest in 1946 and ordering thirty new-build Furies (i.e. not navalised) aircraft which were delivered during 1948 followed by a further twenty-five aircraft. Five T.Mk.20 trainers were also acquired, making sixty in all by 1953. The largest export order came from Pakistan following the division of the country from India. Some ninety-eight aircraft were purchased, eighty-seven as new-build F.60s plus five ex-RN (as F.60A), a further five new-build T.61 trainers and one further refurbished Fury. Also acquiring aircraft was Egypt in 1949 with twelve mostly new-builds, plus NX798 refurbished.

The Sea Fury had entered service some years after the first appearance of jet-powered aircraft in the UK inventory. As had been the case through the Second World War, the Royal Navy's Fleet Air Arm equipment was always some years behind what the RAF could deploy. And so it was that the Sea Fury, superb aircraft that it was, would be the last front-line propeller fighter in service with the FAA (excluding the AS Python turboprop-powered Westland Wyvern). With the decision to acquire the Supermarine Attacker turbojet-powered aircraft as the next front-line fighter, the FAA began retiring the Sea Fury, a number of which had very low hours, having moved directly from Hawker at Langley to storage at AHUs. Seeing an opportunity for further sales of the aircraft abroad, Hawker Aircraft repurchased 251 of those airframes in 1956 and stored them at their own premises at Squires Gate, Blackpool, and later Langley, Chilbolton and Dunsfold.

Refurbishment

From this stock, numbers were supplied firstly to Burma which received twenty-one refurbished aircraft, eighteen ex-RN machines plus three T.Mk.20 trainers in 1957, these being flown out from Squires Gate. Another recipient was the pre-revolutionary Cuba which ordered seventeen aircraft (fifteen FB.Mk.11s and two T.Mk.20s) in 1957 for use against the Castro forces with some being involved in the later Bay of Pigs invasion, although not all aircraft were re-erected before the fall of the Batista regime. (The aircraft were shipped out to Cuba from Liverpool in 1958.) The final recipient was the Federal Republic of Germany which had a requirement for target tugs. Subsequently, sixteen T.Mk.20s and one FB.Mk.11 aircraft were despatched, most with the target-towing equipment fitted, and painted red, from Dunsfold in 1960–63. While the T.Mk.20s offered few problems, the sole FB.Mk.11 was anything but well behaved and, prior to its despatch, it almost despatched Duncan Simpson, innocently carrying out the last manoeuvre of the production flight-test schedule. On 1 August 1963, he had taken WG599 (D-CACY) up for a last check flight before delivery. On looping at around 6,000 feet, Simpson found himself pointing at the ground with the ailerons locked and immovable. Quickly finding himself at between 2,000 and 3,000 feet and unable to bale out, a last-ditch roll-under released the restriction, allowing Simpson to regain control and make a straight in approach to Dunsfold, where the aircraft was left on the ORP for inspection, a loose article being suspected.

The Cuba order was perhaps the least straightforward, embroiling Hawker employees in the revolution then engulfing the country. Len Hersey, of the Repair and Service Department, latterly at Langley remembered his time in Cuba thus:

Sea Fury FB.Mk.11 TF956 at Yeovilton on the occasion of its return to the air in 1972 following extensive refurbishment at Dunsfold. (*Author*)

In September 1958 I arrived in Cuba for the assembly of [seventeen] refurbished Sea Furies which had been crated and shipped to Havana. A colleague, Derek MacKay, and myself, together with Cuban Air Force personnel, started work. This proceeded very well until one evening the manager of our hotel asked if I had heard the news from Venezuela. Naturally I hadn't, and even if I had it probably would have meant nothing to me. He told me that the Freedom Front leader, Señor Castro, had broadcast on Radio Venezuela, quoting my name and room number, holding me responsible for assembling the Sea Furies that were bombing and gunning his troops. He gave me three days to get out of Cuba! That night Derek and I locked ourselves in our room with a bottle of Scotch and the next day moved out of the hotel and into Campo de Columbia, the Air Force Headquarters. We stayed there until our departure after we had more or less completed [twelve] aircraft, then returned to England.[15]

The Fury T.Mk.20 two-seat trainer prototype VX818, first flown in January 1948. The aircraft had been designed for the Iraqi order but was taken over by the Admiralty. Changes from the single-seat version, apart from the second cockpit, included the installation of a tripod-mounted mirror to facilitate the pilot's view of the student's sight and the absence of a tail hook. (*BAE/BL*)

On New Year's Day 1959, Batista fled the revolutionary onslaught and Castro became the de-facto leader of Cuba. Subsequently, around September 1959, another team, again led by the Hawker pilot Don Lucey, arrived in Cuba to erect and test the remaining five aircraft. It appears that the second team comprised Lucey, a local Hawker rep 'Mr Grupe', and two further Hawker technicians. The situation under Castro was utterly chaotic and the team had an enormous task in trying to erect and test the last five aircraft. Lucey subsequently issued a report to Hawker in November 1959 castigating the Castro regime, the remnants of the air force and the general situation in-country.

For a while in the late 1950s and early 1960s the dispersals at Dunsfold Aerodrome were packed with the Sea Furies repurchased by Hawker Aircraft, including those previously in store at Squires Gate and Chilbolton. As these aircraft were slowly refurbished or cannibalised, Hawker became aware that one of the aircraft was in fact the first production

FB.11, serialled TF956. Given its historical importance, it was decided that the aircraft would make a suitable addition to the Hawker Flying 'museum', then at Dunsfold. This eclectic collection of flightworthy aircraft included a Hart, Tomtit and the last Hurricane ever built. With thoughts of adding the Sea Fury, the machine was brought under cover and parked at the back of the flight shed whilst the wheels of higher management slowly turned. However, with work on further Hunters and now also the P.1127 VTOL aircraft keeping everyone busy, the TF956 refurbishment slipped into the background, the aircraft gathering dust in the corner.

However, since work was still also being undertaken on T.Mk.20 Sea Fury refurbishment for the German order, two engineers, Colin Balchin and Don Russell, took it upon themselves to recondition and refit whatever items they could on the aircraft in their spare time. Slowly, the aircraft came back to life until pretty much all was complete, save for a flightworthy engine. At this point, management belatedly woke up to the fact that this Sea Fury was being actively prepared for action and called a halt to proceedings but by now, Duncan Simpson, Chief Test Pilot, had become very interested in the project continuing and pressed hard for the aircraft to be completed and flown. Sadly, it was not

Sea Fury T.Mk.20 WG655 (G-INVN) seen at Dunsfold June 1990. This aircraft subsequently force-landed at Duxford in August 2020 due to engine failure and was severely damaged. (*Author*)

to be, but sanction was obtained for the aircraft to be saved by donating it to the Fleet Air Arm at Yeovilton where, in January 1972, the historic aircraft once more took to the skies and became a much-loved display item until lost in June 1989 in the Firth of Clyde after abandonment by the pilot, having discovered that the starboard undercarriage would not lower.

An abiding theme throughout the life of the Sea Fury and beyond was, and is, the reliability of the Bristol Centaurus engine. The Centaurus was a sleeve-valve 18-cylinder, two-row radial reciprocating engine of 53.6-litre swept volume, which gave some 2,480hp. Production began in 1942 but did not see widespread service use until near the end of the war as early marks of the engine were superseded by the later variants. Hawkers' first use was in the Tempest Mk.II, which used the Centaurus V or VI of some 2,520hp. (Tempest Mk.V and VI used Napier Sabres of various marks.) The Sea Fury used the Centaurus 18 engine of 2,480hp driving a Rotol 12-feet-9-inch five-blade propeller. Importantly, the Centaurus powered two types of aircraft, bomber/transports and fighters, its operational use therefore being quite different between the two types. For the bomber/transport aircraft, engine use tended to be benign, with little change of throttle position once the aircraft had achieved its cruising condition. For the fighter, however, on operational flights, throttle use and therefore demand on the engine was constantly changing and this may point to the origin of the problems that beset the engine throughout its life.

The culprit appeared to be the oil system. Trouble ahead would manifest itself as the oil temperature went through the roof while oil pressure fell through the floor, followed shortly thereafter by the engine coming to an abrupt halt with, if one was really unlucky, a prop blade vertically stopped in one's field of view. Due to the design of the cylinder internal arrangement, lubrication was of the utmost importance. Not only did the cylinder have to constrain the piston's violent reciprocation but, between the piston head and the cylinder wall, the sleeve valve was also in constant movement between the two in a twisting reciprocating motion. To cope with the violence of this activity, a special oil was developed by Shell, called Aero Shell 100U, which appeared to minimise engine seizures but, with the retirement of most sleeve-valve engines by the 1970s, continued production of the special oil has become rare, increasing the risks of running the Centaurus. Modern operators of Sea Fury airframes, particularly in the US, have increasingly replaced the Centaurus with the US Wright 3350 turbo-compound engine or similar, the engine and spares being rather more plentiful.

In the Korean conflict, the Sea Fury's engine was also markedly intolerant of fuel contamination, several being lost when the carriers' aviation fuel tanks became contaminated with water. Captain Alan Leahy, at the time serving as an Air Weapons Instructor on No.738 Squadron, noted that:

The aircraft did not, however, have a fault-free history up to this time (1949–50), as among the first fifty Sea Furies delivered to the Navy there had been at least fifteen engine failures and four pilots had been killed. There was a degree of warning if the Centaurus was in difficulty – the oil pressure would drop off the scale and the oil temperature would go up alarmingly, accompanied by some serious rough running – but whether the warnings came together or separately did not matter as there was nothing the pilot could do to avert an engine failure.[16]

In the UK, Navy Wings at Yeovilton has decided to rest the Centaurus 18 of their Sea Fury FB.Mk.11, VR930, and replace it with a Pratt and Whitney R-2800 Double Wasp radial. This aircraft has not flown since 2007 but it is hoped to have it airworthy for the 2025 show season. This will now be the group's sole Sea Fury, having sold T.Mk.20 VX281 after engine-related forced landings in 2014 and 2021. Chris Gotke, who had been flying the Sea Fury T.Mk.20 prior to its sale, described its handling as 'purely delightful, mainly due to the spring tabs on the control surfaces, it's all very well harmonised'. No doubt he will be more than happy to have the Double Wasp in front of him rather than the Centaurus 18. Gotke was at the controls in 2014 when his Sea Fury T.Mk.20, G-RNHF, developed engine problems, resulting in a forced landing at RNAS Culdrose during the site's Air Show, being awarded the Air Force Cross in 2015 for his safe handling of the situation.[17]

For Sydney Camm, the Sea Fury was surely the ultimate expression of his desire to produce a superlative monoplane fighter which had begun with his designs in 1934 for what became the Hurricane. The Sea Fury was his last propeller-driven fighter; henceforth, motive power for Hawker's creations would come from the new turbojet engines then entering service.

Chapter 6

Sea Hawk

With the advent of jet-turbine-powered aircraft at the end of the Second World War, the Admiralty was seemingly determined not to be left behind in the aerial technology stakes as it had been when called upon to fight at the outbreak of the recent war with outdated machines. The Royal Navy was therefore intent on acquiring suitable jet aircraft, provided of course that it was possible to operate them from an aircraft carrier, which had yet to be proven. To this end, Lieutenant Commander Eric Brown, the Fleet Air Arm officer with probably the most experience of carrier take-offs and landings, was given the task of proving the concept. As the naval representative of the Aerodynamic Flight at RAE Farnborough, Brown was given access to the Jet Flight and its aircraft, from which to choose a suitable mount with which to trial carrier/jet flight, and chose the Vampire as the most suitable.

Once the aircraft had been suitably modified with enlarged flaps and tail hook, Brown worked up his approach at RNAS Ford before making a successful landing aboard HMS *Ocean* on 3 December 1945. Following further landings and take-offs, Brown was happy that jet operation was feasible for the standard squadron pilot once certain modifications were applied to the aircraft to be used. These would allow a high engine RPM to be retained while flaps and airbrakes allowed any lift to be dumped quickly.

Having thus gained a greater understanding of the requirements for operation of jet-turbine aircraft at sea, the Royal Navy set about acquiring suitable aircraft for the fleet. At first, these were derivatives of existing land-based aircraft such as the Vampire and its development, the Venom, which became the Sea Vampire and Sea Venom respectively. Also acquired was a new jet aircraft from Supermarine, the Attacker. This had grown out of an earlier project called the Spiteful, essentially a developed Spitfire with a laminar-flow wing. Its naval equivalent was to be the Seafang but the project was abandoned and the wing applied to a new fuselage to house the RR Nene centrifugal turbojet.

And so it was that, from 1948 to 1953, the Royal Navy placed in service first-generation jet aircraft in order to gain operating experience on the type. The de Havilland Sea Vampire was acquired in small numbers in 1948 but did not see operational squadron service; it was replaced by the DH Sea Venom, a developed version with a more powerful engine which entered service in 1951 as the FAW.20, preceded slightly earlier by Supermarine's Attacker in 1951 although this was obsolescent even as it entered service. It can be seen then that the Royal Navy and the Fleet Air Arm were certainly not wedded to one particular fighter but were determined to cast their net wide in order to ensure that they acquired the most suitable equipment for the post-war years. Thus far, this had entailed designs originating in wartime experience. What was needed was a more modern approach to the problem of operating jet aircraft at sea.

It is unclear just when the DTD first made UK aviation companies aware of the existence of the new jet-turbine powerplant, but what is clear is that the Hawker Design Office would have been an early recipient of this knowledge due to Gloster Aircraft (a subsidiary of the Hawker Siddeley Aircraft Group) being approached in 1939 by DTD with a proposal to build a proof of concept aircraft to carry and test the new engine. It should also not be forgotten that, on the acquisition of Gloster Aircraft in February 1934, Hawker board directors were nominated to sit on the Gloster Board, including T.O.M. Sopwith, Fred Sigrist and Frank Spriggs. That aircraft – the Gloster E28/39 – first flew on 15 May 1941 with the Power Jets W.1A engine installed giving 1,450lb thrust, and in the process wrote a new page in the history of UK aviation. The Hawker Design Office had begun preliminary designs in 1941 for various jet-powered projects against AM.6/41 for an experimental jet fighter. Project P.1010 was based on the then current Hawker fighter, the Typhoon (identified as Typhoon Turbo blower), while P.1011 was a twin-engine heavy fighter/bomber. Neither project proceeded, the specification being covered by the de Havilland Spider Crab (Vampire).

The Hawker Sea Fury was the Fleet Air Arm's last operational propeller fighter in widespread service, although Westland's Wyvern, a turboprop-powered fighter, entered service in small numbers in 1954, only achieving carrier qualification at this late date and remaining in service for just four years. From now on, the defence of the fleet would depend on the jet fighter, the first of which, the Supermarine Attacker, had entered FAA service in 1951 powered by the Rolls-Royce Nene centrifugal flow turbojet engine. The aircraft was somewhat unusual due to Supermarine's insistence on retaining a tailwheel undercarriage, rather than the more conventional tricycle arrangement; the jet pipe exhaust thus impinged directly upon the runway or carrier deck. However, although its performance was somewhat pedestrian, it did allow Royal Navy pilots to acquaint themselves with the operation of jet-powered aircraft from their aircraft carriers and thus prepare themselves for the next jet fighter that would enter widespread service in several air arms. That aircraft would be the Hawker Sea Hawk.

That Sydney Camm and his design team were later than others in promoting a jet-powered aircraft was not because they had not considered such a thing but rather because they *had*. While several preliminary designs were drawn which called upon a jet-turbine engine as the motive power as early as 1941 (i.e. about the same time as the E28/39 first flew), in each case the conclusion was that, at that point in the evolution of the jet engine, power output, efficiency and reliability were not sufficient to allow progress to a workable design suitable for mass production. It was not until 1944 that such a powerplant was offered which would at last fulfil the requirements of the Project Office.[1]

Development

The engine in question was to be available courtesy of Rolls-Royce at Barnoldswick, where Stanley Hooker had been despatched by Ernest Hives, the Rolls-Royce MD at

Derby, to oversee development of Frank Whittle's early work on the gas turbine. In April 1944, a delegation from Rolls-Royce, including Hives and Hooker, had visited Hawker at Kingston to brief Camm and his team on their latest jet engine product. This was the RB.40, a centrifugal design then offering 4,000lb thrust and with development potential to increase this to 5,000lb. Finally persuaded that here at last was a fairly reliable and powerful engine, Camm agreed to look at a suitable design to carry the unit. In the early 1930s, Camm's first point of departure for his revolutionary Hurricane monoplane had been his latest successful creation, the Fury biplane. In 1944, with the possibility of Hawker's first jet now potentially achievable, Camm and his team began with their latest creation, the Fury, but this time the monoplane variant, which had yet to fly!

However, at this period, Hawker was still overloaded with work: the last Hurricane IICs were under construction at Langley, together with continuing development of the Tempest and design work on the F.2/43 fighter project that would mature as the Fury and Sea Fury aircraft and it was not until later in 1944 that the Project Office could concentrate on the jet proposals. At the 6 December 1944 board meeting, during a discussion relating to the post-war reconstruction of the company, Camm raised the requirement for additional test equipment, in particular, a company-owned wind tunnel. Given the slow progress of any approach to the ministry with this item, Camm was keen to push on.

> He felt the delay of two years that must elapse before the ministry issues materialised, would be a period in which the particular needs of this company would be very evident, especially if we were to develop a jet machine.

In the event, MAP responded to the idea by pointing out that they were looking at providing wind-tunnel facilities for industry as a whole via SBAC and that individual action might prejudice negotiations. Suffice to say, Hawker never did get their wind tunnel![2]

In November of that year, discussions between Hawker and DTD and DOR considered an engine claimed to develop 6,000lb thrust and, in response, Hawker sent a scheme to DTD showing a bifurcated jet pipe, presumably to allow for the installation of a jet turbine into an existing airframe without compromising the empennage. The initial design, coded P.1035, appears to have been broadly based on the Fury monoplane with its elliptical-wing design reminiscent of the Spitfire. A more detailed design, P.1040, was created quickly, bearing little resemblance to the Fury, featuring a single cockpit mounted well forward of the centrally-located engine (by now christened RB.41 Nene and developing 5,000lb) to be inserted aft of the cockpit and an empennage consisting of tailplane and elevators mounted partway up a normal fin and rudder arrangement while air intakes were mounted at the wing roots, as per the DH Vampire. So far, so ordinary. What marked out the design from any other was that the jet efflux exhausted either side of the fuselage at the wing trailing edge as discussed at the earlier DTD meeting. By January 1945 Rolls-Royce had agreed to make a mock-up of a suitable bifurcated jet pipe to allow for its testing behind an engine and, the following month, the Hawker board submitted an application for a patent for 'side nozzles for use on jet propelled aircraft'.[3]

The engine developed by Rolls-Royce drew heavily on Frank Whittle's pioneering work on gas turbines and followed his centrifugal design to a large degree. However, Stanley Hooker, whom Lord Hives had championed to develop the new technology, was no slouch at centrifugal-compressor design himself. It was he who had taken the early Rolls-Royce supercharger fitted to the Merlin engine and redesigned it to greatly increase its efficiency.

In 1944 MAP had approached Rolls-Royce with a request for an engine more powerful than the Derwent, itself based on the Whittle W.2B/26. Stanley Hooker took this opportunity to put into practice all the knowledge thus far gained from the Power Jets designs and proposed an entirely new design, still with a centrifugal-flow compressor, which it was hoped would produce a thrust in excess of any so far achieved. The new design, designated RB.40, looked promising but with US engine development already producing similar thrusts, it was decided to redesign the RB.40, which became the RB.41, potentially capable of 5,000lb thrust. This engine, later named the Nene, would become the engine that kickstarted jet engine production globally, though not perhaps in the way that Rolls-Royce had hoped.

The Nene used a double-sided centrifugal compressor driven by a single-stage axial turbine and nine combustion chambers. Within six months of issue of drawings, on 27 October 1944, the engine was running on the test stand, producing 4,000lb which was increased the next day to 5,000lb thrust, a quite remarkable achievement and confirmation that Rolls-Royce had absorbed fully the requirements of gas-turbine technology, at least in the use of centrifugal compression; it would, however, be an entirely different matter when the company sought to move to axial compressors. The Nene first flew as the prime mover in a de Havilland Vampire in March 1946 with the bulk of testing carried out using

P.1040 VP401 under construction in the Kingston Experimental Department. First flown in September 1947, the aircraft was retained at Farnborough for various trials. Withdrawn in 1949 for fitment of Snarler rocket motor for trials carried out Bitteswell, the aircraft was SOC and scrapped at Shoeburyness c.1954/7. (*BAE/BL*)

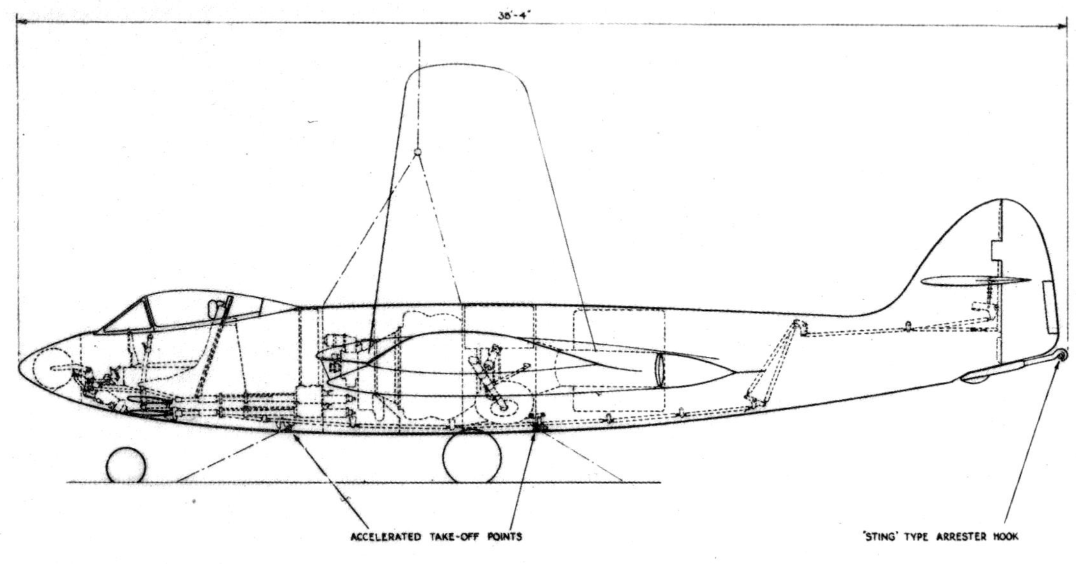

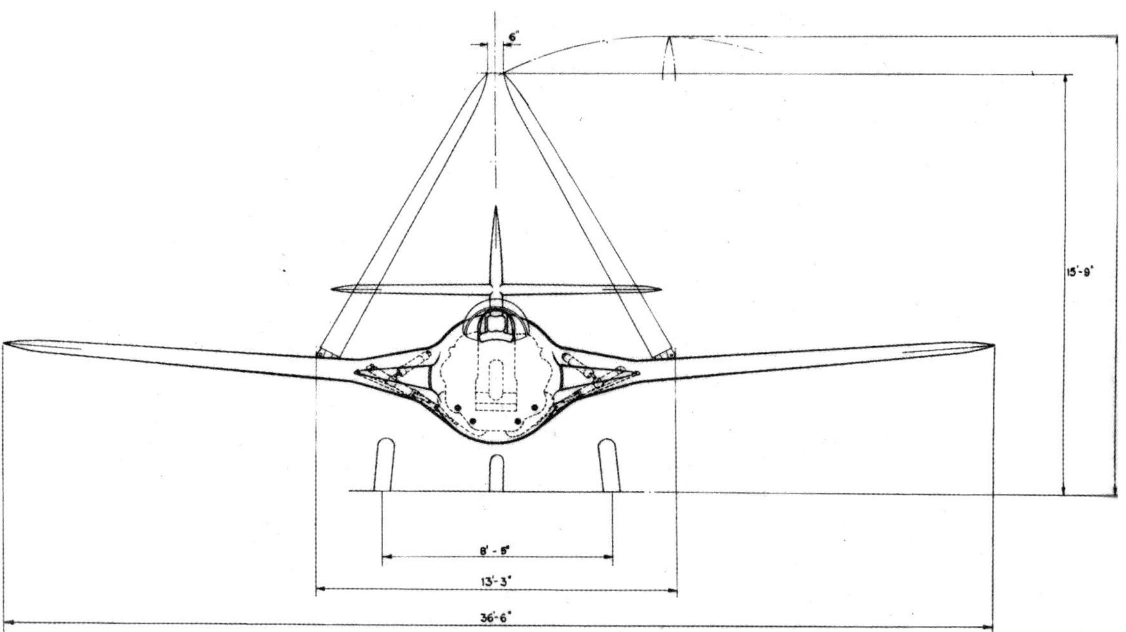

GA of N.7/46 fighter. (*BAE/BL*)

Avro Lancastrians with the engines installed in the outer nacelles. Entering production in September 1946 as the Nene 1, the engine produced 4,850lb thrust for a weight of 1,560lb.

Following visits by various Ministry officials, Hawker submitted a tender for the P.1040 to DTD in February. Having thus established a way forward on the propulsion system, scrutiny fell upon the wing design, specifically the air-intake arrangement, which the

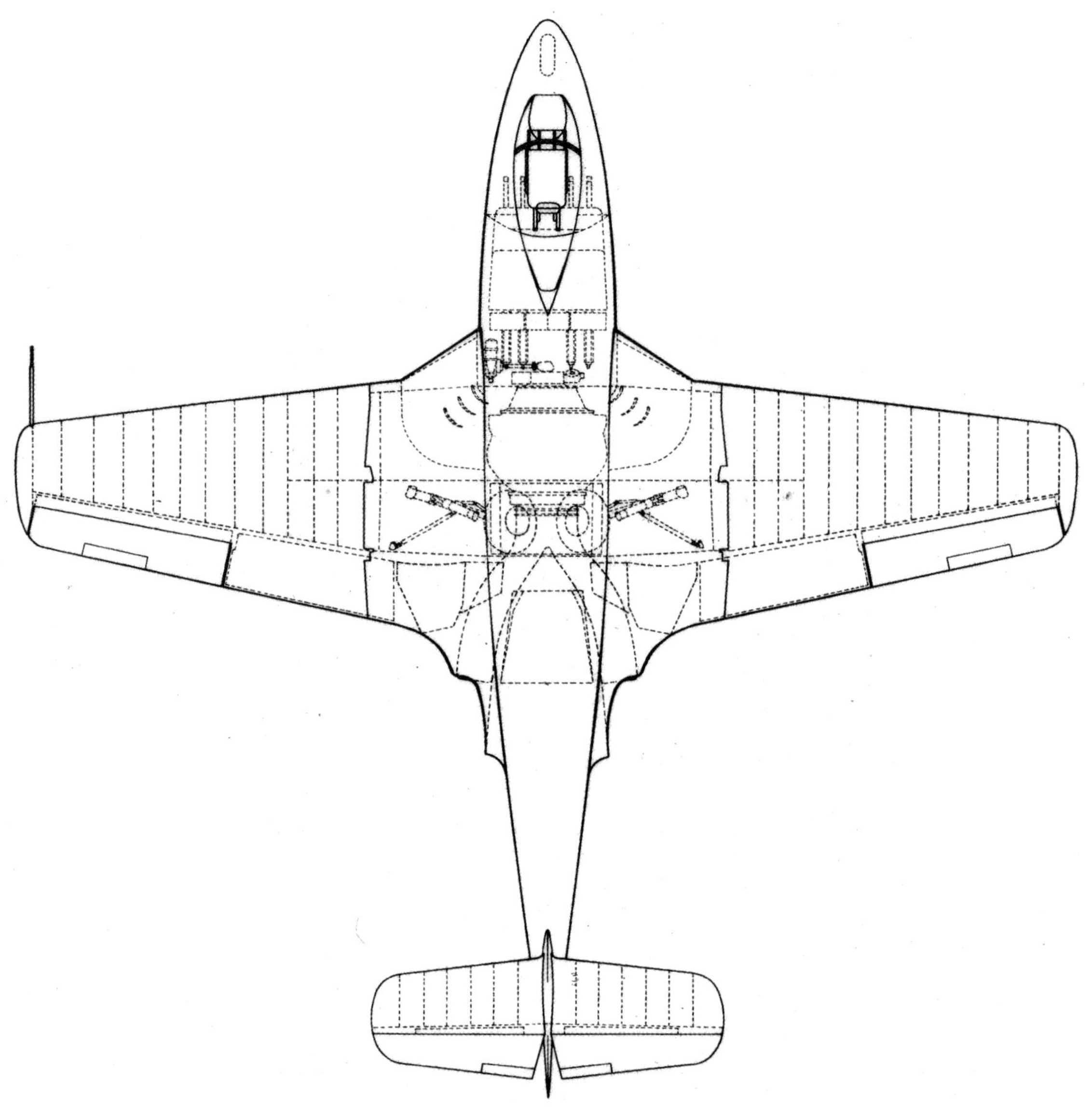

HAWKER NAVAL FIGHTER

SPECIFICATION N.7/46

ROLLS-ROYCE 'NENE' ENGINE.

DTD did not like. A visit to Captain Liptrott at the Air Ministry was thus expedited, the outcome being that, if RAE Farnborough agreed with the intake design, the aircraft represented a significant advance on existing designs. The other concern with which Farnborough could assist was the hope that the wing could be a single-spar arrangement with the loads disposed via heavy-gauge wing skins, the presumed reasoning being that a lighter construction could result. However, in March 1946, Camm appears to have had second thoughts on his single-spar wing arrangement and instructed that a leading-edge spar be added to the centre section and stub-wing assembly to cater for any tendency for torsional deflection.

With RAE confirmation that the intake design was 90 per cent efficient, and with rising confidence that the design team was on the right track, the earlier tender was revised, a new tender covering the P.1040 but including two further types – P.1047, a rocket-powered version with extreme sweep-back and P.1046, a naval version with rocket power – was submitted. In December 1945 Hawker had some good news but some bad news as well. Firstly, the Air Staff decided that the machine did not meet RAF requirements at that stage and would therefore not feature in their future plans. However, the company had recently been visited by Admiral Slattery, who was very interested in the project, the Royal Navy seeing in it the basis of a support fighter, the company being invited to tender for an RAF/Naval interceptor aircraft, this being submitted in January 1946. The tender noted that 'this aircraft has been designed as an interceptor capable of the highest possible speeds and rate of climb while at the same time retaining the ability to carry out the duties of the existing Sea Fury' (yet to enter service). However, since the first prototype had already been schemed as a land-based aircraft, the question of any requirement for wing-fold had not arisen but for naval use this would be expected.

The tender, emphasised this point, noting that 'owing to the very thin wings used (t/c ratio 9.5% as against the Sea Fury of 14.5% at the root) folding problems will be severe and for this reason stowage with wings spread has been given attention'. In an effort to lessen manoeuvring problems with wings spread, the tender offered 'Handling on the deck and in the hangar is eased by making provision for the main wheels to be rotated about the undercarriage leg thus allowing the aircraft to be moved "crabwise".' However, recognising that the novelty of such a scheme might not be to the Admiralty's liking, an alternative was offered.

> If folding is provided, it will be basically similar to that used on Sea Fury, but it will involve an increase in weight of about 300lb, a less clean wing, slightly less stiffness and considerably increased complexity in the hydraulic system. It is difficult to estimate the loss in speed, but it might be of the order of 10–15 mph unless extreme care is taken in maintenance operations.

In the event, this concern did not manifest itself. While the P.1040 with fixed wings had a maximum speed of 505 knots at sea level and M0.815 at height, the production Sea Hawk with its wing-fold was good for 514 knots and M0.823.[4]

The tender was quickly accepted and next month, Hawker was advised that an order had been placed for three prototypes against specification N7/46 for a general-purpose naval fighter, the contract, 6/ACFT/234/CB9(b), being received from Ministry of Supply in May 1946 with the proviso that the order would be built on a semi-private venture basis with the Ministry bearing the first £150,000 of the cost.[5] The first prototype would

The bifurcated jet pipe that attached to the rear of the Nene centrifugal engine. Manufactured by Rolls-Royce, the assembly proved to be something of a headache for the engine company and indeed for Hawker. (*BAE/BL*)

not represent fully the naval requirement, this being an aerodynamic test aircraft, but the full naval requirement would be covered by the second and third aircraft. Also discussed was a swept-wing version of the naval fighter, Hawker submitting a design in June for consideration under their code P.1052, a single research aircraft being agreed in August. With RAE now confirming the structural integrity of the wing design, work in the Experimental Department at Canbury Park Road pushed on apace on the first aircraft, the P.1040, serialled VP401, during late 1946.

With the engine and jet pipe combination finally being received from Rolls-Royce in April 1947, the aircraft was despatched to Langley aerodrome later that month with initial engine runs and taxying trials in June but with the engine temporarily derated to 4,500lb since that was the upper limit of testing completed at Rolls-Royce. Once a further redesign of the jet pipe had been completed at Derby, the engine would then be capable of its full 5,000lb rating. On 25 August the aircraft was despatched to A&AEE Boscombe Down where the revised jet pipe was fitted, ready for its maiden flight which occurred on 2 September 1947, with no major problems revealing themselves. The flight was made by Hawker Chief Test Pilot Bill Humble. The aircraft was then flown up to Farnborough, where Hawker had established a flight test centre from which future testing would be carried out and in October the aircraft was laid up for several days to effect modifications which, it was hoped, might ameliorate the vibration and buffet that had been found during early testing. Also received was confirmation from Rolls-Royce that the full 5,000lb rating could be re-introduced for the engine.

Rolls-Royce Nene centrifugal engine as fitted to all marks of the Sea Hawk. (*BAE/BL*)

With the vibration problems continuing, in November, with no understanding or resolution of the problem, Humble asked Lieutenant Commander Eric Brown to assist by flying the P.1040 and giving his considered opinion. During the war Brown was the naval representative within Aerodynamics Flight and been given access to the Jet Development section at RAE Farnborough; later he was made CO Aerodynamics flight. He therefore already had a wealth of knowledge of the peculiarities of jet-turbine flight whereas Humble had almost none. Brown and Humble had got to know each other well during their development of the Sea Fury and, having flown the aircraft, Brown reported that, in his opinion, the problem was related to engine speed rather than air speed. Modifications made included the replacement of the squared exhaust heatshields with a pen-nib design and the addition of a streamlined bullet fairing at the fin/tailplane junction, these going some way to overcoming the buffet and vibration problems. At this juncture, with Humble's retirement as CTP, Trevor 'Wimpy' Wade took over the test-flying duties associated with the aircraft.

In December, the mechanical test programme revealed a spar failure at lower than anticipated values, the centre section being further beefed up. It would appear that Camm's intuitive concerns regarding wing strength were fully justified. By April 1948 it was reported that the vibration concerns had been completely overcome by the fitting

P.1040 prior to first flight at Boscombe Down with Bill Humble as pilot. The item on the nose is a guide to aircraft incidence fitted for the first few flights. (*BAE/BL*)

P.1040 in flight with Wimpy Wade at the controls. (*BAE/BL*)

The first true prototype N.7/46, VP413, at Farnborough in September 1948. As yet no tail bullet fairing or arrestor hook has been fitted but folding wings and armament have been included. The aircraft was retained by CS(A) at Farnborough and Dunsfold for use in numerous trials, including carrier trials aboard HMS *Illustrious* in 1949. Believed scrapped at Shoeburyness, 1957. (*BAE/BL*)

of leading edge mass balances to the elevators. VP401 was flown to Boscombe Down in June 1948 for an initial assessment as a carrier fighter, the resulting report noting that the tricycle undercarriage and cockpit location provided good visibility for the pilot and general handling was praiseworthy. However, it was also found that stick forces were too low at low speed and too high at high speed. Lack of an airbrake and aileron trimming would be concerns for a carrier fighter while the take-off run was rather excessive at 780 feet with a 40 knot headwind. The first true N7/46 prototype, VP413, made its maiden flight on 3 September 1948, this aircraft being much more representative of the production standard being sought, and including wing fold, arrestor hook and assisted take-off equipment as well as an early airbrake arrangement.

In March 1949 VP413 began initial deck-landing trials at Farnborough prior to actual deck-landing assessment. The trials revealed a rather long-drawn-out take-off distance of 760 feet and a less than acceptable elevator response at low speed. Moving to Boscombe Down in May, VP413 carried out a variety of trials with the Nene 2 developing the full 5,000lb thrust. The early airbrake arrangement was found wanting and a worrying nose drop at high Mach number together with heavy controls, particularly the ailerons, was noted. Prior to actual carrier trials in October, in September VP413 was displayed to the

N.7/46 prototype VP413 at Farnborough in September 1948. (*BAE/BL*)

press at the SBAC Farnborough Air Show by Neville Duke in what might be described as an overly exuberant style which nearly saw the loss of the aircraft. Duke began his display by running in at high speed and low level – inverted. Seeking to roll upright at the end of the run, he let the nose drop, very close to the ground. In a desperate effort to recover, Duke entered a high-speed stall, pulling 10g before effecting a recovery. When the aircraft was examined, the wing and fuselage skins were found to be wrinkled and the nose pick-up spar distorted. Duke recorded that, 'On landing, I walked to the pilot's tent. I found it hushed, and the bar open, early.'[6]

The October carrier trials were generally successful but it was decided that the extended take-off run would need addressing. It was subsequently decided to increase the wingspan by 30 inches and the tailplane by 12 inches. Suggestions for an increase in wing incidence were rejected as too radical at that stage of the design.

In November VP413 returned to HMS *Illustrious* for further trials reflecting the various alterations made in the interim and twenty-five landings were made successfully, apart from the hook hitting the round-down during one landing. Also in November, VP422, the third prototype, took to the air, this aircraft carrying out various trials to perfect a suitable landing-flap and air-brake arrangement to allow for slower landing approaches to the carrier, these being tested aboard in February 1950. This was followed by drop-tank trials and, in June, initial gun-firing trials. Of interest is that in November VP413 was on RAE charge, taking part in 'ventral landing' handling trials whereby the aircraft was catapulted off and landed on without undercarriage, the landing being performed on a rubber flexible deck, design modifications being covered under code P.1043 of April 1945. The reasoning behind this proposal was that, by omitting the undercarriage, some

N.7/46 prototype VP413 at Farnborough showing the extensive array of drag-inducing flaps required to allow a safe approach speed to the aircraft carrier. (*BAE/BL*)

700lb weight saving was achieved that could be put to use for additional fuel or simply lightening the aircraft. What did not appear to cloud the minds of its progenitors was the requirement to manhandle some seven tons of aircraft about a tossing aircraft deck in the thick of a wartime situation when time is everything. Thankfully, the idea went away. Camm appears to have been something of an adherent to the idea in the late 1940s. In an article regarding the development of naval aircraft he stated: 'The elimination of the undercarriage, however, may well enable … a naval fighter to be produced with a superior performance until the (equivalent) shore-based fighter is able to follow suit.'[7]

On 14 November 1951 the first production aircraft, WF143, made its first flight at Hawker's new flight test facility at Dunsfold. Thus, to date, it had taken from November 1944 to November 1951 – six full years – to get the first production machine into the air at a time when the Cold War was warming up rapidly. Why had this taken so long? One could point to a series of delays, the causes of which were diverse. In the early days, the novel engine exhaust layout proved something of a drag on progress, mainly due to hold-ups at Rolls-Royce, upon whom the responsibility for the bifurcated jet pipe rested. Changes to the engine which resulted in various fouls within the airframe did not help. With regard to armament, protracted discussions on the layout of the four-cannon battery brought delays to finalisation of the front fuselage. Design of the production air brake took so long that it was still being finalised as the first production machine was completed while, at a fairly late stage of finalising the design layout, a requirement to make changes to cater for an additional 400lb of naval equipment had Camm figuratively tearing his hair out! The Hawker board was apprised of the Sea Hawk production delay in December 1951 but, by April 1952, no improvement had been noted, the cause being principally assessed as a skilled labour shortage.[8]

However, with the first production machine now airborne, the hope was for a rapid build-up of aircraft for the Fleet Air Arm. It would prove a forlorn hope. The second aircraft, WF144, flew on 21 February 1952 and the third, WF145, on 18 March of that year, allowing WF144 to be sent to Farnborough for carrier proofing trials and WF145 to be sent to A&AEE Boscombe Down for preparation for carrier trials with the Nene 4 and then the Nene 101 fitted. Carrier trials aboard HMS *Eagle* commenced in May 1952 and produced concerns relating to the hook operation, the air-brake jacks (which were considered insufficiently powerful, allowing the brakes to retract partially above 275 knots), the lack of stall warning in the approach configuration and continuous low-amplitude snaking. Meanwhile, armament trials based at Ford on WF149 ended when a wing folded on take-off, killing the pilot and a steward in the officers' mess.

At Hawker's Dunsfold aerodrome, test flights did not always go as planned, the engine in particular giving Frank Murphy, the Chief Production Test Pilot, some hairy moments. On a flight on 12 June 1952 in WF147, following a period of aerobatics which included inverted flight, the engine oil pressure gave cause for concern, falling to zero, a phenomenon that had been observed on other Sea Hawks, and increased vibration from the engine suggesting problems with the powerplant. Following a precautionary landing, flames were seen emanating from the jet pipe, subsequent investigation revealing a completely seized engine. A later flight by Murphy again found him in trouble, this time in WF159 on 19 December 1952. On a test flight to investigate a whistling noise in the cockpit, the engine oil pressure was observed to be dropping, coupled with a smell of hot metal and increased vibration: 'The resonance type of noise appeared to increase in intensity and the previous feeling of uneasiness with the engine changed to a certainty that some failure was imminent.' With a forced landing now likely, he steered for RNAS Ford and carried out a precautionary landing with the engine RPM zero and flames evident from the jet pipe. Subsequent examination showed a seized engine turbine, both incidents likely to have been at least exacerbated by lubrication problems.[9]

At Hawker in the meantime, production rates were causing concerns both with the directors and with the RN. The board was informed at the October 1952 meeting that fourteen aircraft were delivered to Dunsfold for final assembly, of which three were on flight test and a further two were expected to take to the air shortly. By March 1953, only five aircraft had been delivered to the Fleet Air Arm while a further eleven were at various ministry establishments on a variety of trials.

This glacial pace of production was causing much aggravation at the Admiralty. A significant drag on the work was that labour shortages (250 skilled workers were urgently being sought) were exacerbating an already parlous situation in which Hawker Aircraft were attempting to launch two new aircraft programmes simultaneously: the Sea Hawk for the Fleet Air Arm and the Hunter for the RAF. That the FAA was suffering a shortage

N.7/46 VP413 during carrier acceptance trials aboard HMS *Illustrious* in 1949. (*BAE/BL*)

of new aircraft because of their competitor service just added to the rancour. As it became clear that the Hunter would be required in large numbers, a board meeting on July 1952 had discussed plans to off-load the entire Sea Hawk production programme onto another Hawker Siddeley Group company, Armstrong Whitworth at Baginton, to free up labour at Kingston and Dunsfold after the first thirty-five aircraft had been delivered. The situation at Hawker was not helped by the requirement to achieve a build-up of materials and sub-contract work upon which to base the Hunter scheme. This requirement meant that, by July 1953, the company overdraft would amount to some £2,500,000 with the possibility of this rising to £3,500,000 before aircraft deliveries could offset the expense.

However, it was hoped that the complete off-load of Sea Hawk work would be completed by the end of 1952. It would appear that this rosy picture would not be achieved since, at the March 1953 board meeting, Neville Spriggs reported that 'the Sea Hawks were in difficulty again … due to the number of modifications which had recently been put on the shops for making the aircraft suitable for use in the Korean War'. As far as is known the Sea Hawk did not see action in the Korean campaign, being too late to be of operational use in that theatre. The first thirty-five Sea Hawks were duly completed at Kingston by September 1953 and delivered to the FAA from Dunsfold before attention turned to full-scale Hunter production. Henceforth, design and production would be at Armstrong Whitworth at Baginton.

Eventually, the RN order for Sea Hawk Mk 1 was completed as follows: serials WF143-WF161, WF167-WF177 and WM901-WM905, thirty-five aircraft were constructed in the Experimental Department at Richmond Road, Kingston. A further sixty F.1 Sea Hawks were constructed at Armstrong Whitworth at Baginton, Coventry. Thereafter, construction at Baginton turned to the Mk 2 variant, which featured powered ailerons to address the poor roll response exhibited by the Mk 1.

N.7/46 VP413 being serviced aboard HMS *Illustrious* during trials in 1949. (*BAE/BL*)

Meanwhile, work to bring the new jet into service with the Royal Navy was concentrated at RNAS Brawdy in 1953 where No.806 Squadron had been stood up. The redoubtable Eric Brown, by now a Commander, arrived to re-familiarise himself with the Sea Hawk before moving up to Scotland to take command of No.804 Squadron at Lossiemouth which was to re-equip with the Sea Hawk. Since only Brown had any jet experience, this could have been a somewhat accident-prone posting but, in the event, all went smoothly with the squadron pilots soon checked out on the forgiving aircraft. Also at Lossiemouth, No.802 Squadron would follow their No.804 compatriots in effecting a seamless conversion onto Sea Hawk. Other squadrons to receive the Sea Hawk F.Mk.1 were Nos. 898 and 807.

With Sea Hawk production now cleared from Kingston/Dunsfold, all subsequent activity would be centralised at Baginton/Bitteswell where the remainder of the first contract, placed in November 1949, for 151 F.Mk.1 aircraft, was completed though only to the tune of sixty aircraft. This was quickly followed by a contract for forty F.Mk.2 versions in 1954, these featuring power-assisted ailerons to overcome the heavy control problem at high speeds. The FB.Mk.3 version (116 aircraft) was a ground-attack variant of the F.Mk.2, equipped to carry bombs on the drop-tank pylon position, entering service in late 1954. The following mark, the FGA.Mk. (ninety-seven aircraft), was a developed ground-attack version with four weapon pylons rather than two although with a correspondingly reduced performance. This was addressed with the uprated Nene Mk.103 delivering 5,200lb thrust which, when fitted to the Sea Hawk FB.Mk.3, changed its designation to Sea Hawk

A flight of Sea Hawk F.Mk.1s from 806 NAS based at Brawdy over the South Wales coast. (*BAE/BL*)

would become mandatory. Here, the pilot was spoilt for choice; he could either be flung from the deck by catapult or be thrust off forward by rockets (RATO) attached to the fuselage. Neither prospect was particularly attractive since it removed control from the pilot and relied on the relevant piece of equipment functioning perfectly every time, which it didn't. During the Second World War, aircraft carrier catapults had been mainly hydraulically actuated, although some used a cordite charge, an event that applied maximum g-force at the start of the catapult stroke. However, in the 1950s, steam-powered catapults were developed which gave a far smoother acceleration to the aircraft and to the pilot.

The steam catapult was but one of several British innovations that would become commonplace on the aircraft carriers of the second half of the century. Also developed at this time was the angled deck, which allowed the carrier to operate aircraft in both the take-off phase and the landing-on simultaneously. Allied to this revolutionary design was the mirror-landing system that dispensed with the 'batsman' and gave control of the landing phase back to the pilot via a system of light signals. These developments would allow larger and faster aircraft to be operated safely from carriers. Unfortunately, the Royal Navy was still operating ships from the pre-jet era and improvements were urgently required if the Fleet Air Arm was to move effectively into the second half of the twentieth century.

As the Sea Hawk entered service with the Royal Navy, at Kingston work proceeded on schemes to produce a long-range Sea Hawk for which additional fuel carriage would be essential with a consequent increase in all-up weight, which would affect take-off and landing operations. The scheme proposed use of an Attinello-type blowing system or 'blown flaps', whereby engine compressor air was ducted to the wing and thus into a slot in the flap and thence ejected over the flap to energise the airflow and increase wing lift. Using this system, it was estimated that take-off speed could be reduced by some 17 knots and landing speed by 11 knots for a weight penalty of 220lbs but increasing the maximum take-off weight to about 17,900lb. Whilst it offered worthwhile gains, the long-range Sea Hawk proposal never proceeded.

It can be seen from the above that Hawker Aircraft, apparently renowned for producing no aircraft that were truly innovative, had, in the Sea Hawk, produced a fighter which was their first essay into jet propulsion, their first with a tricycle undercarriage, their first pressurised cockpit, and with a novel powerplant layout that used the minimum of internal fuselage volume by reason of the bifurcated intake and exhaust layout. Innovation then was clearly no problem to Sydney Camm and his design team.

Sea Hawk F.Mk.1 WF159, now with the tail bullet fairing in place. This aircraft first flew in November 1952 but, piloted by Frank Murphy, carried out a forced landing at RNAS Ford due to an engine fire the following month. Repaired, it was retained on CS(A) charge until SOC in October 1956. (*BAE/BL*)

The light fleet carriers of late-war design had been an attempt to improve on the escort carrier philosophy but without the expense of the true fleet carrier design. These, such as *Glory* and *Triumph*, had served the country to their best ability during the Korean conflict but didn't really have the speed to keep up with the fleet. Most were scrapped or otherwise disposed of by the early 1960s. Replacing them were larger carriers, laid down during the recent war but not completed until the mid- to late 1950s due to the need to revise design and layout to reflect the new requirements of post-war use.

HMS *Eagle*, laid down in 1942 and accepted into service in 1952, served for a short time before re-entering the dockyard for a comprehensive refit in 1959. Emerging in 1962 the ship had a steam catapult, 8½-degree angled deck, 948 'Searchlight' radar and guided-missile defence system. HMS *Ark Royal*, laid down in 1943, was not completed until 1955. Similar to *Eagle*, she also featured the latest developments including a side lift to facilitate movement of aircraft from hangar to flight-deck. HMS *Victorious* had been laid down in 1937 and served throughout the Second World War, continuing to serve until 1950 when she was taken in for a major refit from 1950 to 1958 to bring her up to the most modern specification. Finally, HMS *Hermes* had perhaps the longest gestation. Laid down in 1944, she was not completed until 1959, such were the new developments required to be incorporated. Like her siblings, she featured an angled deck, steam catapults, mirror-landing system, 948 radar system and side lift. HMS *Hermes* would re-enter the dockyard in 1964 for a further update, emerging in 1966 to serve the Royal Navy for many years to come; just how long will become clear later when her most famous exploits are revealed.

Operational Use

If the Sea Hurricane's operational high point was the epic convoy escort duties of the Second World War, and Korea that of the Sea Fury, surely the Sea Hawk's high point and also its swansong was Suez. While viewed by some as one of the UK's 'colonial' conflicts, the war had rather more to do with commerce. Opened in 1869, the Suez Canal had revolutionised sea transport for European nations, shortening the journey to Asia by thousands of miles. It soon acquired strategic importance, particularly for the UK, which had an extensive empire to administer. Egypt's financial holding in the canal, through whose territory it ran, was relinquished to UK and French interests in 1875 and in 1882 the UK took control of the entire administration of Egypt. In 1888 the canal was declared a neutral zone but attempts to take control of the canal were made during the First World War by the Ottoman Empire, leading to significant numbers of British troops being stationed in the Canal Zone to deter any future aggression.

The discovery of oil in the Middle East increased the importance of the canal still further, a proportion of the UK's supply coming via this route. In the wake of the Second World War, and the stirrings of independence movements throughout the Middle East, the large British garrison at Suez became a source of increasing discontent within Egypt, culminating in a coup orchestrated by Colonel Gamel Abdel Nasser which replaced King Farouk with a Republic of Egypt in 1952. Just prior to this, the then government of Egypt

The first of two P.1052s, VX272, at Dunsfold probably in May 1953 during a visit by HRH the Duke of Edinburgh. The P.1052 was a standard N.7/46 design fitted with swept wings. Of interest is the Hawker Siddeley Group logo on the nose. (*BAE/BL*)

had torn up the Anglo-Egyptian Agreement of 1936, whereby the UK had the right to station troops in the Canal Zone for twenty years, a move received enthusiastically by most Egyptians. By 1953 Nasser had taken effective control of the country and, by 1956, was elected its president.

In this role, Nasser's increasing interventions in the Middle East, which were considered to be contrary to UK interests, led to reluctance in the UK and USA to supply Egypt with modern arms, leading to Nasser turning to the USSR for those, in particular large supplies of modern MiG-15 fighters and anti-aircraft artillery. The concern that this generated within NATO, together with Nasser's other seemingly anti-western interventions, culminated in the UK and USA withdrawing their offer of funding from the Aswan Dam project, an important resource for Egypt. In response, in July 1956 Nasser announced the nationalisation of the Suez Canal Company, which henceforth would be controlled by Egypt, although it should be noted that this did not prevent other nations, including the UK, from using the waterway, although Israel was banned from using it. Fearing for continued access to their dominions in the Far East, Asia and Australasia, France and the UK conceived a plan to recover the Canal Zone by direct attack. In alliance with Israel, France and the UK agreed to 'intervene' in the interests of peace if a war between Israel and Egypt erupted, which it duly did when Israel moved into Sinai in Operation KADESH. The attack began on 31 October 1956.

The British operation, codenamed MUSKETEER, called for the Royal Navy to supply air cover in the region to protect the bombers flying from Cyprus and Malta and, later, ground forces to be landed from naval assets to recover control of the Canal Zone. The carriers HMS *Albion*, with Nos. 800 and 802 NASs, equipped with Sea Hawks, and 809, equipped with Sea Venoms, HMS *Bulwark*, with Nos. 804, 897 and 810 NASs with Sea

Hawks, and HMS *Eagle*, with Nos. 898 NAS (Sea Hawks) and 892 and 893 NASs with Sea Venoms, were despatched together with HMS *Ocean* and *Theseus* in support. On 1 November, the operation began with the Sea Hawks, in the absence of any significant fighter opposition, used mainly in their ground-attack configuration while the Sea Venoms supplied any fighter protection required although, with the majority of Egypt's MiG-15 aircraft either flown out to other Arab nations or destroyed on the ground, this was limited. The Sea Hawk featured four 20mm Hispano cannon under the cockpit with ammunition feed from stowage behind the cockpit. The feeds were rivetted to the fuselage structure, which was not well received by the armourers when there was a stoppage, this proving to be difficult to resolve quickly. The later marks were also well equipped for the ground-attack role, being wired to carry 500lb bombs or RPs under the wings.

Six Sea Hawk squadrons took part in the conflict, flying against shore installations through heavy anti-aircraft fire that damaged several aircraft. Troop landings began two days later at Port Said, this being the first time that large-scale movement of troops by helicopter had been performed. With the operation proceeding smoothly, the forces in theatre were certainly not happy to receive instructions from their respective governments on 6 November to withdraw, due to US pressure on France and UK, not least by threatening

WV908, built as a FGA.Mk.4 and first flown at Bitteswell in February 1955 before delivery to AHU Abbotsinch. Later upgraded to FGA.Mk.6 and based at RNAS Brawdy with 807 and 898 NASs during the 1950s before being allocated to RAF Halton as an instructional airframe. Acquired by SAH Culdrose, the aircraft was returned to flight c.1977 before passing to RNHF at Yeovilton. Further restoration by BAe followed at Dunsfold and the aircraft is currently being returned to flight again by Navy Wings. (*BAE/BL*)

Sea Hawk FGA.Mk.6 WV908 at Dunsfold with wings folded, June 1986. (*Author*)

Sea Hawk FGA.Mk.6 WV908 at Dunsfold in June 1995 prior to its refurbishment. (*Author*)

financial repercussions from any continuation. Accordingly, a ceasefire was announced by the UK government, the two countries, together with Israel, duly ceasing their action, leaving Nasser in control of the canal and the UK and France licking their wounds. During the brief spell of fighting, two Sea Hawks had been lost due to effective anti-aircraft fire as well as two Westland Wyverns and two helicopters. With the humiliating withdrawal of UK forces, Prime Minister Sir Anthony Eden resigned in January 1957.

The Suez conflict was not the last time that the Sea Hawk saw active service, being called upon during the disturbances in Cyprus in the mid-1950s and later in 1960 in Aden. By then most Sea Hawks in the Fleet Air Arm had been relegated to second-line duties but, for other countries, their journey was just beginning.

Export aircraft

With the Royal Navy's contracts completed, no sooner had Armstrong Whitworth dismantled the Sea Hawk jigs at Coventry to make way for other work than two substantial foreign orders emerged for the aircraft. The first was from Marine Luchtvaart Dienst, the air arm of the Royal Netherlands Navy, which ordered twenty-two FGA.Mk.6 aircraft under the designation Sea Hawk F.50 in 1956. These were to form two squadrons for service aboard the former light fleet carrier HMS *Venerable*, which the country had purchased from the UK in 1948 and renamed *Karel Doorman*. The aircraft were delivered between 1957 and 1958.

The second order came from the newly-founded Bundesmarine, the West German Navy, the successor to the war-time Kriegsmarine, founded in 1956. The 1957 order was

Sea Hawk WV911 at Dunsfold as a spares source for the refurbishment of WV908. (*Author*)

again for the FGA.Mk.6, designated F.100, a standard Mk.6 but with enlarged fin and rudder, thirty-four of this version being ordered. The aircraft were assembled at Bitteswell and initially delivered to RNAS Lossiemouth from February 1958 where a West German training squadron was established. Later Mk.100 aircraft were delivered directly to Focke-Wulf at Bremen in West Germany. Also acquired were a further thirty-four Mk.101 aircraft, these featuring an underwing Ecko Mk 34 radar pod as well as the enlarged fin and rudder. Those aircraft were completed between 1958 and 1959 at Bitteswell and were delivered to Focke-Wulf at Bremen or to the squadron at Schleswig.

Given that the German Navy had been required to decommission entirely after 1945, a new aviation arm would need to be created to use the Sea Hawk and the Fairey Gannets which had also been supplied to Germany under MDAP funding. With this aim in mind, Commander 'Winkle' Brown was offered the role of overseeing this resurgent force's introduction to the new aircraft. With his past links to Germany and his excellent language skills, he was perhaps the obvious choice and so arrived in Bonn in 1958 as Head of the British Naval Air Mission, successfully negotiating what could have been a fraught posting, embedded at the heart of his former enemy.

The final Sea Hawk export order came from India. The first batch, new-build Sea Hawk FGA.6s, were delivered during 1961, followed by ex-FAA aircraft, these being FB.Mk.3 and FB.Mk.5s upgraded to FGA.Mk.6 standard, being completed in 1963. Initial deliveries were to FAA bases in the UK to allow for Indian conversion training before the aircraft and pilots moved to India where they were embarked on the INS *Vikrant* (the former UK Majestic-class carrier HMS *Hercules*). A later batch of sixteen ex-FAA refurbished aircraft were acquired direct from FAA stocks rather than via Armstrong Whitworth in 1963–4 and a final batch was acquired from West Germany of twenty-eight ex-Bundesmarine Sea Hawk Mk.100 and Mk.101 machines. The Sea Hawk would remain in the Indian Navy inventory until replaced by the Sea Harrier FRS.Mk.51 in the 1980s.

Intriguingly, some forty-five years after the last Sea Hawk was completed at Dunsfold, in 1995 its familiar shape once again graced the production hangars at the aerodrome. This was WV908, a late series Mk.6, converted from a Mk.4, which had previously been refurbished in 1982 and flown by the Royal Navy Historic Flight in the colours of No.806 NAS at Yeovilton. Grounded in 1989 due to 'lack of funds for its future operation', the airframe languished until a change of operating policy saw funds made available from the Swordfish Heritage Trust and the transfer of the aircraft to BAe Dunsfold in May 1995 for a complete refurbishment and return to flight. Over the next seventeen months, the aircraft was stripped and rebuilt and made its first post-restoration flight at Dunsfold in the hands of Lieutenant Commander David Baddams in October 1996 before flying down to Yeovilton for its official unveiling. Typically, with industry and Navy top brass in attendance for the big day, the Sea Hawk refused to start due to a malfunction with the starter control panel – such is the nature of engineering! Following this hiccup, the aircraft performed on the display circuit for several years before again being grounded due to a cracked jet-pipe and returned to Dunsfold in 1999. Sadly, the rectification work became caught up in the closure of the facility and had to be completed elsewhere but it was then returned to flight before another grounding in 2010. At the time of writing, it is hoped to return the aircraft to flight once more, a superb example of Hawker design.[10]

Chris Gotke has flown both the Sea Fury and the Sea Hawk under the auspices of the now defunct RNHF at Yeovilton and remains impressed with both aircraft although it is clear that, for him, the Sea Fury is the winner. In the air, 'The Sea Fury is a nicer handling aircraft than the Sea Hawk, which needs more trimming with speed changes, but with the powered ailerons, it is a nice aircraft to handle, even with the manual elevator and rudder controls.' In a combat situation, Chris felt that the Sea Fury would be his mount of choice, its manoeuvrability being superior to the Sea Hawk by virtue of its powerful piston engine and better all-round view. Hopefully, he will get to sample the delights of both the Sea Hawk and Sea Fury again soon.[11]

The Sea Hawk was not the first jet aircraft acquired for the Royal Navy but it had given the Fleet Air Arm a simple-to-maintain fighter that had very few vices and could hold its own against whatever adversaries it might meet. That said, it was a straight-wing design that might have struggled to hold its own against the swept wing MiG-15, powered incidentally by the same – albeit reverse-engineered – engine as the Sea Hawk. The Sea Hawk was slowly phased out of first-line service with the Fleet Air Arm as Supermarine's Scimitar became available. Most Sea Hawks had been relegated to second-line use by 1960, with No.806 Squadron the last to give up its mounts. However, it remained in use with training squadrons and FRU until 1969. Not bad for a fighter design from the 1940s and a glowing testament to Hawker's ability to get it right first time. In an inventory dated January 1966, some thirty-one Sea Hawk FGA.Mk.6s were still being held at various naval yards around the UK.

The question may be asked: why did the Fleet Air Arm order the Sea Hawk when it had a comparable jet, the Supermarine Attacker, already in service, from August 1951? Perhaps one may best answer this by examining the opinion of the Royal Navy's primary test pilot at the time, Captain Eric 'Winkle' Brown.

Firstly, the Supermarine Attacker: Brown found the take-off tricky, 'it was not easy to raise the tail off the ground until the aircraft was almost airborne' (the Attacker had a tailwheel undercarriage). In flight, 'The aircraft also suffered from directional snaking in any form of turbulence, which would affect its performance as a gun platform.' For deck landing, Brown found that, 'In the event of a baulked landing full-power could be applied instantaneously but gave a strong nose-up trim change which was dangerous at such slow speed.' His final words on the subject were: 'Thus the Attacker had the distinction of being the Royal Navy's first operational jet aircraft, and for that, if for little else, it will always be remembered.'[12]

Brown's thoughts on the Sea Hawk were of a rather different hue. Having been only the second pilot to fly the prototype P.1040, it is clear that Brown held a special affection for the resultant Sea Hawk.

I now got down to the general handling and deck landing assessment of the N7/46 (the pre-production version of the Sea Hawk) and what a delightful task that proved to be …. The all-round view was excellent … the cockpit layout was first class and the seating very comfortable …. At the conclusion of these tests my assessment was that the N7/46 was undoubtedly an outstanding aircraft and certainly fit to undertake its deck landing trials even in prototype condition, and these were successfully carried out.

And finally, a fitting epilogue from Brown.

It will be obvious that I have a very high regard for the Sea Hawk in all its forms, but that is from the handling viewpoint rather than the performance one. Between my test flying on the Sea Hawk and my operational time with it I had flown the North American F-86 Sabre, which set a standard I still regard as superb …. It says much for the Hawker product that it came out of this analysis with flying colours, although matched against a contemporary fighter of the highest calibre.[13]

Chapter 7

Hawker Hunter

In the Hawker Drawing Office, or the Project Office as it became, it was unwritten law that land-based designs for aircraft were also likely to be offered as a sea-going variant. This did not, however, seem to apply to the Hurricane, perhaps because its vast production for the RAF in time of crisis meant that alternative uses were not envisaged at first. The same might be said of the Hunter, which was also produced in very large quantities to counter the crisis triggered by the Cold War and the UK government's failure to have prepared for it. However, as has been described in Chapter 4, the Hurricane was used successfully by the Royal Navy and, in time, the Hunter would also find its way into the Fleet Air Arm, but not as a sea-going aircraft.

The Hunter was conceived during the turbulent years after the Second World War. The hoped-for peace had not materialised. Instead, a growing and dangerous stand-off between what became NATO and the USSR-led Warsaw Pact meant that a Cold War was fought that presented all of the hallmarks of war bar the actual shooting and bombing, mostly, of the recent conflict. With a successful jet fighter design under its belt, the Sea Hawk, the Kingston Project Office moved to design a second-generation fighter in the transonic realm with which to replace it. Unfortunately, this was a painful period for the design team at Kingston; post-war relaxation of labour restrictions saw a number of its talented members moving on to other vocations, resulting in something of a dearth of quality ability in the team, making progress somewhat slow.

The post-war period was a time of intense experimentation in aircraft design. Encouraged by the opportunities seemingly offered by the new jet-turbine powerplant, all manner of configurations, both airframe and engine layout, were explored, most of which were *culs-de-sac* though others appeared to promise performance benefits for the designer who 'got it right'. In the Hawker Project Office, various studies for a transonic fighter were explored, some ten layouts being assessed including single-engined and twin-engined layouts, but the most promising, at least where Hawker was concerned, was the evolutionary path beginning with the P.1040, N7/46, Sea Hawk design. On the back of this design series, in June 1946, another was quickly offered to the Ministry of Supply featuring the N7/46 fuselage mated to wings swept at 35 degrees, which offered a rise in useable Mach number; this was agreed in June by Deputy Director Aircraft Research and Development (DDARD), but the aircraft would be for research purposes only as there was no enthusiasm for a purchase for service use. The swept-wing P.1052 (two aircraft were produced) was considered to be a successful design, raising the maximum speed from M0.84 at 36,000 feet and time to 35,000 feet of 11 minute 50 seconds for the straight-winged Sea Hawk, to M0.87 and 9 minutes 30 seconds for the P.1052.

Development

Following on this line of reasoning, it was then decided to combine the swept-wing layout with a straight-through jet pipe and all-swept tail surfaces, this being designated the P.1081. This design, with more than a passing resemblance to the Hunter, of which a single example was constructed, increased the maximum speed to M0.89 at 36,000 feet and reduced the time to 35,000 feet to 9 minutes 12 seconds, while also increasing the service ceiling by at least 1,000 feet. Having thus successfully trialled most of the elements that would come together in the Hunter, the project designers then, seemingly inexplicably, abandoned this line of progress and effectively went back to the drawing board. Whether this was influenced by the engine choice is moot. The engine would now be an axial design, the centrifugal powerplant being deemed of limited development potential. Rolls-Royce's new design, the AJ.65, offered far more potential, its small frontal area giving the opportunity to create slim-line designs for the modern jet aircraft and thereby increased performance prospects. The truth was that development of the various experimental aircraft was going on in tandem with the F.3/48 design, which would become the axial-powered Hunter, the straight-through jet pipe arrangement of P.1081 not being flown until 1950 and, therefore, the requisite empirical data were not always available to inform the F.3/48 design.

Thus did Hawker begin the long process of getting their first transonic fighter into the air. Having attempted, unsuccessfully, to design a response to the Ministry's initial OR.228 and its attendant specifications, F.43/46 and F.44/46, for a new twin-engined day fighter and two-seat twin-engined night/all-weather fighter respectively, Camm and his small project office staff decided to abandon a twin-engined approach and start instead on a single-engined layout (Camm's preference anyway) using the Rolls-Royce AJ.65 engine, now coded RA.2 and offering in the region of 5,500lb thrust. Vivian Stanbury, now head of Project Office, began work on this new design in January 1948, seeking to produce an aircraft of around 12,000lb, a wing swept at 42.5 degrees and t/c ratio of around 8.5 per cent, armed with two 30mm cannon. This first layout drawing, dated from 1948, was, as he freely admitted, based on German research data made available to aircraft design teams after the war, and as such featured a planform resembling the later MiG-15: swept wings, unswept T-tail, axial engine fed by a nose-mounted intake and exhausting at the tail and cannon armament in the nose. This design, coded P.1067, appeared to have gained nothing from the varied design work already undertaken on the N7/46 family of aircraft. The fuselage was now 'full of air' from nose to tail, which promised a restricted cockpit and little room for equipment. With the Ministry now feeling happier with progress, OR.228 received the revised specification F.3/48, which called for an aircraft capable of intercepting 'high speed, high altitude bombers in daylight as soon as possible after the bomber is detected on the radar warning system'. The aircraft would need very fast start-up and 'the greatest possible acceleration and highest possible climbing speed'. Max speed at 45,000 feet altitude was to be not less than M0.953 with a time to climb of not more than six minutes.[1]

P.1067 prototype WB188 at Boscombe Down prior to its first flight in July 1951. (*BAE/BL*)

As work progressed on the design, it was clear to Stanbury that the aircraft was some way from these figures (it would never meet them) and, slowly, the design began to falter as demands for greater fuselage fuel capacity (as drawn, the first layout only allowed for 300 gallons), the fitting of a Martin-Baker ejection seat, increased armament, and nose-mounted radar ranging, conspired by mid-1949 to threaten the entire project. At that stage Harold Tuffen laid out a revised scheme comprising wing-root intakes as per the earlier N7/46 aircraft series which solved many of the problems with the front fuselage layout and work proceeded on a more confident note which saw the T-tail abandoned and the tailplane/elevators swept and moved down to a point about a third of the way up the fin as with the earlier N7/46. With the armament relocated to a removeable ventral pack under the cockpit, the design was finally on course to emerge as the world-beating aircraft it would later become. Quite why Stanbury decided on a pitot intake for the Avon engine is lost in the mists of time. He told Roy Braybrook that the Avon, being an axial engine, 'cried out for the straight-through intake', yet designs for P.1065, to F.43/46, also to be Avon-powered, had happily been drawn with wing-root intakes.[2]

In any event, it was this design that moved forward into prototype construction, achieving its first flight at Boscombe Down on 20 July 1951 in the capable hands of Neville Duke, the aircraft being WB188, fitted with the Rolls-Royce Avon RA.7 rated at 7,500lb. Having produced the first P.1067, it was clear that much work would be required to remedy the

P.1067 prototype WB188 showing the elegant lines of what would become the Hunter. (*BAE/BL*)

numerous problems discovered by the company test pilots and at Boscombe Down but, with just three prototypes to carry out the numerous test points and investigations, this work became protracted. Unfortunately, such was the political situation vis-à-vis the Cold War background that production was ordered before those shortcomings could be addressed properly; they included a strong rudder buzz and airframe buffet at high speed, heavy controls at speed, pitch-up at high angles of attack, inadequate air-braking and surge of the engine at high speed/altitude and also during gun firing.

The second prototype, WB195, was used by Boscombe Down to carry out early assessment of performance and control which confirmed earlier deficiencies identified on the first aircraft. The third protype, WB202, was fitted with the Armstrong Siddeley Sapphire engine as an insurance policy against the Avon failing to make the grade. However, a bullet fairing fitted to the rear of the fin/tailplane joint largely cured the high speed

A study in perfection, the second prototype P.1067 Hunter, WB195, first flown on 5 May 1952. (*BAE/BL*)

rudder buzz and buffet while increased powered flying controls improved the lack of roll response and the pitch-up would be largely cured with wing leading-edge extensions. With regard to the air-brake problems, Camm had allowed for this with split flaps as on the Sea Hawk but on the Hunter this imparted a significant trim change that made weapon aiming a precarious process. Work to find a suitable alternative flap design was eventually abandoned and a ventral air-brake designed that offered minimal trim change, this being retrofitted to the early Mk.1 aircraft that had already come off the production line.

However, such were the various new problems emerging and the paucity of prototypes with which to investigate them that CA Release was not achieved until July 1954, as completed F.Mk.1 airframes continued to accumulate at Dunsfold. With a partial CA Release, the aircraft became available for squadron use and soon revealed another problem – short flight duration due to the small fuel capacity. Braybrook understood the specification to call for 1 hr 15 mins but it was often somewhat less, the aircraft being seen as a point-defence asset, and would prove to be an acute embarrassment in RAF service with multiple aircraft losses due to fuel starvation resulting in questions being asked in Parliament. However, with the subsequent production of the Mk.4 variant, with its increased fuel capacity and other modifications, most of the problems were being addressed and the Hunter could emerge as the fine aircraft that it later became. The Mk.6 was perhaps the ultimate fighter variant, much loved by its pilots and very capable with its 10,000 lb thrust Rolls-Royce Avon engine. The aircraft would go on to be produced in a

Third prototype P.1067 WB202 seen at Dunsfold outside the Experimental Hangar. This aircraft was the prototype for the Sapphire-engined Hunter Mk.2. (*BAE/BL*)

fighter/ground-attack variant, the FGA.Mk.9 Hunter, capable of carrying a wide range of bombs and rockets and able to take considerable punishment. As an export aircraft, the Hunter would be supplied to multiple air arms around the world, some 1,972 aircraft being produced as well as hundreds of refurbished, modified and licence-built examples being manufactured.

Naval Use

Given that the Air Ministry foresaw the aircraft being mass produced for service use in the UK, it is strange that no mention of a trainer version was implicit in the original specification. But, even as the first prototype flew, the Project Office, in 1953, was scheming a two-seat version for use in the training role with either tandem or side-by-side seating. With Air Ministry interest evident, work proceeded to design an efficient trainer that lacked nothing in the fighter role and could cover the weapon-training syllabus as well. Hawker's favoured layout was for tandem seating, since this simplified the weapon aiming requirement, but eventually the Ministry settled upon side-by-side seating, this being accommodated in a slightly wider front fuselage which was the only change to the fuselage contours, the design being coded P.1101.

With specification T.157D being issued in 1954, work proceeded swiftly on production of a two-seat prototype based upon the Hunter F.Mk.4 with its 7,500lb thrust engine, this aircraft, XJ615, taking its first flight at Dunsfold on 8 July 1955 and soon revealing severe airflow breakdown around the revised hood contours, governed by a Ministry requirement that the aircraft be identical to the single-seat aft of the front transport joint. That requirement necessitated a severe curtailment of the hood contour, resulting in inevitable airflow disturbance. Many different shapes were considered and trialled and, eventually, by ignoring the earlier Ministry stipulation, a longer hood/dorsal fairing cured the problem completely. The new trainer, designated T.Mk.7, carrying a reduced armament of a single cannon and including a tail-mounted braking parachute, soon attracted a production order while Hawker received authority to proceed with a Mk.6 trainer version using the more powerful 10,000lb thrust Avon, the Mk.203, the prototype, XJ627, flying in 1956 although it was not proceeded with.

Production of the Hunter T.Mk.7 began with a contract for fifty-five aircraft, initially to be built at Hawker's Blackpool factory at Squires Gate, but government cancellation of a large Hunter contract, due to the Sandys White Paper in 1957, resulted in production being moved to Kingston/Dunsfold. Although this first contract was for fifty-five aircraft, the RAF only received forty-five Hunters, ten being diverted to the Royal Navy in 1958, designated Hunter T.Mk.8. Naval interest in the Hunter was first evident in the mid-1950s when it became evident that the existing trainer aircraft available to the Fleet Air Arm, Vampire and Sea Fury, would be incapable of simulating the high speeds and advanced capabilities of the new aircraft being ordered for the service, i.e. the Sea Vixen and Scimitar.

Hunter T.Mk.8

Looking first at the numbers of aircraft acquired, a T.Mk.8 prototype, WW664, was constructed from a repaired F.Mk.4 and trialled at Boscombe Down. Thus successfully completed, production of the ten T.Mk.8 Hunters began, serialled XL580–582, XL584–585, XL598–599 and XL602–604. First flight was by XL580 in May 1958, the batch being completed by January 1959 and the aircraft delivered to RNAS Lossiemouth with Nos. 736 and 764 Training Squadrons between May 1958 and early 1959. These would be the only new-build Hunter T.Mk.8 aircraft received with future requirements met by conversions.

As well as the new-build T.Mk.8 Hunters thus acquired via the RAF contract, further T.Mk.8s were sought and the requirement fulfilled by way of conversions from redundant F.Mk.4 aircraft. As with so much of the Hunter conversions story, accurate numbers of conversions for the Royal Navy are elusive. However, it appears that initially eighteen aircraft were converted to T.Mk.8 standard at Dunsfold and Bitteswell between March and July 1959 from both F.Mk.4 and T.Mk.7 airframes for the Fleet Air Arm Training Squadrons. Those aircraft joined the new-build T.Mk.8s at Lossiemouth, being used to teach applied flying and navigation skills. These eighteen RN conversions comprised the following: the prototype was WW664 and serials were: WT701, WT702, WT722, WT745, WT755, WT774, WT799, WV319, WV322, WV363, WW661, XE664, XE665, XF289, XF322, XF357, XF358.

The prototype naval T.Mk.8 Hunter, WW664. Note the single 30mm cannon mounted on the starboard gunpack and the four drop-tank configuration used to give the naval Hunter longer legs. (*BAE/BL*)

The Hunter T.Mk.8 prototype, WW664, seen during a rather wet display. Following its first post-conversion flight in March 1958, the aircraft was retained by CA at Dunsfold and Boscombe Down for various mods and TIs before allocation to AHU Lossiemouth in July 1961. SOC following engine fire in October 1969. (*BAE/BL*)

Hunter T.Mk.8 XF995 outside the production hangars at Dunsfold. First flown at Dunsfold as T.Mk.8 in June 1964, the aircraft returned to Dunsfold for TI of various modifications. It later served with 764 NAS before returning to 5 MU at Kemble. (*BAE/BL*)

These were followed by four aircraft to T.Mk.8B which were also conversions from T.Mk.7 and F.Mk.4 airframes. Serials were WW664 (prototype), XF967, XF978 and XF994. The aircraft featured a full TACAN fit. Then came a further eleven conversions to T.Mk.8C standard, also from T.Mk.7 and F.Mk.4 airframes and existing T.Mk.8 airframes, with serials WV396, WV397, XF938, XF939, XF942, XF983, XF985, XF991, XF992,

Hunter T.Mk.8 WV363 receives attention. First post-conversion flight was at Bitteswell in April 1959 before issue to 764 NAS Lossiemouth. Later issued to 759 NAS Brawdy in August 1968. It was eventually lost in a ditching in February 1992 following an in-flight fire. (*BAE/BL*)

Another Brawdy-based Hunter T.Mk.8, WT799. First post-conversion flight was at Dunsfold January 1959 before issue to AHU at Lossiemouth. Allocated to RNAS Brawdy in November 1963, believed to be extant. (*BAE/BL*)

XF995 and XL604. Those featured a partial TACAN fit. These aircraft were converted at Dunsfold and Bitteswell in 1963–4 and then delivered to Short Brothers at Belfast, presumably for fit of the TACAN system before final delivery to RNAS Brawdy in South Wales. Thus some thirty-one Hunters were converted to T.Mk.8 standard.

The single to two-seat conversions were finished to T.Mk.8 standard to match the earlier new-build order delivered in 1958–9, the aircraft being Hunter F.Mk.4s which

Hunter T.Mk.8 WT722. which appears to have had its Brawdy designator letters partially removed. First post-conversion flight was at Bitteswell July 1959 before allocation to AHU Lossiemouth. Served with 764 NAS before transfer to RNAS Brawdy in December 1966 and use by 759 NAS and later by FRADU at Yeovilton. Believed to be extant. (*BAE/BL*)

Hunter T.Mk.8 XL598 equipped with four drop tanks but not displaying its base allegiance. This aircraft's first flight was at Dunsfold in October 1958 before allocation to AHU Lossiemouth where it joined 738 NAS, moving to RNAS Brawdy still with the squadron. Later flown by FRADU at Yeovilton, the aircraft was sold to Thunder City Aircraft Co., South Africa, and is believed to be extant. (*BAE/BL*)

Brawdy-based Hunter T.Mk.8 XL580. First flight was at Dunsfold in May 1958 before allocation to AHU Lossiemouth. Served with 764 NAS Lossiemouth. At RNAS Brawdy with 759 NAS by November 1966 and at FRADU Yeovilton by 1972. The aircraft was then returned to Bitteswell for modification to T.Mk.8M standard. Believed to be extant. (*BAE/BL*)

T.Mk.8 XL580 (first flight May 1958), pictured 1962, finished in blue/white FONFT Yeovilton scheme; FONFT standing for Flag Officer Naval Flying Training. To Fleet Arm Museum 1994, believed extant. (*Author*)

had become redundant following the issue of the big-engine Hunter F.Mk.6 to RAF squadrons and therefore featuring the lower-powered Mk.100 series engine of 7,500lb. The factory-based conversion work entailed the removal of the front fuselage back to the front transport joint and its replacement with a new two-seat front fuselage, revised canopy and dorsal fairing. The CA Release for the T.Mk.8 noted the changes from the basic Hunter F.Mk.4: new front fuselage with side-by-side seating, a flying tail, one Aden 30mm gun with 150 rounds on the starboard side, a braking parachute, extended wing leading edge, airfield emergency arrestor hook stressed to 1.5g, naval radio and Avon 122 engine. The aircraft was cleared for day and night use for pilot conversion, gun firing, bombing with practice bombs, air-to-air rocket and RP firing. Aircraft maximum all-up weight would be 17,300lb clean and was cleared for a maximum speed of 620 knots. Of passing interest is a drawing dated May 1959 which shows a twin-Sidewinder missile installation mounted under the wing of the T.Mk.8 at the outboard pylon station. Quite what the naval requirement would have been for this layout is again lost in the mists of time but, clearly, a fighter role was envisaged.[3]

Hunter GA.Mk.11

At a Hawker Aircraft board meeting of 30 March 1960, Sir Sydney Camm had intimated that there was a strong interest in a navalised version of the Hunter that could well lead to a conversion order. This interest became concrete on 27 July 1960 when it was reported by J.T. Lidbury, the managing director, that the Treasury had given authorisation for the conversion of forty F.Mk.4 Hunters for the Royal Navy at a cost of £1,000,000 and, further, that there was a possibility of an order for the conversion of fourteen single-seat Hunters to two-seat versions for naval training purposes, this contract being worth about £750,000. At a meeting on 11 November 1960 at Kingston, between Hawker, Admiralty and MoA representatives, the Royal Navy announced that it intended to acquire some seventy-one Hunter F.Mk.4 aircraft from the Air Ministry, of which some fifty-seven aircraft would remain in basic Mk.Mk.4 specification, and for fourteen aircraft to be modified to T.Mk.8 standard. The numbers were clarified in September when funding for forty Hunter GA.Mk.11 aircraft was authorised by the Treasury. It was further decided that 40 per cent of the GA.Mk.11s would have a RP capability but the remaining 60 per cent would not.

Further to the two-seat conversions, the Royal Navy sought a number of single-seat Hunters for use in the ground-attack training role, this being reported to the Hawker board at the 25 July 1961 meeting where it was noted that an Instruction to Proceed (ITP) for thirty-seven GA.Mk.11 Naval Hunters had been received and work commenced on their preparation. The GA.Mk.11 featured the standard Royal Navy alterations to accommodate an airfield arrestor hook, naval communication and TACAN equipment. In addition, the four-cannon armament package was deleted, the gunports faired over and the radar-ranging equipment removed. On 23 November 1961 it was announced that the order had been increased to forty aircraft, by which time the standard of preparation for the GA.Mk.11 had been settled as: sixteen aircraft to be RP compatible, while twenty-four would not be. The first twenty aircraft would be delivered with the Avon 113 engine and the rest

Hunter T.Mk.8, Yeovilton-based, possibly at Boscombe Down. (*BAE/BL*)

Lossiemouth-based Hunter GA.Mk.11 at Dunsfold equipped with drop tanks on the inner and practice bomb carriers on the outer pylons. Note also the four practice bombs carried on pylons on the centre-line gun-pack location. May 1966. (*BAE/BL*)

Naval Hunters at Dunsfold, 1962; two T.Mk.8s and one GA.Mk.11. The T.Mk.8s carry the FOFNT emblem on the nose. (*Author*)

with the updated Avon 122. TACAN was to be fitted to all aircraft but non-availability of equipment was not to delay deliveries. Equipment to be removed from the GA.Mk.11 included the complete gun-pack installation, DME, VHF and Green Salad and radar-ranging installations. In place of the deleted radio equipment would be fitted UHF main and standby radio sets and IFF, plus ballast to replace the gun installation.

Converted aircraft began deliveries to the FAA from Dunsfold beginning in early 1962. The first aircraft, XE712, converted in late 1961 with first flight in January 1962, was retained at Dunsfold for handling trials and was then transferred to A&AEE Boscombe Down for CA Release trials before finding its way to Lossiemouth in August that year. As the first aircraft arrived on station, the CO, in a letter to Dunsfold CTP Bill Bedford, reported that, 'Everyone is pleased with the aircraft, my ratings are happier and the pilots are like small boys with new toys … . I am extremely pleased with the aircraft … .'[4]

Deliveries continued throughout 1962 and 1963, either to RNAS Lossiemouth for immediate squadron use or to Belfast, to the RNAY or Short Brothers for modification or long-term storage. On the squadron, the aircraft were used to instruct on low-level navigation skills and ground-attack profiles with practice bombs or RPs, the duties being split between RNAS Lossiemouth and Brawdy. As noted earlier, Hunters were not used operationally but first-line pilots did fly the aircraft as part of their training for Sea Vixen and Scimitar operations. The main squadrons involved with the Hunter, both T.Mk.8 and GA.Mk.11, were Nos. 738, 759 and 764 NAS, the aircraft remaining on the squadrons throughout the 1960s until passed to other users in the early 1970s.

Later in their lives, the GA.Mk.11s were operated by Airwork and Flight Refuelling under the aegis of FRADU, the Fleet Requirements and Air Direction Unit, which supplied aircraft sorties to the FAA and RN as simulated targets for interception and tracking exercises. These sorties could be spectacular, with the Hunter approaching ships at very high speed and very low altitude in a simulated missile profile to give tracking practice to the radar and weapon-aiming disciplines aboard ship. Some GA.Mk.11s were fitted with a nose mounted 'Harley' light to facilitate optical tracking. Some five GA.Mk.11 Hunters were fitted with a three-camera reconnaissance nose package, these being redesignated (at least unofficially) as PR.Mk.11.

One unusual job for the Hunter GA.Mk.11 was courtesy of Airwork Services, at the time providing pilots and maintenance for the FRADU tasking, who formed an aerobatic display team in 1975 at HMS *Heron*, alias RNAS Yeovilton, named the Blue Herons with four GA.Mk.11s serialled WT804, WT806, WW654 and XE682. Their first display on 6 September 1975 at Yeovilton Air Day was followed by numerous others at UK air shows for the next five years and a couple of later displays with a reformed team in the early 1980s.

The Hunters operated by FRADU at Yeovilton continued in their role until the early 1990s, an impressive testament to the aircraft's enduring longevity and its ability to adapt to many different roles. However, the FRADU Hunters were not the last of the breed to find a new role, this title going to several of the T.Mk.8 new-build Hunters. Beginning in 1975, three T.Mk.8s were progressively withdrawn from service and returned to Hawker Siddeley Aviation for refurbishment and conversion to Hunter T.Mk.8M. XL602 was

Hunter GA.Mk.11 WV380 in clean configuration disporting off the south coast. First post-mod flight from Dunsfold May 1962, the aircraft served with 738 NAS at Lossiemouth. (*BAE/BL*)

Hunter GA.Mk.11 seen at RNAS Yeovilton in July 1979 while in use with FRADU. (*Author*)

Hunter T.Mk.8M XL602, seen here on Dunsfold's flight line prior to a sortie. The modified nose profile to accommodate the Blue Fox radar is the defining attribute of the T.8M. (*Author*)

delivered to Dunsfold in July 1975 for prototype conversion, the work being completed by March 1978 when the aircraft was on test at Dunsfold. Thereafter, the aircraft was used extensively at Holme-on-Spalding-Moor and Dunsfold on various trials. It was followed by XL603, delivered to Brough in June 1975 for conversion, which was complete by October

Hunter T.Mk.8M XL602 at Dunsfold in June 1990 where it was used as a chase aircraft for other programmes once its use as a Sea Harrier systems trainer was complete. (*Author*)

Hunter T.Mk.8 at RNAS Yeovilton while in use with FRADU in July 1979. (*Author*)

1978, and later by XL580, withdrawn from long-term storage at 5MU and delivered to Brough for conversion in September 1978, the work being complete by June 1980.

As noted, these aircraft were to be used as systems trainers for the forthcoming introduction of the Sea Harrier FRS.Mk.1 into the FAA inventory. While the left-hand side of the cockpit was retained as was, the right-hand side was comprehensively altered to accommodate equipment representative of the Sea Harrier, including a Smith

Hunter T.Mk.8s taxi in at RNAS Yeovilton after another FRADU exercise in July 1979. (*Author*)

Industries Head Up Display and head-down screen and controls for the Blue Fox radar, the aircraft's nose being altered to allow fitment of the Blue Fox radar and processor and pitot static probe to mirror the Sea Harrier nose. XL580 spent most of its life with A&AEE Boscombe Down and later No.899 Squadron at Yeovilton until 1993 when it went into storage. XL603 was allocated to RAE Bedford for radar trials in support of the Sea Harrier programme before moving to FRADU at Yeovilton and storage in 1993. XL602 had the most active life of the three, mainly based at Dunsfold under the aegis of MoD/PE performing a multitude of radar and avionics trials and later being used as a chase aircraft in the Sea Harrier trials. The aircraft passed to FRADU in 1994 before entering storage at Shawbury.

Tony Ogilvy, a naval pilot, recalled his experience on both the T.Mk.8 and the GA.Mk.11 Hunters at RNAS Brawdy:

> From the very first moment that I lifted off in the wonderful little fighter [the Hunter GA.11] I knew that I had been right all along in trying so hard to get into naval fixed-wing aviation … The handling and flight control balance was perfect. It looked beautiful and it flew that way. Nothing, but nothing, will ever compare with the feeling of total freedom and fun that I had in those early days in the GA.11.[5]

In terms of numbers of aircraft acquired, an assessment of the above suggests that a total of eighty-three Hunters of various marks were delivered although later acquisitions probably add to this figure. For example, a number of RAF T.Mk.7 Hunters were transferred to Admiralty charge in October 1976 (retaining the T.7 designation) and delivered to Brawdy before being returned to RAF charge in 1978. A further nine Hunter T.Mk.7 aircraft were passed to the Royal Navy in the 1980s, mainly for use by the FRADU organisation.

Thus the Hunter played a significant role in the Fleet Air Arm. If it never saw active service there, it did contribute greatly to the modernisation and development of tactics for the aircraft in the operational squadrons from the late 1950s until the early 90s. Not a bad testament for an aircraft designed in the 1940s.

Chapter 8

Sea Harrier

Imagine if you will a naval aircraft that had no need of a flight deck from which to take off and land, a deck that required no expensive catapult or arrestor gear, that would therefore allow an aircraft carrier to be built much more cheaply and crewed economically … surely navies around the world would fight to possess such a radical aircraft. The Sea Harrier should have been the fighter that everyone wanted, yet the maritime nations were disinterested and even the Royal Navy lukewarm, to say the least until, that is, the Falklands War of 1982.

'Without the Sea Harrier, there could have been no Task Force.' Thus stated Admiral Sir Henry Leach; he might have added that, without the Task Force, the Falklands War could not have resulted in the most decisive victory for the Royal Navy since the Second World War. The Falklands conflict would finally demonstrate to the naysayers that the Harrier, so long denigrated by more traditional thinking members of the armed forces, was a valuable and potent weapon in the right hands. That it took over twenty years to finally show its true abilities was no fault of Hawker Siddeley, its originator and manufacturer, so much as the inability of those who should have known better, both in government and the Royal Navy, to recognise the potential that its unique possibilities offered and which no other aircraft possessed. It may safely be stated that of all the aircraft that might have entered the FAA inventory, the Harrier was the one that was definitely *not* wanted.

The story of the Sea Harrier had started long before the Falklands War, in fact in 1957. The Hawker Project Office was struggling to make progress with its latest fighter, a large supersonic aircraft to follow the successful Hunter. Current thinking in the corridors of power believed that the future defence of the UK would be achieved not with fighter aircraft, but with guided missiles, this thinking being encapsulated in a White Paper by Duncan Sandys MP, issued in early 1957. By then, Hawker were accentuating the strike aspect of their design, coded P.1121, since the Air Staff had no interest in the aircraft as a pure interceptor. However, as P.1121 morphed into P.1129, it became clear that the project was going nowhere and therefore other ideas were urgently required to fill the hiatus created in the Project Office. One of those was later coded P.1127 and came about following receipt of a concept brochure from Bristol Siddeley Engines (BSEL) which proposed an engine wherein part of the jet thrust could be turned through 90 degrees, allowing a vehicle so equipped to achieve a very short take-off run before swivelling the exhaust thrust to face aft. The brochure piqued the interest of one of the Project Office staff, Ralph Hooper, who was getting bored designing a flying controls test rig for P.1121 and his initial design suggested that a small aircraft could be designed around the engine that might find use as a battlefield liaison vehicle.

Development

As more information arrived from Bristol Siddeley concerning likely upgrades to the engine, slowly a modest vehicle proposal developed around the engine, looking more like a 'normal' aircraft which initially used two swivelling nozzles, and then four, to direct the exhaust thrust down or aft as required, the four-nozzle arrangement allowing an aircraft to rise vertically before proceeding forward as wing lift replaced jet lift, a manoeuvre described as VTOL: vertical take-off and landing. With no other meaningful projects being undertaken at Kingston, design work on P.1127 progressed rapidly towards a prototype with which to explore the possibilities inherent in this novel approach to flight. It might be thought that this concept was so radical that no air force would take it seriously but it was just at this moment that concerns were being raised regarding the vulnerability of national air arms to attack on the ground.

In the beginning: the first three P.1127 prototypes up from Dunsfold showing a variety of minor differences reflecting evolution of ideas as the first six aircraft were built. XP831, the first aircraft, is in the foreground. Note the skin wrinkling evident behind the hot nozzles; this area was significantly beefed up on the Harrier GR.Mk 1. (*BAE/BL*)

In the background of this story was the Cold War between NATO and Warsaw Pact forces facing each other across the centre of Europe. It was widely accepted within NATO doctrine that the West's airfields were vulnerable to early attack which risked neutralising NATO air strength, and that wide dispersal of air assets was one way in which to counter the threat. Allied to dispersal was the acknowledged requirement to be able to operate aircraft from semi-prepared surfaces such as roads if/when airfield runways were destroyed. Thus it was that, in the eyes of Hawker staff at least, the P.1127 offered the perfect start for an aircraft capable of wide dispersal that needed no runway at all; surely Air Staffs across NATO would be clamouring for such an aircraft …or not. Initial interest at the Air Ministry was polite but disinterested even in funding a prototype. All eyes were turned to the latest bigger, faster, shinier, career-enhancing aircraft project – TSR-2 – which would do everything in one airframe. The tactical strike reconnaissance machine being developed by BAC, an amalgamation of Vickers-Armstrong and English Electric, promised all things to all men, but was turning out to be ferociously expensive. A small experimental VTOL machine was not going to make a name for career-minded officials at the Ministry: TSR-2 was the project to be involved with.

However, finance for two aircraft was latterly forthcoming such that, with funding for engine development being supplemented by the US-funded MWDP, the first prototype was ready for trials by July 1960. With the P.1127 successfully, if somewhat tentatively, hovering over the grid at Dunsfold on 21 October 1960 for the first time, courtesy of 'Bill' Bedford, progress during 1961 was rapid with the aircraft's envelope being explored in both hovering and conventional flight, aided by orders for further prototype/development aircraft being forthcoming. Ultimately, six P.1127 aircraft would be built and flown (although two were lost in non-fatal accidents). By now, such was the interest in VTOL ability within NATO as a means to preserve and use aircraft in wartime that a requirement was circulated to member countries for the design for a supersonic fighter with VTOL capability which offered the tempting reward of large orders for the successful design. This chimed nicely with work being undertaken at Hawker Kingston by Ralph Hooper.

Dispirited by attempts to develop the existing P.1127 to meet the Air Staff's domestic OR.345 for a VTOL fighter, which had theoretically been written around the P.1127, Hooper had started afresh on a much more ambitious design for a supersonic V/STOL (vertical/short take-off and landing) fighter coded P.1150. Minor work was required to match this design with the NATO requirement, NBMR-3, which resulted in Hawker Siddeley submitting its tender, coded P.1154, in January 1962 for a Mach 2 capable fighter equipped with a form of reheat called plenum chamber burning which burned fuel in the cold airstream of the front nozzles. The competition had by now become a major project within Western Europe which attracted all the baggage of national economic, political and military partisanship which attends such competitions. Ultimately, while the Hawker Siddeley proposal was considered the best on technical merit, because it did not involve multinational participation, it was placed on a par with the French proposal, which did. With France announcing that they would pursue their own project in any event and with no NATO budget to actually purchase P.1154, the entire edifice collapsed.

P.1127 XP831 arrives aboard HMS *Ark Royal* to a bemused reception from the 'Goofers Gallery'. (*BAE*)

Meanwhile, back at Kingston, V/STOL design was at a crossroads. With interest being shown in P.1154 by the RAF and with the possibility of naval interest, John Fozard was given the job of developing the supersonic V/STOL proposal, while Hooper continued with his work on developing the basic P.1127 concept and also to produce an improved version for use by a three-nation team to develop an understanding of the operational techniques required for V/STOL in the field. The result, the Kestrel FGA.Mk.1, was a more capable aircraft which featured an upgraded engine, improved aerodynamics (not least a more capable wing) and wing pylons for drop-tank carriage. The three nations, UK, West Germany and the USA, each contributed finance for a total of nine aircraft, together with pilots and ground crew to enable the Tripartite Evaluation Squadron to function as a stand-alone unit based at West Raynham in Norfolk from where, in 1965, dispersed operation in the field was extensively tested and procedures developed which would stand the UK in good stead in later years. While all this was going on in the wilds of Norfolk, other, rather more nautical activities were proceeding at Kingston.

A flight of Harrier GR.Mk.1 aircraft, c.1970, showing a rather more capable aircraft than the preceding image. (*BAE/BL*)

In the early 1960s the Admiralty was fielding the Supermarine Scimitar as its primary strike aircraft and the DH Sea Vixen as its carrier-based fighter, neither capable of true supersonic performance. As is normal practice, as a new aircraft enters the inventory, its replacement is already being considered; Sea Vixen would require replacement in the late 1960s or early 70s, while the RAF would need to replace the Hawker Hunter and English Electric Lightning in the same time period. The Treasury and Chancellor thus saw a good opportunity for cost saving and proposed that the next fighter for the RAF and FAA should be a common design. With the P.1154 design still 'warm' from the abortive NBMR-3 competition, the RAF was most interested in a strike version of the aircraft while the Admiralty was also prepared to consider an interceptor version *if* it would result in a less expensive purchase, the development costs being shared with the RAF. With the release of Specification OR.356/AW.406 in April 1962 the possibility of a common service aircraft became a distinct possibility and Hawker project team members met with Air Ministry and Admiralty figures to begin the process of gathering data on a preferred specification. The RAF wanted an aircraft able to provide strike/reconnaissance from dispersed sites in support of the Army, broadly reflecting the earlier NBMR-3 requirement for which V/STOL ability was paramount. On the other hand, the Royal Navy required

Harrier GR.Mk.1 XV742 aboard the cruiser HMS *Blake* during trials in 1969. (*BAE/BL*)

a two-seat, high-altitude supersonic interceptor with powerful radar and guided-missile armament, any strike role being purely secondary. The RN saw no use for V/STOL capability since at that time it was also in the throes of seeking authority for a new class of large and powerful carrier of which the first, CVA-01, was expected to be launched in the late 1960s for completion in 1973 and for which the Royal Navy wanted an aircraft with McDonnell F-4 Phantom II capabilities, ideally by purchase of Phantom IIs!

That the Royal Navy had a fight on its hands to acquire large new carriers is something of an understatement. At the Treasury, aircraft carriers were perceived as large and very expensive luxuries which the country could no longer afford; even refits of the existing carriers had to be fought for tenaciously. The Royal Navy however insisted that it needed new vessels with which to police the 'East of Suez' area of the Middle and Far East and furthermore required fast and sophisticated aircraft with which to do its job. With the East of Suez argument being accepted by the government, the Treasury had very reluctantly approved funding for a single new carrier with an option on a second. However, these would be expected to replace existing carriers – they were not to be regarded as additions. So it was that what the Navy certainly did NOT want was an aircraft which required no special equipment or vast areas of flight deck for its operation since this would surely

Harrier GR.Mk.1 XV758 receives some attention while aboard HMS *Bulwark* during carrier trials. (*Author*)

bring into question the entire CVA-01 concept. With this less than promising background, Hawker designers met with a Royal Navy contingent at Kingston to hear just what the FAA 'shopping list' might contain.

After various design ideas had been floated, eventually the Hawker Project Office offered a large swept wing V/STOL strike fighter capable of supersonic speeds which it was hoped did not compromise either service's requirement too much. Initial design offered an airframe with 80% commonality but, with constant modification to accommodate RN requirements, by May 1963, this had dropped to 20%. With constant disagreement over the naval design bogging down progress, Hawker was instructed by government to go back to basics and produce one common design for both services. Inevitably, neither RAF nor FAA could accept the design, the entire project by now floundering and at risk of cancellation. However, secretly, the Admiralty had been pursuing a means of acquiring the Phantom II and ultimately, having announced its withdrawal from the P.1154 project, this was achieved in 1964, though it would be a Pyrrhic victory. Within two years, the CVA-01 carrier project was itself cancelled and the FAA Phantoms and Buccaneers would ultimately be passed to the RAF for land-based use, a bitter pill for all naval staff to swallow.

With the Royal Navy out of the picture, the RAF version of P.1154 was reinvigorated and design quickly moved forward, though now with costs increased due to the wasted years attempting to fit a RN quart into a RAF pint pot. It also meant that all development

Harrier GR.Mk.1 XV281 descends to the hangar deck while aboard HMS *Eagle*. (*Author*)

costs would fall to the RAF. The Air Ministry need not have been overly concerned for, with a change of government, the incoming administration of Harold Wilson cancelled P.1154 and for good measure AW.681 and TSR-2 as well! So it was that the Royal Navy got its cherished Phantoms (though powered by Rolls-Royce Spey engines, the development costs of which were far in excess of obtaining the engines used in US aircraft), and for a short period was able to operate them from the remaining fleet carrier, HMS *Ark Royal*, before she was decommissioned in 1979. With the retirement of HMS *Ark Royal*, the Royal Navy finally lost its fixed wing aircraft capability; henceforth, the air component would be helicopter based aboard commando carriers and the newly constructed trio of 'Through Deck or Anti-Submarine Cruisers' intended as anti-submarine vessels and commando carriers of which the first – HMS *Invincible* – was launched in May 1977.

Writing in 1969, as the Harrier entered service with the RAF, W.G.D. Blundell, in his book *British Aircraft Carriers*, in attempting to divine the future of naval aviation commented:

British defence policy remains the same and fixed wing flying in the Navy will come to an end in the early seventies. However, it is almost certain that the remaining aircraft carriers will have an extension of service by utilising them as commando carriers. There is talk, too, at the time of this book going to press, that a more powerfully engined Harrier – a single seat VTOL fighter – may be developed for service with the fleet.

As a contributor to *Jane's Fighting Ships*, he was right on the money![1]

As was seen above, the Royal Navy had fought hard to resist pressure to take a V/STOL fighter for which it believed it had no requirement that could not more efficiently be answered by the F-4 Phantom and thus throughout the 1960s, the use of Hawker's V/STOL technology had no operational basis upon which to base the idea of a maritime version of the aircraft. What experience there was had mainly been accrued not by the FAA but by Hawker Siddeley Aviation and the RAF. In connection with the proposed P.1154 (RN), however, the Royal Navy had played host to the first use of fixed-wing

HMS *Hermes* hosting seaborne Harrier trials in the late 1970s, courtesy of Hawker Siddeley Aviation's Harrier demonstrator G-VTOL. (*BAE/BL*)

Speculative studies of ship designs to accommodate a ski-jump bow for operation of V/STOL aircraft. (*BAE/BL*)

V/STOL when the P.1127 prototype XP831 had demonstrated deployment aboard a carrier, carrying out a number of landings and take-offs aboard HMS *Ark Royal* in February 1963 with no problems at all. Indeed Bedford and Hugh Merewether agreed that vertical landing was even easier than ashore since the carrier's island superstructure gave excellent height cues to the pilot. Later, in June 1966, a Kestrel had been used in trials aboard the commando carrier HMS *Bulwark* in connection with a plan to employ RAF Harriers as part of an amphibious assault force, these trials being repeated in 1969 with a Harrier on *Bulwark* and aboard HMS *Eagle* in 1970.

So it was that a small body of research was generated in the UK which showed the feasibility of V/STOL deployment at sea. But it was in the US, specifically with the USMC, that evidence of the advantage that fixed wing V/STOL use bestowed was fully demonstrated. Of all the US armed forces, only the USMC had not participated in the Tripartite Evaluation Squadron trials at West Raynham but when the US Kestrels were shipped to the US after the trials, USMC pilots were able to experience the exciting new technology and understand the benefits that it could bestow for an amphibious force. So impressed was the USMC that, beginning in 1969, that service eventually took delivery of 110 aircraft designated AV-8A (and eight TAV-8A trainers), a minimum change version of the Harrier GR.1 supplied to the RAF. Over the next few years, USMC and US Navy built up a body of experience concerning V/STOL in close support that eventually led to a decision for USMC to become an entirely V/STOL equipped fighting force.

So it was that, despite its best endeavours, the Royal Navy found itself effectively painted into a corner. With no large conventional carriers left, the RN could resign itself to the loss of fixed-wing aircraft deployment for the first time in over fifty years or it could look to the impressive body of evidence that had built up regarding maritime V/STOL and decide whether there was sufficient requirement to embrace the technology and regain an embarked fixed-wing complement. This is indeed the path that was ultimately pursued though, given the animosity regarding aircraft carriers at the Treasury, the RN had to tread extremely carefully to avoid any suggestion that the forthcoming 'Command Cruisers' and later, the possibility of acquiring aircraft had anything at all to do with resurrecting the aircraft carrier.

While the P.1154 had not answered the need of the Royal Navy in 1964, perhaps the Harrier could go some way to answering the needs of the FAA in terms of close support for the fleet. An assessment of the new 'Through Deck Cruisers', of which HMS *Invincible* would be the first, showed that, although not optimised for Harrier deployment, the ships would be capable of carrying a mixed force of the aircraft and helicopters. These light cruisers had their origins in a requirement for helicopter-equipped cruisers to accompany the new CVAs planned in the 1960s as part of the anti-submarine screen. Though the big carriers foundered on the treacherous reef of politics, the cruiser design had continued quietly and would emerge as the Invincible-class carrier of which HMS *Invincible* was commissioned in 1980, *Illustrious* in June 1982 and *Ark Royal* in 1985.

It must be said that Hawker Siddeley was nothing if not tenacious in its belief that the Harrier was perfectly suited for maritime operations and therefore continued its modest campaigning for such an aircraft throughout the trials and tribulations attending the CVA debacle. In 1966, shortly after the decision to proceed with P.1127 (RAF) – later named Harrier – it issued a brochure titled 'P.1127 for Naval Operation', highlighting the potentialities of the aircraft in the maritime environment and the modest changes required to operate the aircraft in an interceptor and strike role armed with Sidewinder AAM and Martel ASM. Suggestions for improving take-off at high weight included a gridded platform to duct away exhaust gas or a modified RATO pack on the centre-line of the aircraft. Additional equipment was envisaged as a modest radar capable of detecting a cruiser sized target at 80 miles, radio altimeter system and wide-band homer and retention of the inertial navigation system of the RAF aircraft. It was hoped that, with deletion of certain equipment, navalisation would add just 130 lb weight which, if possible, would be a remarkable achievement.[2]

With the Harrier GR.Mk.1 in service with the RAF and USMC experience expanding, a further brochure of 1974 continued the campaign for a maritime Harrier. Titled 'Sea Harrier – The Shipborne Combat Aircraft', the advantages of Harrier at sea were actively promoted; capability for short or vertical take-off, no requirement for wind-over-deck for launch and recovery, no requirement for catapult or arrestor equipment and the ability to land on any convenient portion of the deck. It may be said here that the brochure was aimed as much at smaller navies not currently possessing full-sized carriers as much as at the RN and the eventual advent of maritime Harrier did lead to smaller navies acquiring the aircraft later.[3]

With opinion at the Admiralty and the Treasury now coalescing around the idea of taking Harrier to sea, Specification 287D&P was issued together with Naval Staff

The first Sea Harrier FRS.Mk.1 to fly, XZ450 in 1978, was also the first to be lost during the Falklands campaign in 1982. (*BAE/BL*)

Sea Harrier XZ450 demonstrates a ski-jump launch at the 1978 SBAC Farnborough Air Show. (*BAE/BL*)

Requirement 6451 calling for a minimum change Harrier suitable for maritime operation. This acknowledged, in January 1970, the agreement of ministers that 'a V/STOL option capability should be incorporated in the design for the new cruiser'. With political acceptance of the ability of the Harrier to complement the helicopter in fleet protection, in 1972 Hawker Siddeley Aviation was awarded a study contract to investigate a ship-borne variant of the Harrier and in May 1975, finally an order for twenty-four Sea Harrier FRS. Mk.1s was announced, later bolstered by orders for a further ten and several T.Mk.4N trainers. Also in 1972, a Royal Navy engineering officer – Lieutenant Commander Douglas Taylor – was finalising his thesis at Southampton University entitled 'The Operation of V/STOL Aircraft from Confined Spaces' (completed 1973). This rather dry sounding work proposed the theory that inclining the flight deck of an aircraft carrier or other surface at the end of an aircraft's travel would allow substantially greater loads to be carried due to the

A rather scruffy Sea Harrier XZ440 at Dunsfold sporting a pair of dummy AMRAAM missiles. (*BAE/BL*)

upward trajectory imparted to the aircraft on take-off. This idea was assessed by the Royal Navy and Hawker Siddeley Aviation and found to be sound, leading to HMS *Invincible*, then in build, receiving an interim 'ski-jump' ramp of six degrees added to its bow. Such was the success of this innovation that it would be applied to all carriers in the Invincible-class and also to the two Queen Elizabeth-class carriers of the twenty-first century.

The first flight of the Sea Harrier FRS.Mk.1, serialled XZ450, occurred at Dunsfold on 20 August 1978 in the hands of John Farley, this aircraft being demonstrated to the public at Farnborough Air Show the following week together with the ski-jump, erected especially for the show. The Sea Harrier differed considerably from the RAF Harrier whilst retaining an overall similarity as was required in the original requirement – minimum change was the order of the day!

The most obvious change was to the cockpit area, this being raised by 11 inches, producing a larger cockpit with much improved all round visibility, and the nose was reconfigured to accommodate a Blue Fox radar system optimized for air-to-air and sea-search capability. All components that might be subject to saltwater corrosion were replaced or suitably protected and tie-down points added to the undercarriage. Because of difficulties of aligning an inertial navigation system at sea, the Ferranti 541 was replaced by an attitude-heading reference system coupled to a doppler radar and the head-down moving map display of the Harrier deleted. Armament comprised AIM-9 Sidewinder and twin 30mm cannon for air-to-air combat, a range of bombs (including nuclear) and rockets for the strike role and an F.95 camera mounted in the nose which supplemented the reconnaissance role in combination with the radar. An updated and enhanced electrical system with twin alternators and much modified cockpit displays made the Sea Harrier a much more user friendly environment for the pilot compared to the RAF Harrier.

Sea Harriers from 800 NAS about to begin their display at the 1980 SBAC Farnborough Air Show. (*Author*)

With deliveries to the Royal Navy triggered by the handover of the first aircraft, XZ451, at a ceremony at Dunsfold on 18 June 1979, aircraft were flown down to RNAS Yeovilton to form the first squadron – No.700A – which would act as the Trials Squadron from September 1979 to allow work-up to operational status. Meanwhile HMS *Invincible* had begun her own trials in March 1979, embarking her first Harriers in October for combined sea trials. As more Sea Harriers arrived at Yeovilton, No.899 Headquarters Squadron formed, followed by Nos. 800 and 801 NASs as the two carrier deployment squadrons. Thus it was that, as 1982 dawned, the FAA and Royal Navy were well placed to deploy operationally should the need arise.

By the 1970s the Royal Navy's fleet of aircraft carriers was badly depleted. HMS *Victorious* had been decommissioned in 1968 and *Eagle* in 1972. HMS *Triumph* had been converted in 1965 to heavy-repair ship and entered reserve in 1975. The Centaur-class carriers, HMS *Centaur*, *Bulwark* and *Albion*, completed in the 1950s, were either scrapped or converted to commando carrier. This left just HMS *Ark Royal* and HMS *Hermes*. *Ark Royal* had been laid down in 1943 and commissioned in 1955 and was the Royal Navy's largest carrier in the 1960s and 70s, operating the McDonnell F-4 Phantom and Hawker Siddeley Buccaneer S2. Decommissioned in 1979 and scrapped the following year, this left

HMS *Invincible*, the first of the new 'through-deck cruisers', about to launch a Sea Harrier, c.1980. (*BAE/BL*)

just HMS *Hermes*. *Hermes* had been a long time building: laid down in June 1944, she was not completed until November 1959. Thus by the 1970s she was distinctly showing her age and considered too small to operate the FAA's F-4 Phantom safely. In the early 1970s she was converted to commando-carrier status and later to anti-submarine warfare carrier and finally, in 1980, a ski-jump ramp was added to her bow before recommissioning in 1981. Despite this extensive work, the ship was slated for decommissioning in the Defence

Hermes-based Sea Harrier XZ492 overflies the 32,000-tonne Soviet carrier *Kiev*. On deck can be seen two examples of the Soviet VTOL Yak-38 Forger. (*BL*)

Review of 1981 while talks began to sell HMS *Invincible* to Australia, which agreed to the purchase in February 1982.

Operational Use

When the world awoke on 2 April 1982 to news that Argentina had invaded the Falkland Islands and South Georgia UK dependencies, it was widely expected that the UK government would offer little short of official protest at the UN since it no longer had the resources to retake the territory by force. However, Argentina's president and armed forces had failed to understand UK intentions and commitment and, within days, the government of Margeret Thatcher had despatched a task force with the intention of regaining the islands. Central to these plans were the two carriers available for service (just).

Sea Harriers on the deck of HMS *Hermes* during rough-weather trials. Given the relatively high freeboard of the carrier, it certainly appears that the trials team found some. (*BL*)

The first development batch Sea Harrier, XZ438, in the hangar at Dunsfold equipped with the BAe Sea Eagle anti-ship cruise missile. Its large size is readily apparent. (*BAE/BL*)

Sea Harrier XZ438 in flight with two Sea Eagles under the wings. The weapon was not deployed during the Falklands conflict as it was still undergoing trials at the time. The Sea Eagle was a generation ahead of the Exocet used during the Falklands conflict. (*BAE/BL*)

Intensive servicing activity on a Sea Harrier aboard HMS Invincible during the Falklands conflict, 1982. (*BL*)

HMS *Hermes* and HMS *Invincible* quickly took aboard their embarked squadrons of Sea Harriers (No.800 to *Hermes* and No.801 to *Invincible*) and Sea King helicopters and put to sea as the kernel of the UK Task Force for Operation CORPORATE. Armchair pundits aplenty claimed that the Sea Harriers would have little chance against the supersonic Mirage fighters of the Argentine Air Force – the *Fuerza Aérea Argentina* – especially since the Fleet Air Arm would be outnumbered by some 10:1 in any aerial engagements.

Hostilities erupted on 25 April 1982 with the retaking of South Georgia and on 1 May East Falkland came under air attack from a high-level Vulcan and low-level Sea Harriers attacking Port Stanley airfield in an attempt to neutralise the threat of aircraft using the runway and facilities. The same day, the Sea Harriers of No.801 Squadron began their successful attrition of the supersonic Mirage IIIs, the main Argentinian air defence fighter. In the subsequent encounters, no Sea Harriers were shot down in air-to-air combat although a few were lost to ground fire and unrelated accidents in the appalling weather of the South Atlantic winter. By mid-May, with British troops ashore in numbers, the retaking of the islands was only a matter of time as the Army and Royal Marine Commandos relentlessly tightened their grip on the Falklands and Port Stanley in particular. With Port Stanley in sight and the final battle about to begin, the Argentinian forces' surrender was accepted on 14 June 1982.

Sea Harriers aboard HMS *Invincible* prior to a launch. The nine aircraft in this image all appear to be loaded for air defence duties. (*BL*)

HMS *Hermes* hosts a mixture of Sea Harrier and Harrier GR.Mk.3 aircraft during the Falklands conflict, 1982. The GR.3 in the foreground sports a pair of Paveway II laser-guided bombs. (*BL*)

During Operation CORPORATE, twenty-eight Sea Harriers were deployed to the South Atlantic, generating 1,190 sorties comprising CAP and strike operations. During this period the Royal Navy Sea Harriers shot down twenty-three Argentine aircraft, of which eleven were Mirage III/Dagger supersonic interceptors, while losing no aircraft in air-to-air combat. This remarkable result completely upset the received wisdom that in a

The crowded deck of HMS *Invincible* as a Sea Harrier launches. A mixture of bombs and Sidewinder missiles litter the forward deck, 1982. (*BL*)

one-on-one attack, supersonic would always best subsonic, an argument that ignores the importance of manoeuvrability and experience in the clash.

The Sea Harrier had been able to operate in often atrocious weather conditions that would have grounded any other fixed-wing aircraft at sea and win the one-on-one encounters with the supersonic Mirage. For all those who had damned the Harrier with faint praise in the preceding decades, here at last was the proof of the efficacy of the aircraft. As noted at the head of this chapter, 'Without the Sea Harrier, there could have been no Task force.' The unique abilities of the Sea Harrier had long been recognised by the CO of No.801 Squadron – Nigel 'Sharkey' Ward. He had been 'Mr Sea Harrier' while at the MoD planning the aircraft's entry into service and, once in command of No.801, had worked relentlessly to turn its remarkable attributes to good use as an air defence

HMS *Ark Royal* post Falklands conflict with Sea Harrier FRS.Mk.1 and Sea King Mk.2 (AEW) escorting, c.1990. (*Author*)

fighter. If the Falklands War was won thanks to the Sea Harrier, it was also thanks to the aggressive training of Ward that his squadron was able to take on the modern Argentine fighters – and win.

One often overlooked aspect of the Falklands War was the immediate and sustained uplift in national morale that proceeded from its successful conclusion. The era of national

A Sea Harrier from each of the three squadrons show off the new colour scheme applied during the Falklands conflict. 800 NAS in the foreground, 801 NAS in the centre and 899 NAS to the rear. (*BAE/BL*)

history comprising the post-war period had seen a steadily declining internal assessment of the country's abilities in the political and social climate culminating in the Winter of Discontent of 1978/9 under the Labour administration of James Callaghan. With the return of a Conservative administration under the UK's first woman prime minister, Margaret Thatcher, there was no real feeling of having turned a corner. However, the Falklands War saw this negative view of the UK wiped out and a new optimism surface which saw the 1980s and early '90s as a period of economic and social progress under Thatcher's determined control that witnessed *inter alia* the ending of the Cold War with the disintegration of the USSR in 1989.

With post Falklands War production returning to normal, development of the Sea Harrier continued with the various trials aircraft based at Dunsfold and Boscombe Down. Included in these trials were those required for deployment of the WE177 nuclear store to be carried operationally by the Sea Harrier. Handling and bombing sorties were flown at DTEO West Freugh in Scotland on the instrumented bombing range at Luce Bay. The aircraft chosen for the trial in May 1984 was XZ440, the release trials being flown by Heinz Frick. Describing the event, Frick recalled:

> I remember that this trial was all a bit secret and we had a new head up display to assess the weapon aiming etc. The plan was to run in as low as possible to avoid enemy radar contact and at about five miles from the target pull up for a roll off the top and smartly disappear in the opposite direction to avoid the bang. I had to use the controls to follow a line on the head up display and press the bomb release button, the computer would then decide when to release the weapon. After about five seconds I rolled to the right; all went as planned and I felt a slight thud as the weapon parted company. After about five seconds I rolled to the right again expecting to look down and see the bomb on its way. I was a bit shocked to see it only about 100 feet away travelling still at my speed (and height). I then also realised that there was no defence against this dastardly piece of kit.[4]

Luckily, the store eventually peeled away and ended its days in the bay below.

Notwithstanding the success of the Sea Harrier in 1982, it was also recognised that the minimum change requirement that had seen the Harrier fitted for maritime duties had compromised its ability to oppose modern fighters successfully. The inability of the Blue Fox radar to look down over land (it had been optimised for sea search) and the need to get in close to ensure a kill with the AIM-9 Sidewinder were two obvious areas that needed to be addressed. Proposals were duly drawn up by British Aerospace (BAe) designers (HSA and BAC had been nationalised in 1977) that would answer these needs and several others as well, whilst retaining the basic airframe via a Mid-Life-Update (MLU) programme; there was also the more basic need for attrition replacements for those aircraft lost in battle. The design submitted included a new Blue Vixen radar capable of multi-mode jam-resistant function with a fully developed look-down shoot-down capability against multiple targets and a new 'beyond visual range' guided air-to-air missile – the Hughes AIM-120 AMRAAM – of which four could be carried on wing and fuselage pylons. Also planned was carriage of the BAe Sea Eagle anti-shipping missile, a generation ahead of the French Exocet, under the wings and an AN/ALE 40 chaff and flare self-protection system, the major sub-systems being connected and controlled via a MIL-STD 1553B databus.

Phase 1 of the MLU saw the introduction of the AN/ALE 40 system, MADGE (microwave aircraft digital guidance equipment) and Sea Eagle and twin Sidewinder capability and improved electrical generation; these aircraft retained the FRS.Mk.1 designation. Phase 2 of the MLU saw the aircraft returned to Kingston and Dunsfold for more radical surgery, including a fuselage extension of 13.5 inches to accommodate a lengthened avionics bay and reshaping of the nose profile to take the Blue Vixen radar package. The first of these aircraft, ZA195, emerged at Dunsfold in September 1988

The first FRS.Mk.2, ZA195, launches from HMS *Ark Royal* in November 1990. The aircraft carries the full complement of AIM-120 AMRAAM BVR missiles. (*Author*)

as the FRS.Mk.2 and began its development flying trials, soon followed by the second development aircraft, XZ439. With the introduction of the heavily modified aircraft into service with the Fleet Air Arm, the designation changed to F/A.2 to mirror the loss of the nuclear strike role, the aircraft being no longer wired to take the WE177c nuclear store. As well as the FRS.1 aircraft returned to works for upgrade to F/A.2 status (eventually all suitable aircraft were cycled through this upgrade), the Royal Navy ordered a further eighteen new-build Sea Harrier F/A.2s as well as a small batch of two-seat trainers converted from ex-RAF and RN T.Mk.4 Harriers and designated T.Mk.8 Harrier, seven being converted. The conversion added most of the F/A.2 instruments to the front cockpit and included the Doppler radar but not Blue Vixen.

Much of the flight testing of the new F/A.2 Sea Harrier was carried out by Lieutenant Commander Rod 'Fred' Frederiksen, who joined the team at Dunsfold in 1989. Frederiksen had joined the Royal Navy in 1966, flying Sea Vixens with No.893 NAS from HMS *Hermes* in 1970 and later F-4 Phantoms from HMS *Eagle*. Following an ETPS course at Boscombe Down in 1977, he remained onsite as a test pilot and was still there when the Falklands War erupted. He managed to get a posting to No. 800 NAS and embarked HMS *Hermes* for the journey south. During the subsequent action Frederiksen was credited with the destruction of an Argentine Dagger in air-to-air combat as well as several aircraft

Sea Harrier FRS.Mk.2 XZ439 completes a successful launch from HMS *Ark Royal* in November 1990. (*Author*)

destroyed on the ground. He was also Mentioned in Despatches for his role in driving an Argentine patrol vessel ashore whilst attempting to land reinforcements for the enemy. After the war, Frederiksen returned to Boscombe Down prior to a posting as CO of No.800 NAS embarked in *Illustrious* in 1988. Fred's bonhomie was legendary, a skill no doubt honed in the wardroom on various postings. Frederiksen died in September 2009.

Lieutenant Commander Taylor Scott was another Fleet Air Arm pilot to join the Sea Harrier test team at Dunsfold. Joining the Royal Navy in 1964, Scott flew Sea Vixens before attending a 'Top Gun' course in the USA, followed by an F-4 Phantom posting aboard HMS *Ark Royal* in 1974. Posted to Dunsfold on secondment in 1977 to assist in the testing of the Sea Harrier FRS.Mk.1, Scott returned to Yeovilton in 1982 as the Falklands conflict developed, to assist in the formation of No.809 NAS as a temporary additional Sea Harrier squadron to reinforce the South Atlantic squadrons. Returning to

Dunsfold, Scott was promoted to DCTP in 1987. That year he was killed when testing a Harrier GR.Mk.5 when the seat malfunctioned and he was thrown from the aircraft over Salisbury Plain.

Having demonstrated to the doubters in the Treasury, but also within the Service itself, the capability and flexibility that a carrier air group represented during the Falklands crisis, the Sea Harrier was again in harm's way in 1992 as the break-up of the former Yugoslavia resulted in bitter ethnic and partisan warfare. A UN force was despatched which included UK troops and in early 1993 a naval task group built around HMS *Ark Royal* sailed for the Adriatic to provide additional support with eight Sea Harriers and a complement of AEW and troop-carrying helicopters, with ASW helicopters spread around other ships in the group. In August HMS *Invincible* took over the Adriatic role before handing back to *Ark Royal* at the end of the year, now part of a NATO force. As the situation on the ground deteriorated, the Sea Harriers provided protection for the UN forces by enforcing a no-fly zone over the region, losing a Sea Harrier shot down by a SAM over Goradze.

Sea Harrier XZ439 launching from the ski-jump at RAE Bedford during proving trials. AMRAAM missiles are being carried on the outer wing pylons but the fuselage stations are empty. (*BAE/BL*)

As the situation in Bosnia continued to deteriorate, NATO forces launched strikes as part of Operation DELIBERATE FORCE on targets in Bosnia with Sea Harriers, this time from HMS *Invincible* with laser-guided bombs. In 1999, with the conflict in the former Yugoslavia continuing, this time in the former Serbian region of Kosovo, *Invincible* was back in the Mediterranean flying support missions with its Sea Harriers over the disputed territory in support of NATO forces but, meantime, the situation was hotting up in the Arabian Gulf with Iraq causing friction and resulting in the carriers being tasked with trade protection in the unstable Gulf waters.

Away from the disturbances in Bosnia and Serbia, in 1994 the Royal Navy carried out an experimental deployment of RAF Harrier GR.Mk.7s aboard HMS *Invincible* as an exercise aimed at improving carrier capability by adding a dedicated strike element to the existing Sea Harrier fighter complement. This small deployment would later re-emerge and reshape the form and function of the carrier air component. In part, this deployment was part of a longstanding plan to include the RAF in naval planning in an effort to gain support at the Treasury for future plans regarding new carriers and indeed had formed part of the thinking of the Strategic Defence Review of 1998. Sure enough, in April 2000 it was announced that henceforth, the Royal Navy's Sea Harrier squadrons would join with the RAF's four Harrier GR.7/9 squadrons to form Joint Force Harrier, resulting in future carrier deployments consisting of a mix of Sea Harrier F/A.2 fighters and GR.Mk.7/9 strike aircraft to provide greater flexibility and punch to carrier air groups. Some sceptics in and out of the Senior Service saw this as a threat to the Sea Harrier, and this received apparent confirmation in 2002: as the ever present pressures on the Defence Budget came to the fore again, hints were abroad at the Admiralty that the Sea Harrier would be retired in 2006 while HMS *Invincible* would be placed in the reserve in 2005.

In the event, Sea Harrier squadrons began the retirement process in 2004 with the temporary disbandment of No.800 Squadron at the end of March; it would reform in 2006 on the Harrier GR.Mk.7/9 at RAF Cottesmore. No.800 NAS was the oldest FAA squadron, stood up in April 1933 flying Hawker Nimrod and Osprey aircraft. The next squadron to retire was No.899 NAS, the headquarters squadron, in March 2005 leaving just No.801 NAS to carry on until 2006 when the last Sea Harrier squadron was officially retired. The retirement of the Sea Harrier resulted in the Royal Navy being unable to deploy with fighter cover, future operations using only the RAF Harrier GR.Mk.7/9 and helicopters and relying on land-based fighters for any protection required, a situation that would normally have been anathema to their Lordships at the Admiralty. However, in the background, plans were advanced for radical new carriers to join the fleet, matched by new aircraft in the form of what was known variously as JCA and JSF and would finally emerge as the F-35 Lightning 2.

Export Aircraft

Despite the success of the Sea Harrier in the hands of the Royal Navy, its export success was modest indeed, only India seeking to obtain the aircraft. In 1957 India had purchased the Majestic-class carrier HMS *Hercules* from the UK while still under construction and,

USMC AV-8A aircraft aboard the USS *Saipan*. The USMC was the first service to take the Harrier to sea operationally. (*BAE/BL*)

A USMC AV-8A is marshalled prior to launch aboard the USS *Saipan*. (*BAE/BL*)

on completion in 1961, renamed it INS *Vikrant*. Commissioned in March 1961, *Vikrant* carried a squadron of Hawker Sea Hawks of No.300 INAS which would remain in service until replaced by the Sea Harrier. With the Sea Hawk fast passing into obsolescence and following displays of the Harrier (actually the two-seat demonstrator G-VTOL) by John Farley aboard *Vikrant* in July 1972, plans were laid to acquire a version of the Harrier for operation afloat. These plans finally came to fruition in 1980 and the first six aircraft, designated Sea Harrier FRS.Mk.51, were delivered in 1983, followed by two T.60 trainer versions. These were later followed by further batches of FRS.Mk.51 and T.Mk.60 aircraft in the later 1980s/early 90s, making a total of twenty-three FRS.Mk.51s and four T.Mk.60s. Unlike the Royal Navy, India did not obtain the F/A.2 variant of the Sea Harrier, possibly because of restrictions on the sale of Blue Vixen, but limited upgrades were added to the existing aircraft to keep them current. With the retirement of *Vikrant* in 1997, the carrier was replaced by the former HMS *Hermes* as the INS *Viraat*, which India had purchased in 1987 and finally decommissioned in 2017.

Although only one country sought to acquire the pure Sea Harrier, two European countries acquired versions of the US AV-8A and AV-8B for use at sea. Spain identified a requirement for the basic Harrier in the early 1970s but could not purchase directly from Hawker Siddeley because of political differences with the Spanish dictator, General Franco. Instead, they were ordered through the USMC although still manufactured in the UK. Six AV-8S and two TAV-8S Harriers were ordered (identified by HSA as Mk.55

The Spanish version of the Harrier, the AV-8S Matador, seen at Dunsfold in June 1980. (*Author*)

Spanish AV-8S and TAV-8S on the flight line at Dunsfold in June 1980. (*Author*)

Indian Sea Harrier FRS.Mk.51s lined up at Dunsfold prior to their deliver flight April 1991. (*Author*)

The replacement of the Spanish AV-8A Matador is pictured here at Dunsfold. The EAV-8B was based upon the USMC AV-8B with minor changes. The later EAV-8B Plus was ordered in the 1990s. (*BAE/BL*)

The Italian *Marina Militare* also plumped for the USMC AV-8B, based upon the AV-8B Plus standard, as can be seen here with radar and FLIR in the nose and defensive aids systems installed in front of the dorsal fin. (*BAE/BL*)

and Mk.56 and named Matador in the UK) and delivered during 1976 to Spain via the US. Further aircraft were ordered in 1977, five being delivered in 1980, although with Franco gone, they were delivered directly from Dunsfold. Following those orders, further aircraft were requested but based on the AV-8B and manufactured and delivered in the US. Twelve aircraft were obtained and delivered in 1987, a further eight being acquired in the early 1990s. All operated from the only Spanish carrier *Dedalo* (the former USS *Cabot*) until a new carrier was commissioned – the *Principe de Asturias* – operated from 1989, this carrier incorporating a ski-jump bow.

The final country to take the Harrier to sea was Italy. Due to a pre-war treaty, Italy's navy had been forbidden to possess a fixed-wing contingent, instead operating various helicopter carriers. The commissioning of a new carrier, *Guiseppe Garibaldi*, in 1983, however, made clear an intention to acquire fixed-wing aircraft, the carrier displaying a ski-jump bow! Following evaluation of the UK Sea Harrier and the US AV-8B in the late 1980s, the AV-8B was chosen and sixteen aircraft together with two TAV-8B trainers

Harrier GR.7/9 ZD351 resplendent in its 800 NAS decommissioning colour scheme in December 2010. 800 NAS was part of Joint Force Harrier and, as such, took the Harrier II to sea after the Sea Harrier F/A.2 had been decommissioned. (*via Bill Anderson*)

ordered. Thus, although the Sea Harrier missed out on these orders, the potential of the maritime Harrier had been understood and applied to the smaller nations' air arms, just as Hawker Siddeley had hoped.

Sea Harrier, then, was probably the last all-British fighter; it was certainly Hawker/ Hawker Siddeley Aviation Kingston's last fighter despite efforts to the contrary. Its eventual success was perhaps out of all proportion to expectations in many quarters and showed that V/STOL/STOVL was a concept that perfectly fitted the maritime environment. A new design built with STOVL at its centre but with more power and greater weapons ability would certainly be a system sought after by future navies. That weapon system would be developed, although it would not emanate from the Kingston Project Office, but from the USA. Kingston's pioneering input would, however, underlie design decisions in many respects, if for no other reason than that it had the greatest knowledge of V/STOL/ STOVL design in the world.

Chapter 9

The Future

In 1997, as the government announced its intention to carry out a strategic defence review, the Admiralty began to shape its arguments for this to include the purchase of two large modern carriers to replace the now elderly Invincible-class ships. The resulting review in July 1998 confirmed the amalgamation of Sea Harrier and RAF Harriers into one force, Joint Force Harrier, and also the intended purchase of two CVF carriers to replace the Invincible-class, the price paid by the RN being yet further reductions in the surface fleet. Slowly, the Invincible-class 'carriers that never were' had been decommissioned, HMS *Invincible* in August 2005, HMS *Ark Royal* in March 2011 and lastly HMS *Illustrious* in August 2014. With the Sea Harrier retired as from 2006, carrier-based organic fighter protection ceased for the Royal Navy. All hope of a resurgence now lay with the promise of two new carriers that would commission sometime in the future and would, in the meantime, be hostages to fortune in the high-stakes game of service politics.

To the surprise of many both within and without the Royal Navy, the new CVF carriers were not only launched but commissioned into service. HMS *Queen Elizabeth*, ordered 2008, was laid down in 2009, launched in 2014 and commissioned in December 2017. At 65,000 tonnes she is the largest ship to serve in the Royal Navy and is the name ship for the class. HMS *Prince of Wales* was also ordered in 2008, was laid down in 2011, launched in 2017 and commissioned in December 2019. Also displacing 65,000 tonnes, neither ship has thus far covered itself in glory, being plagued by mechanical breakdowns that have seen both return ignominiously to port with various defects requiring the tender services of the manufacturer, a consortium of BAE Systems, Babcock International and Thales Group, and the dockyard mateys. Even before the launch of the *Queen Elizabeth*, politics was busily intruding with the government of the day deciding (on whose advice one can only speculate) that the carriers should be fitted out for conventional aircraft operations, i.e. by the addition of catapults and arrestor gear at a cost running into several billions, only to reverse that decision later.

It had always been envisaged, and intrinsic in the design, that the carriers would operate STOVL aircraft which would have no requirement for catapults and arrestor gear, thereby achieving significant cost savings both in plant and maintenance costs. The aircraft chosen was always likely to be a variant of the Lockheed Martin F-35 Lightning II; in the event, the F-35B STOVL variant was selected, these being operated by a mixed RAF/RN team. Squadron strength would be twelve to sixteen aircraft but the carriers are capable of taking up to twenty-four with squadrons crewed jointly by RAF and FAA. The first squadron stood up was No.617, followed by No.809.

Lockheed Martin F-35B Lightning II – the future of the Royal Navy's air component in the twenty-first century. (© *MoD/Crown Copyright 2025*)

While the F-35B design was the work of US-based aviation consortia, the Kingston Project Office design experience hovered like a ghost behind the scenes, input into the project coming from individuals formerly employed not only in the Project Office but in the Flight Test environment, together with former BAE Systems test pilots via constant design reviews known as 'Greybeard' meetings. Also central to the F-35B design was work carried out by BAe and RAE (later QinetiQ), based at RAE Bedford on the so-called 'VAAC Harrier'. The cockpit workload of the Harrier had always been a difficulty, particularly the transition between jet-borne and wing-borne flight when the adjacent controls for engine speed and nozzle position could, in the heat of the moment, be mixed up with catastrophic consequences. Using the second T.2 Harrier built, a programme titled 'Vectored Thrust Advanced Flight Control' was initiated in 1982 to change the Harrier mechanical/hydraulic controls to fully fly-by-wire electronic control. After much research both in the UK and the USA, it was not until 2002 that a final decision was taken to install a system called Unified in JSF, an algorithm-based control system that uses just two 'inceptors', a left-hand control that governs aircraft speed (faster/slower) and jet-borne or wing-borne flight and a right-hand side-stick that governs direction (left/right/up/down). This system is now used in the F-35B Lightning II and has proved far simpler to operate than the mechanical systems of the Harrier.

The Sea Harrier has rightly been dubbed 'the last all-British fighter'; henceforth front-line aircraft design and manufacture will be undertaken by consortia of nation states, with all the advantages, and disadvantages, that attend, Eurofighter Typhoon being a good example. This multinational collaboration between manufacturers in the UK, Germany,

Italy and Spain, with France dipping in and out, saw initial work in the 1980s stretch out over the succeeding decades which saw entry into service only in August 2003. Similarly, the Lightning II or JSF has seen a protracted design and development phase stretching from the 1990s to service introduction in 2015. Although both aircraft are excellent examples of their type, these long lead times tend to produce an aircraft threatened with obsolescence even as it enters service and require expensive upgrades to remain current.

Finally, it is worth returning to Sir Sydney Camm's philosophy regarding the design of naval aircraft since this was the over-riding control of so much that Hawker produced. His approach was that the naval fighter should not be disadvantaged in comparison to land-based aircraft merely because of its operational environment. Writing in 1949 (*Hawker Siddeley Review*, pp.3–9) he said:

The naval fighter must of course embody all the desirable features of the land fighter plus special requirements associated with its work with the fleet, as follows: i) special facilities for landing, ii) special facilities for take-off, iii) longest possible duration of flight, iv) ability to be folded to small dimensions so that the maximum number can be carried, v) best possible pilot's view, vi) good slow flying qualities.

HMS *Queen Elizabeth* and HMS *Prince of Wales* working up together, a rare view given the teething problems associated with their introduction into service. (© *MoD/Crown Copyright 2025*)

If one could design a fighter which included all of these attributes then it could be a winner, and this is what the Project Office strove for.

Looking at the fast evolution of the naval fighter, Camm noted:

Prior to 1930 stalling speeds were low enough to enable landing and take-off operations to be carried out unassisted. Note that the approach speed of the Fairey Flycatcher was about 50 knots. By 1932, the year when the Nimrod was introduced, the approach speed had increased to 60 knots …. The stimulus of war forced increased wing loadings so that the later types of Hawker Sea Fury … have approach speeds of about 87 knots.

While those speeds were within the bounds of fairly straightforward control, the introduction of jet-powered aircraft changed the situation completely. Camm again:

The introduction of jet engines has introduced severe problems due to the absence of airscrew slipstream. The latter contributed greatly to the handling of the aeroplane during the approach and landing operations, as it could rapidly be turned on and off. With the jet engine the control over the variation of engine power is much less rapid, and further, has no effect on lift at all …. The approach speeds have increased alarmingly, being over 100 knots for modern jet fighters.

This was written in 1949 when the Sea Hawk had yet to join the FAA. Later naval fighters continued this upward trend, culminating in the Royal Navy with the F-4 Phantom's landing speed of 140–150 knots.

Of course, this upward trend did have an alternative: the Sea Harrier. Taking Camm's points above, i) special facilities for landing – none required; ii) special facilities for take-off – none required; iii) longest possible duration of flight – with drop-tanks and in-flight refuelling, theoretically infinite; iv) ability to be folded to small dimensions – not required, the Harrier was a very small aircraft; v) best pilot's view – Harrier had almost 360-degree viewing ability; vi) good slow-flying qualities – can fly at zero knots if required. What a machine! The F-35B Lightning II embodies all these qualities and, therefore, as far as Camm would have been concerned, represents the perfect naval fighter for the twenty-first century and maybe beyond. That it is not British can only be mourned but the knowledge that it embodies much UK experience and, as importantly, Hawker experience, is perhaps some consolation.

Appendix 1

Aircraft Specifications

Type Specification – Sopwith Aviation Co Ltd.

Where possible, numbers constructed are derived from *Royal Navy Aircraft Serials and Units, 1911–1919* by Ray Sturtivant and Gordon Page, published by Air Britain in 1992; *British Military Aircraft Serials 1911–1971* by Bruce Robinson, published by Ian Allan in 1971 and *Sopwith Aircraft* by Mick Davis, published by Crowood Press in 1999. The numbers below should not be read as definitive since aircraft were built, rebuilt, cannibalised and swapped between services, rendering accuracy something to be aspired to rather than achieved. Lastly, numbers shown are for up-take by the RNAS only. In many cases far more were built for the RFC and Allied forces.

Schneider
Description – Single-seat scout/reconnaissance floatplane.
Construction – Biplane, wooden structure, fabric covering.
Powerplant – 100hp Gnome Monosoupape 9 rotary engine.
Wingspan – 25 feet 8 inches.
Length – 22 feet 10 inches.
Weight – Empty 1,220lb. Loaded 1,700lb.
First Flight – 1913.
Performance – Maximum speed 87mph. Ceiling 7,000 feet.
Armament – Single Lewis gun or 20lb bombs.
Number constructed – 136.

1½ Strutter
Description – 9,400, two-seat general-purpose scout/reconnaissance and 9,700, single-seat bomber.
Construction – Biplane, wooden structure, fabric covering.
Powerplant – 110hp Clerget 9J rotary engine (later 130hp Clerget 9B).
Wingspan – 33 feet 6 inches.
Length – 25 feet 3 inches.
Weight – Empty 1,160lb. Loaded 2,205lb. (depending on type).
First Flight – December 1915.
Performance – Maximum speed 96mph. Ceiling 15,500 feet.
Armament – Single fixed synchronised Vickers gun (pilot), single free Vickers machine gun (observer).
Number constructed – 459 plus 70 specifically issued as Ship's Strutters.

Baby
Description – Scout/bomber floatplane.
Construction – Biplane, wooden structure, fabric covering.
Powerplant – 110hp Clerget 9Z or 130hp Clerget 9B rotary engine.
Wingspan – 25 feet 8 inches.
Length – 23 feet.
Weight – Empty 1,226lb. Loaded 1,715lb (depending on engine).
First Flight – September 1915.
Performance – Maximum speed 100mph. Ceiling 8,000 feet.
Armament – Single fixed synchronised or overwing free Lewis gun. Two 65lb bombs,
    Le Prieur rockets.
Number constructed – 465.

Pup
Description – Single-seat scout.
Construction – Biplane, wooden structure, fabric covering.
Powerplant – 80hp Le Rhone 9C, 80hp Gnome mono, 80hp Clerget, Monosoupape
    100hp rotary engine.
Wingspan – 26 feet 6 inches.
Length – 19 feet 3¾ inches.
Weight – Empty 787lb. Loaded 1225lb (depending on engine).
First Flight – February 1916.
Performance – Maximum speed 112mph. Ceiling 20,000 feet (depending on engine).
Armament – Single fixed synchronised Vickers gun.
Number constructed – 226 plus 30 specifically issued as Ship's Pups.

Triplane
Description – Single-seat scout.
Construction – Triplane, wooden structure, fabric covering.
Powerplant – 110hp Clerget 9Z or 130hp Clerget 9B rotary engine.
Wingspan – 26 feet 6 inches.
Length – 18 feet 10 inches.
Weight – Empty 993lb. Loaded 1,415lb (depending on engine).
First Flight – May 1916.
Performance – Maximum speed 117mph. Ceiling 20,500 feet.
Armament – Single fixed synchronised Vickers gun.
Number constructed – 199 plus two fitted with Hispano-Suiza engines.

Camel
F.1 Camel
Description – Single-seat scout.
Construction – Biplane, wooden structure, fabric covering.

Powerplant – 130hp Clerget 9B, 110hp Le Rhone 9J, 170hp Le Rhone 9R, 150-hp Bentley BR.1.

Wingspan – 28 feet.

Length – (Clerget) 18feet 9inches, (Le Rhone) 18 feet 8 inches, (Bentley) 18 feet 6 inches.

Weight – Empty (Clerget) 962lb, (Le Rhone) 889lb, (Bentley) 977lb. Loaded (Clerget) 1,482lb, (Le Rhone) 1,422lb, (Bentley) 1,508 lb.

First flight – December 1916.

Performance – Maximum speed (Clerget) 104.5mph, (Le Rhone) 118.5mph, (Bentley) 111mph. Ceiling (Clerget and Bentley) 18,000 feet, (Le Rhone) 21,500 feet.

Armament – Twin fixed synchronised Vickers guns.

Number constructed – 102.

2F.1 Naval Camel

Description – Single-seat shipboard scout.

Construction – Biplane, wooden structure, fabric covering.

Powerplant – 130hp Clerget or 150hp Bentley BR.1.

Wingspan – 26 feet 11 inches.

Length – 18 feet 9 inches.

Weight – Empty 1,036lb. Loaded 1,530lb.

Performance – Maximum speed 122mph. Ceiling 17,300 feet.

Armament – Single fixed synchronised Vickers gun, single free Lewis gun.

Number constructed – 661.

Type Specification – HG Hawker Engineering Co Ltd.

Performance specifications below via *Hawker Aircraft Since 1920* by Frank Mason (Putnam 1991 from company documents). (Note that performance figures achieved by A&AEE Martlesham and Hawker often differed.) Totals via *British Military Aircraft Serials 1911–1971,* by Bruce Robinson, published by Ian Allan 1971.

Woodcock

Description – Mk II, single-seat night-interceptor fighter.

Construction – Biplane, wooden construction, fabric covering.

Engine – 380hp Bristol Jupiter IV.

Length – 26 feet 2 inches.

Wingspan – 32 feet 6 inches.

Weight – empty 2,083lb, loaded 3,023lb.

Performance – maximum speed 141mph at sea level. Climb to 10,000 feet 8 minutes 18 seconds. Endurance 2¾ hours approximately. Service ceiling 22,500 feet.

Armament – 2 x synchronised Vickers guns.

No built: Woodcock I – 3 . Woodcock II – 67.

Hedgehog
Description – Three-seat fleet reconnaissance.
Construction – Biplane, wooden construction, fabric covering.
Engine – 398hp Bristol Jupiter IV.
Length – 30 feet 8¾ inches.
Span – 40 feet ½ inch.
Weight – Empty 2,995lb. Loaded 4,791lb.
Performance – Maximum speed 120½mph at sea level. Climb to 10,000 feet 23 minutes 59 seconds. Endurance 2½ hours. Service ceiling 13,500 feet.
Number built: 1.

Horsley
Description – Two-seat day-bomber or torpedo-bomber.
Construction – Biplane, composite wooden/metal construction, fabric covered.
Engine – 665hp Rolls Royce Condor IIIA.
Length – 38 feet 10 inches.
Wingspan – 56 feet 5¾ inches.
Weight – Empty 4,958lb. Loaded 9,270lb.
Performance (Mk. II torpedo-bomber) – Maximum speed 118mph at 5,000 feet. Climb to 5,000 feet 12 minutes 30 seconds. Service ceiling 11,200 feet.
Number built: Horsley torpedo-bomber variant – 48. Export (Greece and Denmark) 8.

Hoopoe
Description – Single-seat naval interceptor.
Construction – Biplane, metal construction, fabric covered.
Length – 25 feet 4 inches (Mercury). 24 feet 6 inches (Panther).
Wingspan – 2-bay 34 feet 6 inches. Single bay 33 feet 2 inches.
Engine – 450hp Bristol Mercury II radial. 560hp Armstrong Siddeley Panther III radial.
Weight – (Mercury II) Empty 2,490lb. Loaded 3,550lb. (Panther) Empty 2,785lb. Loaded 3,910lb.
Performance – (Panther III) maximum speed 196.5mph at 12,500 feet. Climb to 10,000 feet 6 minutes 40 seconds. Service ceiling 23,600 feet.
Number built – 1

Nimrod
Description – Single-seat carrier-borne fighter.
Construction – Biplane, all metal structure, metal and fabric covering.
Powerplant – 477hp Rolls Royce Kestrel IIS or 608hp Rolls Royce Kestrel VFP water-cooled in-line engine.
Wingspan -33 feet 6¾ inches.
Length – 26 feet 6½ inches.
Weight – Empty 3,115lb. Loaded 4,059lb.

Performance (landplane). Kestrel IIS – Maximum speed 196mph at 12,000 feet. Climb to 10,000 feet 6 minutes 8 seconds. Ceiling 26,900 feet. Kestrel VFP – max speed 193mph at 14,000 feet. Climb to 10,000 feet 5 minutes. Ceiling 28,800 feet.

Armament – Twin fixed synchronised Vickers guns.

Number built: 87 plus 4 export.

Osprey

Description – Two-seat carrier-borne fighter reconnaissance aircraft.

Construction – Biplane, all-metal structure, metal and fabric covering.

Powerplant – 630hp Rolls Royce Kestrel IIMS.

Wingspan – 37 feet.

Length – 29 feet 4 inches.

Weight – Empty 3,405lb. Loaded 4,950lb.

Performance (landplane) – Maximum speed 168mph at 5,000 feet. Climb to 10,000 feet 7 minutes 40 seconds. Ceiling 23,500 feet.

Armament – One fixed synchronised Vickers, one moveable Lewis gun.

Number built: 132 plus 7 export.

Type Specification – Hawker Aircraft Co Ltd.
Sea Hurricane

Description – Single-Seat fighter

Construction – Monoplane, all-metal frame with fabric covering. Wing initially fabric covering, later stressed skin.

Powerplant – Mk I Rolls Royce Merlin II or III 1,030hp. Mk II Rolls Royce Merlin XX 1,280hp or Merlin 22 1,460hp.

Wingspan – 40 feet.

Length – Mk II 32 feet.

Weight – Mk I empty 4,670lb. Loaded 6,600lb. Sea Hurricane Mk.IIC empty 5,880lb loaded 8,100lb.

Performance (Mk IIC) – Maximum speed 336mph. Climb to 20,000 feet 9.1 minutes. Ceiling 35,600 feet.

Armament – Sea Hurricane IA, IB, IC – 8 x 0.303-in Browning machine guns. Sea Hurricane IIC – 4 x 20mm Hispano cannon. Sea Hurricane IIC – 2 x 250lb bombs or 2 x 500lb bombs, 8 x 3-in rocket projectiles.

Number built: Sea Hurricane all Marks – 405.

Sea Fury

Description – Single-seat carrier-borne fighter-bomber.

Construction – Monoplane, all-metal stressed skin.

Powerplant – Bristol Centaurus 18 radial air-cooled engine, 2,480hp c/w 5-blade Rotol propeller.

Wingspan – 38 feet 4¾ inches.

Length – 34 feet 7 inches.

T/C ratio – 14.5% root, 10% tip.

Weight – Empty 9,240lb. Loaded: 12,350lb.

Performance (FB.11) – Maximum speed: 380mph sea level, 460mph at 18,000ft. Climb to 20,000 feet 5.7minutes. Ceiling: 37,800 feet.

Armament – 4 x 20mm Hispano cannon. Various bombs up to 1,000lb, 3-in unguided rockets.

Number built – 911.

Sea Hawk (Mk.3)

Description – Single-seat carrier-borne strike fighter.

Construction – Monoplane all-metal stressed skin.

Powerplant – RR Nene RN.4 (Mk.101) rated at 5,000lb thrust. Later Nene Mk.103 rated at 5,200lb.

Wingspan – 39 feet.

Length – 39 feet 10½ inches.

Weight – empty 9,187lb, loaded 13,225lb.

Performance – Maximum speed at sea level 514 knots. M.823 at 36,000 feet. Climb to 35,000 feet 12½ minutes. Ceiling 43,000 feet.

Armament – 4 x 20mm Hispano cannon with 200 rounds per gun. 2 x 1,000lb bombs or 3-in or 5-in RPs or 2 x 90 gall drop tanks. Mk 6 – Up to 4 x 500lb bombs or 4 x 90 gall. drop tanks.

Number built – 542.

Hunter T.8 and GA.11

Description – Single- and twin-seat fighter/ground-attack trainer.

Construction – Monoplane all-metal stressed skin.

Powerplant – RR Avon RA.7 and 21 series, (GA.11) Mk.113 or Mk.122. (T.8) Mk.122 of 7,500lb thrust.

Wingspan – 33 feet 8 inches.

Length – T.8 – 48 ft 10½ inches. GA.11 – 45 feet 10½ inches.

Weight – T.8 - empty 13,482lb, Loaded 17,210lb. GA.11 (post mod 228) - empty 12,767lb, loaded 16,145lb.

Performance – (RA.7 rating) Maximum speed M0.93 at 36,000 feet (single seat). M0.92M at 36,000 feet (twin-seat). Climb to 45,000 feet 9.8 minutes (single-seat), 12½ minutes (twin-seat). Ceiling 48,800 feet (single-seat), 47,000 feet (twin-seat).

Armament – T.8 - 1 x 30mm Aden cannon, 150 rounds, 2 x bombs up to 1,000lb, multiple rocket batteries, drop tanks, practice bomb carriers.

Number built: 83 aircraft – 43 T.8 new-build or conversion. 40 GA.11 conversion.

**Type Specification - British Aerospace plc and later BAE Systems
Sea Harrier FRS.1, FA/2, T.8.**

Description – Single-seat carrier-borne V/STOL all-weather/night fighter/strike/ reconnaissance. Twin-seat systems trainer.

Construction – Monoplane all-metal stressed skin.

Powerplant – Rolls Royce Pegasus Mk 106 vectored trust turbofan, 21,500lb thrust.

Wingspan – 25 feet 3 inches.

Length – 47 feet 6 inches.

Weight – empty 13,444lb, loaded (max) 26,200lb

Performance – Maximum speed 740mph at sea level, M0.98 at altitude. Service ceiling 51,000 feet.

Armament – 2 x 30mm Aden cannon, Sidewinder AAM (max of four), Hughes/Raytheon AIM120 AMRAAM (max of four). 1,000lb bombs on four wing and one fuselage station (max of five). Matra rocket pods, Lepus flares, drop tanks.

Number built: 109: 75 x single-seat FRS.1/FA.2 and 7 x twin-seat T.8 (not including T.4N) for UK. 27 x FRS.51 and 4 x twin-seat T.60 for India.

Appendix 2

Squadron Use and Embarked Carriers

Nimrod
Squadron Use:
Initial distribution: No.408 Flight aboard HMS *Glorious*; No.402 Flight aboard HMS *Eagle* and No.409 Flight, all 1932. Re-organisation resulted in the following disposition: No.800 Squadron in HMS *Courageous*; 801 Squadron in HMS *Furious* and 802 Squadron in HMS *Glorious*, all 1933. Later further squadrons equipped: No.702 Squadron in HMS *Glorious*; Nos. 757 and 803 Squadrons.

Other squadrons equipped with one or more: Nos. 713 Naval Air Squadron, 759 Naval Air Squadron, 780 Naval Air Squadron, 781 Naval Air Squadron and Nos. 404 and 408 (Fleet Fighter) Flights FAA.

Osprey
Squadron Use:
No. 800 Squadron in HMS *Courageous*, 801 Squadron in HMS *Furious*, 802 Squadron in HMS *Glorious*, 803 Squadron in HMS *Eagle* and HMS *Hermes*. Nos. 711, 713, 714, 715, 716, 718, 758, 712, 810 and 780 Squadrons.

Nos. 404, 405, 406, 407, 409, 443, 444 and 447 Flights.

Sea Hurricane
Squadron Use:
No.800 Squadron. Formed 1933. Acquired Sea Hurricanes June 1942. Present on *Biter* for the TORCH landings. Disbanded 1945.

No. 801 Squadron. Reformed August 1941 acquiring Sea Hurricanes. In May 1942 sailed in *Argus* to Mediterranean and transferred to *Eagle* to cover Malta convoys. Hurricanes replaced by Seafires. Disbanded 1946.

No.802 Squadron Formed 1933. Reformed 1942 acquiring Sea Hurricanes. Arctic convoys aboard *Avenger*. Re-equipped with Sea Hurricane IIBs and re-embarked *Avenger* for TORCH landings. Reformed 1945 on Seafires. Disbanded 1959.

No.803 Squadron. Formed 1933. Acquired Sea Hurricanes 1941 for operation in Egypt, Western Desert and Palestine. Replaced with Fulmars, then Seafires. Disbanded 1969.

No.804 Squadron. Formed 1939. Acquired Sea Hurricanes 1941. Assigned to catapult Merchant ships 1941. Present at TORCH landings 1942. Replaced by Hellcats 1943. Disbanded 1944.

No.806 Squadron Formed 1940. Acquired Hurricanes 1941 for use in North Africa. Disbanded 1947.

No.807 Squadron. Formed 1940. Acquired Sea Hurricanes 1942 aboard *Argus* providing convoy protection. Re-equipped with Seafires 1942. Disbanded 1955, recommissioned 1958–1962.

No.813 Squadron. Formed 1937. Acquired Sea Hurricanes 1941, operating from *Eagle* covering Malta convoys. Carrier sunk during Operation PEDESTAL 1942 and all Hurricanes lost. Disbanded 1945.

No.824 Squadron. Formed 1933. Acquired Sea Hurricanes in 1943 to provide fighter cover for the TSR Swordfish, transferred to *Striker* 1943. Replaced by Wildcats 1944. Disbanded 1944.

No.825 Squadron. Formed 1934 as 824 Squadron. Acquired Sea Hurricanes 1943 and joined *Furious* on convoy escort. Hurricanes withdrawn 1944 and replaced by Wildcats.

No.835 Squadron. Formed 1942 as a TBR squadron. Acquired Sea Hurricanes 1943 aboard *Battler*, previously with 804 Squadron. Also served aboard *Argus* 1943 and *Ravager*, all on convoy escort duties. Replaced by Wildcats 1944. Disbanded 1945.

No.877 Squadron. Formed 1943. Acquired Hurricane IIBs (not Sea Hurricanes) and operated at Tanga in Tanzania, then in Kenya. Does not appear to have gone to sea. Disbanded 1943.

No.880 Squadron. Formed 1941. Fleet Fighter Unit; acquired Sea Hurricane IAs, then IBs in 1941. Boarded *Indomitable* for West Indies duties, then Cape Town. Supported landings on Madagascar (Operation IRONCLAD) 1942. Convoy duties for Operation PEDESTAL to Malta. Replaced by Seafires 1942.

No.883 Squadron. Formed 1941. Acquired Hurricane IBs 1942. Embarked *Avenger* for Arctic convoy duties 1942, accompanying PQ18. *Avenger* torpedoed during North African landings and sank with squadron aboard.

No.885 Squadron. Formed 1941. Reformed 1941 at Yeovilton with Sea Hurricane IBs and embarked *Victorious* 1942 for Arctic convoy escort. Operation PEDESTAL Malta convoy duties 1942. Replaced with Seafires 1942. Disbanded 1945.

No.889 Squadron. Formed 1942. Acquired Hurricane IIBs (not Sea Hurricanes) for operations in the Western Desert. Disbanded 1943. Reformed 1944 with Seafires. Disbanded 1945.

No.891 Squadron. Formed 1942. Acquired Sea Hurricane IBs 1942. Embarked *Dasher* with Sea Hurricane IIBs to support North African landings. Partially embarked *Dasher* for Iceland convoy protection duties but ship blew up in the Firth of Clyde 1943. Disbanded 1943. Reformed 1945 with Hellcats. Disbanded 1945.

No.895 Squadron. Formed 1942. Acquired Sea Hurricane IBs 1942. Replaced with Seafires 1943. Disbanded 1943.

No.897 Squadron. Formed 1942. Acquired Sea Hurricane IBs 1942. Replaced with Seafires 1943. Disbanded 1944.

Although mainly used by the 800 series operational squadrons, Sea Hurricanes were also used by training and fleet requirements squadrons in the 700 series. These included:

No.728 Squadron Fleet Requirements Unit; No. 731 Squadron Deck Landing Control Training; No.748 Squadron Pilot Refresher Training; No.759 Squadron Fleet Fighter School; No.760 Squadron Fleet Fighter Pool; No.761 Squadron Fleet Fighter School; No.762 Squadron Advanced flying Training School; No.768 Squadron Deck Landing Training School; No.770 Squadron Deck Landing Training Squadron; No.775 Squadron Fleet Requirements Unit; No.776 Squadron Fleet Requirements Unit; No.778 Squadron Service Trials Unit; No.779 Squadron Fleet Requirements Unit; No.788 Squadron Fleet Requirements Unit; No.789 Squadron Fleet Requirements Unit; No.794 Squadron Air Firing Unit.

Sea Fury
Squadron Use:
No.801 NAS on HMS *Vengeance* and *Glory*.
No.802 NAS on HMS *Ocean*, *Theseus* and *Vengeance*.
No.803 Squadron RCN on HMCS *Magnificent*.
No.804 NAS on HMS *Glory* and *Theseus*.
No.805 Squadron RAN on HMAS *Sydney*.
No.807 NAS on HMS *Theseus*, *Ocean* and *Glory*.
No.808 Squadron RAN on HMAS *Sydney* and HMS *Vengeance*.
No.898 NAS on HMS *Ocean*, *Theseus* and *Glory*.

Sea Hawk
Squadron Use:
Embarked in HMS *Albion*, *Ark Royal*, *Bulwark*, *Centaur* and *Eagle*.
Operational squadrons: Nos. 800, 801, 802, 803, 804, 806, 807, 810, 811, 895, 897, 898, 899, plus three RNVR squadrons, five training squadrons and use by FRU units from Hurn.

Hunter
Squadron Use:
Nos. 700, 738, 759 and 764 NASs. Then passed to FRADU units.

Sea Harrier
Squadron Use:
Nos. 800 and 801 NASs, embarked on HMS *Invincible*, HMS *Hermes*, HMS *Illustrious*, HMS *Ark Royal*. No.899 NAS, Headquarters Squadron, shore-based at RNAS Yeovilton. No.809 NAS, temporary commissioning as additional squadron for support during the Falklands War.

Notes

Introduction
1. *Flight*, 28 December 1956.
2. *British Aviation*, Vol.3, Putnam, 1973, p.427.
3. Fozard, John (ed), *Sydney Camm and the Hurricane*, Airlife, 1991, p.29.
4. Sturtivant, Ray and Page, Gordon, *Royal Navy Aircraft Serials and Units, 1911–1919*, Air Britain, 1992.

Chapter 1
1. In November 1910 in the USA, Lt Eugene Ely USN had taken off from the foredeck of the USS *Birmingham* and, early the following year, landed on the USS *Pennsylvania*, later taking off again to fly back to base. All flights were made with the ships stopped.
2. From *Sea to Sky*, Sir Arthur Longmore, Geoffrey Bles, 1946. p.36. Penrose gives the figure of 50 aircraft and six airships. Penrose, Harold, *British Aviation – The Pioneer Years*, Cassell 1980, p.281.
3. Ibid., p.46.

Chapter 2
1. *British Aviation*, p.205.
2. *British Aircraft Before the Great War*, SOP/AIC/001, courtesy of Brooklands Museum.
3. Sopwith Brochure, SOP/GEN/011, courtesy of Brooklands Museum.
4. Penrose, *British Aviation*, p.243.
5. Layman, R.D., *Naval Aviation in the First World War*, Chatham, 1996, p.161.
6. *Prop Swing* Summer 2017.
7. Jarrett, Philip, *The Royal Naval Air Service in the First World War*, Pen and Sword, 2015, pp.127–90.
8. Floor Space, Employees, Output, SOP/GEN/011, courtesy of Brooklands Museum.
9. Layman, *Naval Aviation in the First world War*, pp.206–7 (these numbers only account for Naval equipment and personnel. Aircraft numbers are for operational aircraft only).
10. Hawker Intelligence Unit calculated over 18,192 although this included post-war aircraft.
11. Interview with Robert Parke, SOP/GEN/001, courtesy of Brooklands Museum.
12. Formation of HG Hawker Engineering Co., HAL/HIS/040, courtesy of Brooklands Museum.

Chapter 3
1. *British Flight Testing. Martlesham Heath 1920–1939*, Putnam 1993, pp.64–6.
2. Ibid., p.219.
3. Ibid., p.220.
4. Nimrod papers, HAL/NIM/001, BAE Systems, courtesy of Brooklands Museum.
5. *Prop-Swing* Summer 2016, pp.4–10.

Chapter 4
1. The oft repeated statement (not least by Frank Mason) that the Hawker board authorised go-ahead of planning for 1,000 Hurricanes is not supported by the Hawker board minutes of April 1936 or indeed any date in 1936.
2. Robertson, Bruce, *British Military Aircraft Serials 1912–1966*, Ian Allen 1967 and Sturtivant, Ray, and Burrow, Mick, *Fleet Air Arm Aircraft 1939–1945*, Air Britain 1995.

3. *Hurricane Derivatives, Hawker Aircraft*, HAL/HIS/037, BAE Systems, courtesy of Brooklands Museum.

4. *Hurricane: The War Exploits of the Fighter Aircraft*, William Kimber, 1982, pp.213–14.

5. 'Mason, Tim, *The Secret Years, flight testing at Boscombe Down 1939–1945*, Hikoki Publications, 1998, pp.160–1. Poolman, Kenneth, *Escort Carrier – HMS Vindex at War*, Book Club Associates, 1983, p.71.

6. Crabb, Brian James, *Operation Pedestal. The Story of Convoy WS21S in August 1942*, Shaun Tyas, 2014, p.25.

7. Popham, Hugh, *Sea Flight*, William Kimber, 1954, p.126.

8. Robertson, *British Military Aircraft Serials 1912–1966*. Sturtivant and Burrow, *Fleet Air Arm Aircraft 1939–1945*.

9. Interview with Frank Chapman, *The Aeroplane*, August 2024, p.108.

10. Lloyd, F.H.M., *Hurricane – The Story of a Great Fighter*, Harborough Publishing, 1945, p.135.

Chapter 5

1. Mason, *The Secret Years – Flight Testing at Boscombe Down 1939–1945*, p.60.

2. 'John, Fozard (ed.), *Sydney Camm and the Hurricane*, Airlife, 1991, p.68.

3. Dennis, Richard, *Royal Aircraft Establishment at War*, Tutor Publications, 2008, p.14.

4. Ibid., p.16.

5. 'Sheddan, Sqn Ldr C.J., c/w Norman Franks, *Tempest Pilot*, Grub Street, 2011, p.50.

6. Ibid., p.131.

7. *Camm Diary*, March 1943, HAL/HIS/081, BAE Systems, courtesy of Brooklands Museum.

8. Hawker board meeting, 4 February 1943.

9. Ibid., 1 December 1943.

10. Ibid., 11 July 1945.

11. *The Secret Years. Flight Testing at Boscombe Down 1939–1945*, p.208.

12. Brown, Capt. Eric, *Wings of the Weird and Wonderful*, Airlife, 1983, pp.135–40.

13. Between 1943 and 1948, aircraft mark numbers transitioned from Roman to Arabic numerals. For Hawker Aircraft, the changeover occurred between 1946 and 1948, the Sea Fury Mk X being manufactured in 1946, entering service in 1947 while the FB.11 entered service in 1948.

14. Brown, *Wings of the Weird and Wonderful*, p.138.

15. Budgen, Christopher, *Hawker's Secret Cold War Airfield*, Pen & Sword, 2020, pp.74–5.

16. Leahy, Alan J., *Sea Fury – From the cockpit*, Ad Hoc Publications, 2010, p.21.

17. Chris Gotke, personal communication, August 2024.

Chapter 6

1. Sea Hawk jet precursors – Budgen, Christopher, *Hawker's Early Jets*, Pen and Sword, 2021. Complete list of jet related projects – Budgen, Christopher, *Hawker's Secret Projects*, Pen and Sword, 2023.

2. Hawker Aircraft Ltd board meeting, 6 December 1944.

3. Ibid., 21 February 1945.

4. N7/46 (Sea Hawk) tender, HAL/SHK/001, BAE Systems, courtesy of Brooklands Museum.

5. Hawker Aircraft Ltd board meeting, 12 November 1946.

6. Duke, Neville, *Test Pilot*, Wingate, 1953, p.193.

7. John, *Sydney Camm and the Hurricane*, p.34.

8. Hawker Aircraft Ltd board meetings, 20 December 1951 and 3 April 1952.

9. Frank Murphy Flight Test Reports, HAL/SHK/026, BAE Systems, courtesy of Brooklands Museum.

10. *Aeroplane*, January 1997.

11. Chris Gotke, personal communication, August 2024.

12. Brown, Capt. Eric, *Wings of the Weird and Wonderful, Vol. 2*, Airlife, p.115.

13. Ibid., p.40.

Chapter 7
1. Specification F.3/48, HAL/HUN/017 and 061, BAE Systems, courtesy of Brooklands Museum.
2. Harold Tuffen recalled to Braybrook that it was primarily the abandonment of wing fuel cells which triggered this revision, rather than restricted space around the cockpit, the fuel all being squeezed into the fuselage instead. Braybrook, Roy, *Hunter*, Osprey, 1987, pp.59–62.
3. Hunter GA.11 papers, HAL/HUN/032, BAE Systems, courtesy of Brooklands Museum.
4. Ibid.
5. McLelland, Tim, *The Hawker Hunter – A Complete History*, Crecy, p.84.

Chapter 8
1. Blundell, W.G.D., *British Aircraft Carriers*, MAP Technical Publication, 1969, p.13.
2. *P.1127 for Naval Operation* brochure, HSA/SHR/005, BAE Systems, courtesy of Brooklands Museum.
3. *Sea Harrier – the Shipborne Combat Aircraft* brochure, HAS/SHR/003, BAE Systems, courtesy of Brooklands Museum.
4. Heinz Frick, personal communication, August 2024.

Index

Sopwith/Hawker/HSA/BAE Personnel: